HOLLYWOOD DIRECTORS 1941-1976

Richard Koszarski

NEW YORK
OXFORD UNIVERSITY PRESS
1977

Copyright © 1977 by Oxford University Press, Inc.

Library of Congress Cataloging in Publication Data

Main entry under title:

Hollywood directors, 1941-1976.

Includes index.
1.   Moving-pictures—Production and direction—Addresses,
essays, lectures.
2.   Moving-picture producers and directors—United
States—Biography.
I.   Koszarski, Richard.
PN1995.9.P7H64   791.43′0233′0922   76-51716
ISBN 0-19-502217-3
ISBN 0-19-502218-1 pbk.

Printed in the United States of America

One more book dedicated to
WILLIAM K. EVERSON

ACKNOWLEDGMENTS

Again I would like to thank my editor, Sheldon Meyer, for having faith in these old articles in the first place. Martha Browne and Victoria Bijur copyedited the manuscript, a particularly thankless task.

My wife Diane produced another amazing index, and managed to provide even *more* inspiration and support.

The stills were supplied by the Museum of Modern Art Film Stills Archive, The George Eastman House/International Museum of Photography, the British Film Institute, Mr. Samuel Fuller, and the author's collection.

For the usual invaluable assistance, my thanks to George Pratt in Rochester, and David Bradley in Hollywood.

And of course the most obvious thank you to those directors who created these articles in the first place—as well as the world of film that goes with them.

CONTENTS

CONTENTS

CONTENTS

CONTENTS

INTRODUCTION

Throughout the 1914-40 period the basic structure of the American film industry was still under development. The creators of this industry investigated widely divergent approaches to the theory and practice of filmmaking, and discussed their opinions in fearless and often foolhardy fashion, samples of which we observed in the first volume of this anthology. With the Hollywood system still abuilding, the attentions of filmmakers were expansive and outward-directed, and prophetic or theoretical writings flowed freely from the pens of Hollywood directors. This trend is largely reversed in the period covered by the present volume, and the reasons can be traced directly to the status of post-1940 Hollywood itself. By this time the American film had established itself as an elaborate and well-diversified industry, with a capital investment in excess of two billion dollars. The production/distribution/exhibition machine had been completed, and was operating with smoothly-oiled efficiency. This establishment seemed as comfortably self-perpetuating as the steel industry or the food distribution chain, and like these operations it welcomed no innovation or reform. Its industrial conservatism was matched by an aesthetic self-satisfaction which derived also from the final perfection of a long evolutionary development. André Bazin has pointed out that the break in Hollywood's artistic history comes not with sound, but with the triumph of *mise en scène* over montage, which he dates as beginning around 1940. Late 30's cinema had achieved a state of stylistic equilibrium resulting from the ultimate perfection of shot-counter-shot editing techniques, and by 1939 had reached a comfortable impasse.

INTRODUCTION

In tracing an outline of Hollywood history since that point we are charting two parallel courses: the awkward unraveling of a seemingly impervious industrial base, and a concurrent tendency on the part of filmmakers to conserve what they can of this shaky establishment. A comparison of this volume of *Hollywood Directors* to its predecessor reveals a dramatic drop in the number of "think" articles and a corresponding increase in "nuts-and-bolts" articles. It is the early directors who felt it useful to develop theories of comedy, theories of the audience, theories of sound, theories of color. More than a few went crystal-gazing and came up with television, specialized art-house cinemas, and so forth. In this volume there is little of such speculative writing, and the reasons are too complex to elaborate fully here. Certainly a sense of artistic and industrial fulfillment was generally shared in Hollywood, and so there was little impetus to investigate new areas of thought. Motion pictures had arrived, and there was no need to prove anything to anyone—either in print or up on the screen. That situation especially was quite different in the early days, when filmmakers were seeking status and recognition of almost any sort. When the business end of the industry began to totter in the late 40's, defense mechanisms began to arise, and the filmmakers expended their energy on a wide variety of "how to" articles. These fall mainly into two categories. Most apparent are the production histories, the "how I made such-and-such" articles which are so prevalent here. Discussions of the making of *The Best Years of Our Lives,* *Rebel Without a Cause,* or *The French Connection* tell us a great deal about the development of filmmaking processes in general, as well as about a few specific films of interest. But they are basically inward-directed, exposing the workings of the industry instead of expanding its horizons in newer and perhaps better directions. They are three times as common here as in the first volume. The second category is the "how you can make such-and-such" article. For example, throughout the 40's and 50's there was a great move of screenwriters into direction, and information about this process is exchanged at some length. It is debated pro and con (mostly pro) and explained in detail in both personal and general terms. Other articles along this line tell us how to make an independent feature, how to shoot European locations, and other useful pieces of information. This again is all very pragmatic, aimed at developing useful skills for the here and now. But there seems little desire to explore issues outside the immediate sphere of the industry, or even to relate industry matters to some larger concern. Of course there are still a good many conjectural pieces here, if somewhat fewer than in the first volume. Orson Welles's second thoughts on Hollywood are delightfully revealing, and comments by such diverse directors as Chuck Jones, Samuel Fuller, and Josef von Sternberg provide ample indication of the quality of Hollywood thought in these years. And due to the rise of critical journals and specialized industry publications, the level of discourse apparent in these articles is substantially higher than the general level achieved in the first volume.

So the history to be traced in these articles hugs the surface of events in Hollywood very closely. One can trace the reactions to an event like ripples spreading across a pond, and it is useful to watch how they crowd in on one another and often provoke counter-responses. As an example, a crucial theme that runs throughout the book is that of the "film author," the idea that one person should be responsible for the artistic integrity of any film. This argument is a way of attacking the factory system of production (the producer system) by promoting greater personal control on the part of one individual. But this is discussed from many different perspectives, sometimes the director being elevated, sometimes the writer, and sometimes (in articles by producer-directors) even the producer! But no one reading these articles can ever again say that the idea was first developed by French critics and imported here only recently. From the first page the seeds of this argument are blowing around furiously, and the very phrase "film author" comes up at an insistently early point. Less noticeable are reactions to such technical developments as TV, CinemaScope, and 3-D, but each is duly dealt with in turn. Of the major political trauma of the day, the House Un-American Activities Committee investigations of J. Parnell Thomas, we hear very little, and that only by indirection. The few vaguely political statements in the book are nearly all from the lips of men like Rossen and Milestone who were directly involved in the turmoil. The reasons for this general silence in print (from the right as well as the left) are not difficult to understand, and should provide a useful lesson in historiography for the attentive reader. An anthology such as this, which consists entirely of period articles, will necessarily stress certain developments and suppress others. It might be expected that forthright discussions of HUAC activities by Hollywood directors will be quite rare, while articles on the creative aspirations of screenwriters will be much more common. So while *Hollywood Directors 1941-1976* does provide a first-person history of American filmmaking over these turbulent years, the kind of history it presents is governed by what sort of articles actually made it into print.

A quick study of the contents here will show that certain kinds of directors are more fully represented than others, and this is primarily a function of the published material available. Obviously directors like Huston or Brooks who also write their own screenplays will tend to go into print with their thoughts more frequently, but there are stranger biases at work here as well. There is a distinct shortage of examples from American action directors, and we have nothing from John Ford, Howard Hawks, or Raoul Walsh (although we do have Aldrich, Fuller, and Corman). Instead there is an absolute wealth of material from directors of central European origin. It seems that half the directors in Hollywood started out in Budapest or Vienna, putting in at least an appearance at the German UFA studios. And half of *these* seem to have worked on the film *Menschen am Sonntag*! We are talking not just about a few big shots here, like Lang, Wilder, and Curtiz, but about a whole range of directors functioning at all levels of the industry; Siodmak, Zinnemann, Benedek, Dieterle, Koster. Why these directors should be so much better represented in print than their American cousins I do not know, but the sheer number of these emigrés in Hollywood during the 40's and 50's goes a long way toward establishing the source of the dark *film noir* style which pervades American films of the period—a clear holdover from the German UFA style. While no one specifically addresses himself to this point, the conclusion arises inevitably from the cumulative presence of so many UFA graduates.

In the introduction to the first volume I wrote of the selections: "Some of this thinking was productive, some fruitless, some merely screwball." As we have seen, such an assessment will not work here, for we are dealing with another and much more pragmatic period. Better to see these writings as a collective journal of Hollywood history, firmly rooted in the realities of day-to-day existence. For the authors, filmmaking was an ongoing and all-consuming passion, and there was little time left over for speculation on the future or recollection of the past.

HOLLYWOOD
DIRECTORS
1941-1976

ORSON WELLES
(1915-)

Published right in the middle of the pre-release squabbling over *Citizen Kane*, this article seems either hopelessly brave or irretrievably foolish. Beyond a certain degree of self-satisfaction, what could Welles have hoped to gain by so vehement an assault on producers, agents and studio heads? The destruction of the Hollywood system? A more effective voice for himself within that system? It is hard to see this as anything more than a sardonic throat-cutting exercise, with the blood pressure rising in every producer, agent and studio head who might chance across it. That it was issued while delicate negotiations over the fate of *Kane* were still underway, and *before* Welles' films had suffered any insult at the hands of Hollywood hacks, makes it seem not merely petulant, but downright rash as well. Von Stroheim also issued denunciations of the Hollywood studio system, but he at least waited until there was a corpse on hand for evidence. In Welles' case the corpses would pile up only afterwards: *The Magnificent Ambersons, It's All True, The Lady from Shanghai, Macbeth, Touch of Evil*— a series of films all gleefully dismembered by studio functionaries with small regard for Welles and smaller reason to harbor any such regard. Recent critics have speculated on a self-destructive streak in Welles' career, and this characteristic seems particularly in evidence here. Hollywood was able to tolerate a variety of eccentric talents, local as well as imported, but only Welles chose to spit in the eye of his new employers. Given the first opportunity they were all quite willing to spit right back.

ORSON WELLES WRITING
ABOUT ORSON WELLES

This article will probably make me no friends in Hollywood, but I haven't been making friends there at a rapid rate, and since my recent lectures on the motion pictures, it would be hard to say how I could make any new enemies.

I know it's a mistake to talk about Hollywood at all, but it can't be helped. As a matter of fact, I appear on the lecture platform only when I am flat broke. The money is easy, but it's hardly worth the trouble I get into.

I mention these personal matters because I'm here about to strike out at certain Hollywood institutions, and I'd like it understood that I'm not striking back at Hollywood.

I couldn't if I would. Hollywood has more to say against me, and says it, than I have to say against Hollywood. This is because I have proposed and contracted to do more work on a movie than anyone on the regular assembly line of the industry is allowed to do, and as though this weren't enough, for some time I didn't make the movie.

That's why I'm broke, and that's why I had to make that lecture.

I had the same trouble last year in New York. Almost everybody in the metropolitan area had failed to share my enthusiasm for a stage production of mine, which cost me everything I had made on the radio. I therefore spoke on "What's Wrong with the Theatre." The proceeds, together with additional sums even more dishonestly come by, were dedicated to another flop. A second lecture—called "What's Wrong with the Theatre"—provided the money for a trip to Hollywood.

This year I am a movie producer. But since I've only just produced a movie and don't get paid until I do, I've found it necessary to lecture on "What's Wrong with the Movies."

From *Stage*, February 1941.

4

Orson Welles (with pipe) rides the camera boom during the shooting of *Citizen Kane* (1941). Director of photography Gregg Toland is just visible at extreme lower right corner.

Neither topic was my choice. The Lecture Bureau, which ought to know about such things, assures me that nobody at all wants to hear what I have to say about ancient Chinese ceramics, the origin of waterfalls, or regional planning, subjects on which I am fully as well grounded and informed as I am on motion pictures, as anybody in Hollywood will admit.

I'm told that people will only pay money to hear me say something I shouldn't. My lectures, it would seem, are mainly attended by the same elements which support those more pointless and most reckless of sporting exhibitions, whose expectation of disaster is very high. If this is so—if getting myself into trouble is the sum of my appeal as a public speaker—then in candor I must admit that I seldom disappoint my audiences.

The newspapers, to pay tribute where tribute is due, have contributed whole-heartedly to my success as a lecturer, by sharpening and polishing what they swear they heard me say. For instance, I take little credit for having said last year: "The theatre is dead." My own words, which were: "The theatre will never die," can scarcely be called a sizeable contribution to those immortal lines. The press, however, generously overlooked my negligible collaboration. Walter Winchell took the opportunity to point out that *I* was dead in the theatre, and George Jean Nathan proclaimed eloquently that "The theatre will never die." Others, excoriating me for my ingratitude, were kind enough to record all my flops as smash hits and a widely syndicated cartoon showed me gorging myself at an expensive restaurant, attended by a skeleton dressed as a waiter and labeled "The Theatre."

The waiter motif appeared again this season when my "Actors are the servants of the public" was translated by the newspapers (somewhere between my lecture and the linotypes) into "Actresses should all be waiting on table." At this, Miss Bette Davis, in a special interview, leaped to the defense of waitresses, who, she said by way of rebuttal, are very nice people. Miss Ann Sheridan, surely in a moment of temper, stated for publication that I was no better than a Harvard undergraduate. The general feeling against me in the movie community, in fact, reached such an intensity of unfriendliness that I felt obligated to spend what I had made on the lecture advertising my apologies in the trade papers.

And so I'm broke again.

And so I'm writing this article—very glad indeed for the chance to state my sentiments in print as clearly as I can. And before I begin, I'd like to assure any readers I may have that any opinions I may express are prejudiced as little as possible by my own curious record in the movie business. I shall not deal with that record nor attempt to explain it since I am not the subject of this article, and anyone who cares to say I am is simply changing the subject.

Out of consideration for my feelings, I'm not going to talk about myself any more. I'm going to talk about Hollywood because *Stage* invited me to, because I've retired from the lecture field, and I've got to eat.

Also, there are a few things wrong with Hollywood. . . .

I've been here quite a spell now (long enough for the circumstance of my not making a movie to have become more generally interesting than my movie contract—which still exists—and my beard—which does not).

But I haven't lived here long enough to admit that I live here. Nobody ever does. The movies, that is, may be here to stay, but not the movie makers. The notion of permanent residence is the assumption only of the California tax-gatherers, and citizens of twenty years' standing have scarcely unpacked. I myself know some of the oldest inhabitants of this Athens of the Southwest, whose possessions include estates, children born on the premises, and furniture imbedded in the heaviest of cement, whose delusion it is that they're occupying a hotel bedroom, not necessarily with bath, just passing through. Hollywood, apparently, is as hard to leave as Tahiti. Its inhabitants, deeply tanned but unresigned to the sunshine and the flowers, all confidently expect to take the next boat home—to write a novel, play another part on Broadway, resign, or commit suicide. But if nobody lives here, nobody leaves.

The gold rush is still on, for one thing. The boom town is in its second generation, and the dirt—figuratively speaking at least—is still paying. Walter Wanger's fifteen-year-old description of Hollywood—"A western mining camp with service from the Ritz"—is still pretty accurate.

Grand Luxe on the frontier is certainly the peculiar and considerable charm of the good life as we know it in the movie colony. But whether the good life is what keeps us here is an interesting question. The Grand Luxe is beguiling all right, but even the softest of our Hollywood species—the highest flier, let us say, no matter how deeply and contradictorily immersed in his swimming-pool—is bound to be intrigued by the other half of the combination: the frontier part of it. As it happens, the worst that can be said by the movie-buying public of movie-making Hollywood recommends it most to us who make movies (and, I hasten to add, we who have just made one). Hollywood is still a frontier. That it should be after all these years (the motion picture is an older institution in our time than the professional theatre was in Shakespeare's) is to the movies' shame and our advantage.

Bigger money or a bigger market can never be offered an

art form, and the form itself is for every art a new hemisphere.

The actor is just now in possession of the means to act without the necessity to project. The closeup is the first new thing he's had to play with since he took off his mask three thousand years ago and added his face to his voice.

The dramatist, mostly impotent since the invention of the novel, has a new dimension now, a new thing to write besides words. Newly equipped with an imagery which is simply the image itself—more literal than sight and more eloquent than modern language—he is again capable of poetry.

A public is drafted for serious music whose composer (starving these days in opera and ballet, those monetary unfeasibilities, and worse: esthetic bankrupts) now finds himself, unbelievably, with a paying job and availed of a fresh and flexible narrative form.

Finally the director's art becomes a major art. It was a new art, apparent only just before the movies were invented, and its importance was exaggerated, and still is, in the theatre. But if an actor can do without a director, a camera can't. Call directing a job if you're tired of the word "art." It's the biggest job in Hollywood. (It should be anyway, and it would be, except for something called a producer.) If you don't like artists, call a movie director a craftsman. He won't mind. He's the world's happiest man, and if he isn't, it's because there are producers in the world.

I'm coming to producers in just a minute.

For the craftsman, the motion picture is a field of beautiful opportunity. The opportunity is just as beautiful for the merely crafty. Precisely according to the tradition of frontiers, Hollywood, with everything to offer anybody with anything to offer, has failed to restrict itself against the nobodies with nothing. The mere takers swarm. There is always room, on any frontier, for the untalented.

Beauty is syndicated for its own sake.

Power and glory, never cheaper than here, are obtainable without the nuisance of an utterly heartless exploitation of labor. Thus the extremely great among studio executives get more might for their money than all the other industrialists in history—a king's portion at cut-rates.

And it's always Christmas morning for the percentage boys.

These last (they would like to be called artists' representatives, but they will not be called artists' representatives by me) are many of them as comfortably situated as the average Maharajah; all are more accurately certain of their future.

Boom money has always cheerfully subjected itself to a good bit of finger-sifting by interested third parties, none less deserving or better organized than the Hollywood agent.

Not that some agents aren't honest. (I heard one of the biggest tell another, "My office ain't been unethical in two years!") But even the hungriest stragglers in the pack strike every attitude of respectability—an attribute previously unmentioned in the record and richly undeserved.

Some agents do sometimes bring together someone who wouldn't otherwise get a job and someone else who wouldn't otherwise give it to him; but the majority of ankles into which these artists' representatives have clenched their parasitic teeth belong to people who need agents as much as a street-car needs an attendant stationed on its step to announce that for a fare the street-car will carry passengers along the track.

Other tolls are exacted in the movie industry: compulsory charities and space ads in the trade papers, but nothing hurts more than that tidy missing ten percent of your earnings that indicates you have somewhere, with your eyes open, voluntarily swallowed a tapeworm. It hurts because the money is likely to be worse than wasted. Unless your agent wraps you up in a package with a couple of other clients, involves you, that is to say, in some sort of swap or combination offer, he is telling you the truth when he tells you he's working in your interests. But your interests represent only a small percentage of the interests of your representative—less than ten percent, invariably. Your agent needs the goodwill of the studios more than you do, and so he can't afford to fight as hard for you as you could. He's either afraid of getting in bad with a producer, which makes him useless to you, or he's useless to you because he's in bad with a producer.

Sometimes an agent leaves the racket and gets a job as a producer. You can't blame him for trying to better himself. It's just too bad that anyone ever was an agent to begin with. Now that we're finally on the subject, it's too bad anybody ever gets to be a producer.

Only a little less superfluous than the agent and almost as successful, unlike certain others among Hollywood's middlemen (the publicity man and the columnist, for instance) the producer is not a necessary evil. He's unnecessary, and he's an evil.

The functions of the agent, with minor exceptions (appropriate payment for which could then be arranged for), could all be handled by a clerical bureau with a small fee above the cost of maintenance. The functions of the producer are already taken care of, and if they aren't they should be, since they're all somebody else's functions. Simply stated, the producer's functions are none of his business. The producer as a functionary is thus, naturally enough, hard to define.

In England, a producer is a man who stages a play; on Broadway, he is the man who finances a play; in Hollywood, he is the man who interferes with a movie.

I say nothing against the executive head of any studio. I wouldn't if I dared.

Several studio executives are seriously ignorant and some are absolutely foul. A lot of them are just old-fashioned small-time showmen who got in cheap on a new thing that turned out to be a sure thing and were shrewd enough to hang on.

With a few outstanding exceptions, none of them is very smart or very very stupid. They are part of a success story. They had all the regulation Horatio Alger pluck and luck. Nimbly they stayed at the top of one of the world's fastest growing industries. They helped it grow, but it's also true that it couldn't help growing. It's grown too big for them—that's all right, if they're no longer young enough to grow, they're old enough to die. Let them die rich. They found more gold than they earned, but it's all theirs. None will outlive the boom, and nobody wants them to. Few are equipped to face an increased possibility of failure, very few deserve a new success. There are these few, I admit, a very few, in the valley of the shadow of prosperity, who've kept their eyes on the horizon. There are also men in charge of big studios who are undeniably gifted, honest, and even amenable to progress. The existence of these men cannot be overlooked. There are about three of them.

But a studio head is only occasionally, incidentally, and never properly speaking a producer.

A studio head is to the motion picture industry and the motion picture art what a publisher is to the book business and to literature.

A producer has no equivalent in any other craft or profession, which is one of the good things about any other craft or profession.

It's true there is such a thing in journalism as the editor, but an editor dictates policy—at the worst—and stops at that. He buys writers, but he lets them write. He collaborates very rarely, he tells you what he wants only if he knows what it is, and then he leaves you alone. When this article was commissioned, for example, no special functionary was delegated to supervise its execution. These words are not offered up as they're written down to somebody who thinks he could write better if he could write. Your (average) writer of movies knows such freedom only in his dreams, and then only if his producer leaves his dreams alone. Your (average) writer of movies is scarcely allowed to sign his name without submitting it to a story conference, and often begs permission not to sign it at all.

Like the writer—the actor and the designer of sets, and the composer of music, the cameraman, the wardrobe man, the make-up man—all are subjects of his undeniable highness, the Hollywood producer.

Please understand, I think a movie needs a boss. There has never been a motion picture of consequence that has not been, broadly speaking, the product of one man. This man has been the producer, could be the writer, has been and usually should be the director. Certain pictures are rightly dominated by their stars or even their cameramen.

Good pictures and even bad—like paintings—bear the signature, though it be unwritten, of this dominant personality—items: Selznick, Zanuck, Thalberg, Guitry, Von Sternberg, Von Stroheim, Vidor, Capra, Ford, Menzies, Sturges, Chaplin, Sol Wurtzel.

Not that the dominating personality of one picture is necessarily the dominating personality of another, though he be part of the second set-up. A motion picture dominated by Sol Wurtzel, for example, bears the Wurtzel stamp, but this can be eradicated in another picture of which he is officially the producer but in which, say, John Ford is the personality.

This dominant personality is the essential of style in the motion picture art. When it is absent, a motion picture is a mere fabrication of the products of various studio departments from the set builder to the manufacturer of dialogue, as meaningless as any other merchandise achieved by mass production.

Let's have more personalities in the picture business and let them dominate all they want to, but let them be the personalities of those who really make pictures. What we can do without is the dominating personality of a high-salaried official with nothing to do except dominate, and no other talent.

Actually and exactly this is the producer's only real function. Of course, he also "coördinates." He administers finances and schedules shooting, but so does an obscure, very efficient member of the studio system known as the unit manager.

What the unit manager can't do, the producer shouldn't.

It is argued that somebody is needed to pick the story for a picture, decide on its casting, and determine its esthetics. The director would seem a pretty obvious candidate for these jobs, and when he can, he claims them as his right.

When the director or somebody else nominally in the producer's charge manages to dominate the producer, the producer is harmless enough, but most producers manage, through the exercise obviously of the devious abilities which made them producers in the first place, to negate all other potential dominant personalities. The resultant motion picture at best is a coherent interpretation by the craftsmen he employs of what the producer, as dominant personality, asks for but can't execute.

At worst, what emerges is the worst that can ever be said of the Hollywood product—a motion picture without any personality at all.

As I leave this sketchy discussion of the motion picture producers, I feel it essential to point out that being a motion picture producer myself, I am utterly without bias on the subject.

I must further admit that producers, agents, and other personal grudges are merely contributors like myself to what's wrong with Hollywood, which is finally, absolutely and simply the scarcity of good movies.

There have been, I anticipate the answer, four or five pictures recently of truly adult excellence, but Hollywood makes almost six hundred feature pictures a year, and every year for almost twenty years has presented a public with at least a couple of pictures good enough to make it look as though Hollywood had come of age.

There is, I think, a moral or a conclusion to be drawn from this.

Ten years ago one of these pictures of truly adult excellence was Milestone's superb *All Quiet on the Western Front*. A serious thinker attended the opening of this picture with Lionel Barrymore, and on their way to supper spoke passionately to Mr. Barrymore on the theme that pictures had finally hit their stride, that from now on—witness *All Quiet on the Western Front*—to deal with pictures would be to deal with a mature, a serious, and an important art. Mr. Barrymore was just as enthusiastic about the picture, but he asked our mutual friend not to forget the age-old situation to be encountered the world over in high-class brothels. Four or five times a year, beyond doubt, a patron would show up, said Mr. Barrymore, who would both ask for and listen respectfully to the Suite from *Peer Gynt*, or even the *Symphony in D Major* by Mozart. The rest of the year it was far more likely that the customers would get and like *Frankie and Johnnie*.

ROUBEN MAMOULIAN
(1898-   )

In the first volume of this anthology we included an essay by Rouben Mamoulian on the color design of *Becky Sharp*, the first complete feature in three-color Technicolor. Six years later Mamoulian's first impressions on the use of color in film—developed from his work on stage productions like *Porgy*—had become remarkably specific, and were realized to their fullest in his production of *Blood and Sand*, of which he writes here. While previously he had spoken in general terms about the supposed psychological effects of different color tones, his examples here are concrete and typically imaginative. Mamoulian was lucky enough to have made his film for Twentieth Century-Fox, whose wartime Technicolor releases were the industry's most sophisticated. Ernest Palmer and Ray Rennahan won a well-deserved Oscar for their photography of *Blood and Sand*, but the peculiar stylization involved, notably the evocation of El Greco, Velasquez and the other Spanish masters, is very much the contribution of the director. Indeed, the color design here is so memorable that one tends to forget the narrative and remember only such electrifying chromatic effects as the scarlet mouth of Rita Hayworth. An American expressionist of the first order, Mamoulian was a pioneer in the stylization of such formal elements as sound and color, always seeking new devices to project the inner dramatic values of a scene. That his expressionism has gone largely unrecognized by critics and historians is ironic—as if all such stylization in Hollywood must necessarily arrive direct from the UFA studio. For Mamoulian, the only important realism was "psychological realism," and if that entailed spraying the hospital corridors green, so much the better.

CONTROLLING COLOR
FOR DRAMATIC EFFECT
ROUBEN MAMOULIAN

For more than twenty years, cinematographers have varied their key of lighting in photographing black-and-white pictures to make the visual impression enhance the emotional mood of the action. We have become accustomed to a definite language of lighting: low-key effects, with sombre, heavy shadows express a sombrely dramatic mood; high-key effects, with brilliant lighting and sparkling definition, suggest a lighter mood; harsh contrasts with velvety shadows and strong highlights strike a melodramatic note.

Today we have color—a new medium, basically different in many ways from any dramatic medium previously known, whether the stage or previous black-and-white pictures. And in color, we have not only a new dimension of realism, but also a tremendously powerful means of expressing dramatic emotions. Is it not logical, therefore, to feel that it is incumbent upon all of us, as film craftsmen, to seek to evolve a photodramatic language of color analogous to the language of light with which we are all so familiar?

This has, at least, been my conviction since the introduction of the present Technicolor three-color process made color in its modern sense possible. It was my privilege to direct the first feature production ever made in this process, *Becky Sharp*, some seven years ago. While this assignment carried with it the excitement of pioneering in a new medium, it was not altogether a satisfactory one. My own connection with the picture, it will be remembered, followed upon the tragic death of the very capable director[1] who began it; and no creative artist, whether director or cinematographer, cares to take over an assignment that way, with inadequate preparation. Moreover,

[1] Lowell Sherman–R. K.

From *The American Cinematographer*, June 1941. Reprinted by permission.

Rouben Mamoulian.

the story was, I am convinced, none too happily chosen as a vehicle for launching the color medium; many of the characters were British officers, and had necessarily to appear in scarlet uniforms: and red is the most aggressive of all colors.

Nevertheless, I enjoyed making *Becky Sharp*, and in that first pioneering effort we all of us learned valuable lessons about color and its use.

During the intervening years, the Technicolor process has

made many improvements, especially in efficiency and technical smoothness. For my own part, I have tried to advance with it in my understanding of color in all its uses. Hoping for an opporutnity to direct another color production, I have tried to study color from every angle—the history of color; the psychology of color; the artistic application of color as four thousand years of painters have taught it to us; and something, at least, of the scientific aspects of color as regards color in pigments and light-values. In addition, I made it my business to see each successive Technicolor production, watching with interest the work in color of directors, cinematographers and art directors.

Finally Darryl F. Zanuck of 20th Century-Fox gave me the privilege of directing a Technicolor production, *Blood and Sand*. In it, with the invaluable collaboration of cinematographers Ernest Palmer, A.S.C., and Ray Rennahan, A.S.C. (my pioneer partner with *Becky Sharp*), art directors Richard Day and Joseph Wright, and of course the technical cooperation of the entire Technicolor organization, I have tried to put into practical use some of the things I have learned about color.

The first and most obvious step, as I saw it, was to develop a color-plan which would coordinate the emotional aspects of action and dialog with the physical production and with the fact of color. The coloration of the setting and costumes for each scene and sequence must be keyed to the emotional mood of that particular action in exactly the same way a cinematographer keys his lighting to match the mood of the action. In the same way, the color-treatment of each sequence must be keyed to the dominant mood of the production, and planned so that the production, when assembled, will form a dramatically and chromatically coherent whole. Above all, every detail—sets, set-dressings, props and costumes—must be carefully coordinated with this plan and with each other.

How herculean a task this is, none of us realized until we attempted it. In making a black-and-white film, we are all too accustomed to accepting a chair as a chair, so long as it is of the correct design for a given set, and of somewhere near the correct tone of photographic gray to harmonize photographically. In Technicolor, the color, even more importantly than the form of the chair must be actively considered: it must harmonize with set and costumes both physically and psychologically. In a black-and-white scene, we can use, for example, a red-upholstered chair in reasonable confidence that its dark-gray rendition on the screen will not be objectionable. In Technicolor, that aggressively red-upholstered chair could very easily dominate not only set, but action, not merely distracting attention from the action, but very probably inducing in the audience an unanticipated, and possibly undesired emotional response, far different from the intended dramatic mood of the scene. It is the same with every smallest detail, even down to a handkerchief.

Fortunately, the story of *Blood and Sand* divides itself into six or seven clearly-defined sequences, each of which is sufficiently distinct so it can be seen to have its own specific dramatic mood, and which can be given its individual color-mood as well. The first of these is the prologue, in which the character of Juan Gallardo as a little boy—poverty-stricken but self-assured and resolved to become the greatest of matadors—is established. Then comes that depicting Gallardo, ten years later, as a rising young bull-fighter, culminating in his triumph in the Seville arena. Next comes his bedazzlement by the wealthy and worldly-wise Doña Sol. There is, too, a definitely individual mood set in the sequence in Juan's dressing-room immediately before the bull-fight. Following this, and recurring at the close of the production, are the sequences in the arena chapel. Similar, yet entirely different in mood, is the scene of El Nacional's death. Likewise, though they are related to some of the other sequences, the street and market scenes carry a distinctive flavor all their own.

Since *Blood and Sand* was a Spanish story, I was anxious to capture the authentic atmosphere of the country, not only in its literal, every-day reality, but also in its poetic essence. This atmosphere has been best expressed pictorially by the great Spanish painters. It was only fitting, therefore, that we should turn to them for inspiration.

After all, in making a motion picture, and especially a motion picture in color, we are essentially making a series of paintings. What does it matter if we are not painting our picture with water-color or oil paint, but with colored light projected on a white screen? What does it matter if our picture moves and speaks: it is still fundamentally a picture. To what better source of inspiration could we turn than to the greatest masters of painting?

Not that any of us made a slavish attempt to imitate them! That would have been fatal. We were working in a different medium, expressing different thoughts. But we could—and did—turn to them as fellow-artists who knew the country and its emotions, for guidance in expressing similar emotions in our own medium. Their use of color, proven by centuries of approval, could guide us in choosing the colors we used in expressing similar emotions, painting comparable scenes.

Therefore for the early sequences of Juan's poverty-ridden childhood, we turned to the character paintings of Murillo. He set the mood for our sequence in such paintings as his "Young Spanish Beggar"; bronze-browns and blacks dominated.

The next sequence built progressively to the bull-ring scenes. For this, and for all scenes of violent action, we followed the style of Goya, with his dramatic and vivid colorings.

The scenes in the luxurious home of Doña Sol tried to capture the essential flavor, though not the detail, of Velasquez, the great master of light and shadow, who so flashingly depicted the richness of court life.

El Greco, the outstanding religious painter of Spain, supplied the inspiration and color-mood for the sequences in the chapel.

For the death-scene of Nacional, we sought to capture the flavor in form and composition of the 14th century primitives. This treatment happens to fit not only the mood of the action, but the character of El Nacional. He was himself a primitive— a simple, unlettered man, whose dying regret was that he had never learned to read or write.

For the scenes in Juan's dressing-room, we for once turned from Spain to the Italian, and particularly the Venetian painters of the 16th century. We tried to capture something of the luxury of color and strong suggestions of bustling movement that such painters as Titian and Veronese put on their canvases.

For the street and market scenes, we essayed to capture something of the mood of Sorolla. And as an interesting sidelight, for the bull-fight posters used in the picture we used originals by Carlos Ruano Llopis, the outstanding painter of matador and corrida scenes today.

In the costuming, we tried to express something of the essential qualities of each character. For example, there was Juan's childhood sweetheart, later his wife, Carmen, played by Linda Darnell. Many of her costumes were white—universally recognized as the color of purity. Another, when she found herself losing her husband, was black, which suggested not alone sadness, but also formed a subtle contrast with the more brilliant costumes of Doña Sol. Yet another, worn during two of her most important sequences, was blue—recognized for ages as symbolic of "true blue" constancy and faithfulness.

Doña Sol (Rita Hayworth), on the other hand, was throughout the patrician seductress. She made her first appearance in a neatly-tailored suit of purple—the patrician color, as evidenced by the phrase, "born to the purple." Later, increasing use was made of more vivid colorings in her costume. In the sequence at the dinner where she first ensnares Gallardo, she is first seen in a white evening gown. Later, as she sings to him, playing the guitar, a close-up of her fingers highlights the scarlet paint on her nimbly-flying finger-tips. In another scene, where she and Tyrone Power play their most passionate love-scene, we see her in a close-up, after which the camera dollies back to reveal the flaming orange bodice she wears, as her scarlet-tipped fingers entwine themselves in Power's black hair. (The combination of red and black has always been symbolic of danger—passion—and evil menace.) This costume, incidentally, forms an effectively dramatic contrast with the simple black dress worn by Linda Darnell when she enters the scene later.

Power himself—always the "Spanish beggar" at heart, is dominantly costumed in various shades of brown, with of course the inevitable exception of his matador costumes which in the various sequences include blue-and-gold in the first bull-fight and finally a pure white outfit in the last, avoiding any reds except in the inevitable and necessary cape, with which he plays the bull.

His mother—Nazimova—is throughout the dominant note of tragic foreboding: she is seen mostly in funereal black and grays, and once in burnt terra-cotta. Nacional, too, is always in black save in his ring trappings, for he is the plain man—the primitive, protesting always against the life of the bull-ring.

Coordinating these concepts with the detail requirements of motion pictures was no small task. For a single example, there is the scene in which Juan's wife, knowing already something of her mate's dalliance with Doña Sol, endures the whining complaints of his leech-like sister and brother-in-law for as long as she can, and finally bursting into anger, drives them furiously from the room, after which she has recourse to utterly feminine tears.

As she passively endured the complaints of her sponging relatives, she was clad in a blue costume. But it seemed impossible to me that she—or any actress—could convincingly play a scene requiring a display of passionate rage such as followed, while clad in cold blue. A crimson note—no matter how tiny—would highlight that surge of anger. The problem was solved with a scarf. During the early part of the scene, she kept it rolled in her hand. When her anger finally broke forth and she denounced the hangers-on, I had her unroll the scarf—a natural action for in gesticulating angrily, you might expect her to lossen her grip on it. Finally, as she rushed to the wall, seized a sword, and angrily beat the intruders from the room, the scarf, still in her hand, painted flashing streaks of crimson with every movement.

But then—she must weaken and dissolve in tears. The blue note should now dominate. The crimson of the scarf would again be intrusive. How to get rid of it? First I tried having her toss it on a desk as she turned back into the room. But there was no guarantee it would be concealed from the camera. Finally I had a small lead weight sewn into the corner of the scarf, and instructed her to toss the scarf on the desk so that the weighted corner fell over the edge. That worked perfectly;

the weight whisked the bit of crimson lace out of sight behind the desk, thus effectively removing its now dramatically discordant note of red.

It may seem that these details are affected—unnatural. Well, so, too, are many of the conventions we recognize as important dramatic aids in black-and-white cinematography. For example, suppose our script establishes that a man's wife has left him; he is alone, broken-hearted, and contemplating suicide. Every cinematographer in the world would play such a scene in low-key lighting. Yet in real life, a man might feel those emotions in a brilliantly-lit room—perhaps even amid the gayety and bright lights of a night-club. Yet to get the fullest dramatic effect on the screen, we would do the unnatural thing, and present the scene in low-key cinematography.

Unnatural, yes. But more truly expressive of inner emotion. And that is what we who as directors or as cinematographers are striving to picturize emotions on the screen must do in conveying a visual impression of those emotions, whether we do it in monochrome or in color.

There were many things we did in making *Blood and Sand* which were unnatural. On the set, they looked incredibly artificial. But on the screen, they gave the effect we desired; often they proved more realistic than reality its literal self.

In this, we had excellent precedent in the methods of innumerable painters from the dawn of time. If El Greco or Velasquez painted a cardinal, or a king, he strove to depict not only *a* cardinal or *a* king, but one who typified the regal. The crimson robe was not merely a crimson robe, but a crimson robe which typified the splendor of all imaginable regal habiliments.

In its general impression, that is; If you study such a painting in minute detail, you will see that the painter, to gain his effect, used almost every imaginable color from deepest black through purples, greens, yellows, and so on to create his highlight-and-shadow effects. We repeatedly strove for similar effects, by similar means. I kept a spray-gun with an unusually wide range of paints constantly standing by on the set, so that we could spray any prop or any costume to get the desired effect.

I recall, for example, the way we sprayed a white shirt worn in one scene. It was supposed to be white; but we sprayed it with traces of many other colors—greens and gray-greens, even touches of blue and blue-greens. I am sure that most of the people in the studio thought my senses had taken leave of me when they saw what I had done to that shirt. But when we screened the rushes, that shirt took its exactly right place in the scene, and appeared much more real than if it had remained a literal white shirt!

In the same way, in the hospital scene of El Nacional's death, the dominant colors were gray-greens and blues. The studio had provided some excellently authentic hospital accessories—white sheets, a bed and surgical instrument-cases immaculate in white enamel. They would have proved a jarring, discordant note in the scene. But when they were sprayed a dull gray-green, they fitted perfectly—and I am sure none except possibly the most super-critical medico will notice that they are not the regulation white.

In the chapel scenes, we again heightened the mood by spraying the altar-ornaments, the crucifix, and so on, a green like the patina of old bronze. We heightened this hue, which followed out the sombre green-gray of the set, by doing much of the lighting with green filters over the lamps. Of course, in the closer shots, we kept the green light away from the players, though in the longer shots, we let players and set alike show traces of the greenish light. I have not as yet found any people who noticed this artificiality—but I've found many who complimented me and the cinematographers on the emotional feeling of that sequence.

Cutting, too, is something which must be learned all over again in a true color film. In some instances, the fact of color makes for faster cutting; in others, for slower. There can be no general rule, for as in everything else in cinematics, each scene must set its own rules. But things which are of little or no importance in black-and-white becomes vital to either make or break a sequence in color.

For example, I recall that some years ago one of the art-directors at Paramount experimented with sets with red walls. The shade chosen was one which in black-and-white photographed as a pleasing, neutral dark gray. They were used through the whole production. In a Technicolor picture, I would hesitate to use such a set for any but the shortest flash.

In *Blood and Sand*, we introduced Power, playing Juan as an adult, in this fashion. His cuadrillo is travelling in a fourth-class railway carriage. The other three discuss their progress at some length. His voice is heard offstage. Finally we cut to a full-screen shot of a newspaper, which he is pretending to read. The paper comes down, and we have a big-head close-up of the young matador, reclining in his seat, his head resting against the folds of his brilliant red muleta. In monochrome, we could hold that close-up for almost any footage—one hundred, three hundred, a thousand feet if need be. In color, the emotional impact of that red background is so strong that the shot could only be held for a few seconds. Yet it was necessary: it gave Juan's first appearance the necessary impetus which helped him build and carry his vivid characterization throughout all the ensuing reels.

On the other hand, there are times when color must be cut for far slower tempo than we would do in monochrome to obtain the same, or rather a similar dramatic effect.

All told, controlling color in this manner, for dramatic effect, is a matter of being unnatural—often supremely unnatural, in order to produce psychologically natural *and emotional* visual effects. It is at present a matter of exploring a new medium—trying to learn to express ourselves in a new language. But as we film craftsmen—directors, cinematographers and art directors together—learn how to express ourselves in that new language, I am confident we will discover that we have gained an invaluable new means of expression, both pictorial and dramatic.

ALBERT LEWIN
(1894-1968)

Albert Lewin was for years Irving Thalberg's resident intellectual, an English professor whose Harvard M.A. lent
an aura of respectability to Metro's production board. He
served as script doctor on many of Thalberg's pet projects,
and *The Guardsman, Mutiny on the Bounty* and *The Good
Earth* were typical of the literate properties he produced
for the studio. After Thalberg's death Lewin moved to
Paramount, and then with David Loew began independent
production through United Artists. *So Ends Our Night*
was the last Lewin film to be directed by another, for as an
economy move he directed their next production, *The
Moon and Sixpence* (1942), by himself. While this article
is literally a producer's view of producing (and as such an
interesting contrast with Orson Welles' comments) there is
clearly a director inside all this just waiting for the opportunity to burst out. When that opportunity did come
Lewin certainly made the most of it, directing six of the
most obsessive and exotic films ever seen in Hollywood.
Lewin had considerable impact on the West Coast art scene
as a promoter of such surrealists as Dali and Man Ray, and
later as a major exponent of primitive and pre-Columbian
art. These concerns are not merely *apparent* in the films he
directed, they typically serve as the focal point of the work.
A reverence for the act of artistic creation and the sacred
quality of art underlies all his finest work (especially *The
Picture of Dorian Gray* and *Pandora and the Flying Dutch-
man*), while artists and aficionados often serve as central
characters. Although Lewin's films were occasionally over-
deliberate or even fussy, at their best they achieved a ba-
roque grandeur without parallel in the history of American cinema.

"PECCAVI!"
THE TRUE CONFESSION OF A MOVIE PRODUCER

ALBERT LEWIN

When, after Homeric effort, a picture is at last exhibited, the critics have their unhomeric say. If they observe that the screenplay is narrative rather than dramatic, that it rambles where it should run, repeats points already made, and at last bogs down in an obvious anti-climax, the stream of the story imperceptibly disappearing in a desert or arid dialogue; if they reproach the director for his plodding pace, his unimaginative attack on individual scenes, his commonplace characterizations; if they belabor the film editor for tiresome redundancies: the conscientious producer has an irresistible impulse to rush forward crying, "Peccavi!," exposing, like the minister in *The Scarlet Letter*, a mystical guilt branded upon his bosom. If, on the other hand, generous and deserved applause is heaped upon the director and the screenplay, the actors, the sets, the photography and the musical score, the ecstatic producer does not bare his head for the laurel, but remains diffidently in the background, like an insect with protective coloring, admiring the singing birds and the bright plumage, and very glad not to be devoured.

This is as it should be. The responsibility is the producer's; the glory belongs to the artist. Perhaps on some moonlit night, seated on a terrace above the gleaming Pacific, where the mountains fall like enchanted waves upon the sea, he may, encouraged by a sequence of dry martinis, indulge himself so far as to allow an adorable and ambitious female hypocrite to whisper what his heart so longs to hear—that he, too, is a creative artist. Let it for once be announced with trumpets, let the heralds proclaim it not in the market-place but in the salons where fame is publicly delivered like the Dauphin, let the truth appear naked and noble—the producer, too, is a creative artist. Nevertheless, the producer knows that the responsibility is his—the glory, if

From *Theatre Arts*, September 1941.

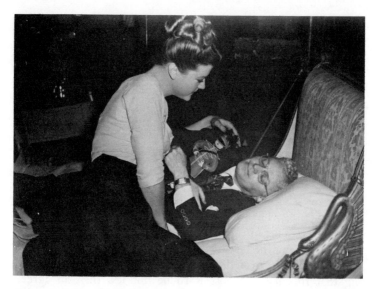

Albert Lewin with Angela Lansbury during the shooting of *The Private Affairs of Bel Ami* (1946).

any, belongs to the others. If the screenplay is feeble, then the producer failed to give the writer the necessary guidance; if he gave the necessary guidance and the screenplay still lay lifeless, then it was his duty to find another writer. There is no escaping the collaborative nature of the movies. If the director, the writer, the actors, the technicians fail, it is because the producer has failed them as an effective collaborator; or has lacked the courage, where he found effective collaboration inadequate, to change his man. His job is to find the best people available and collaborate with them so creatively that they work all together at the top of their bent.

This is unfortunately not the current conception of a producer, popularly visualized as a horrible man with money who, because he is financing the production, assumes the privilege of encumbering it with his assistance, dragging the artistic efforts of the clever people he has engaged down to his own vulgar level. Out of this misconception the producer emerges as a legendary illiterate, at worst disgusting, at best funny, an outlandish tree in which the bright malapropisms build their nest. And yet even the most naive have a suspicion that there is more to it than that, for the inevitable question seems to be, "But just *what* does a producer do?" One replies cryptically, "A producer is a kibitzer with authority." It is an illuminating figure, but like all metaphors calls for explicit exegesis. Nothing can be more explicit than a case history. Here then is a narrative of what the producer did, in this case a team of producers—David L. Loew and Albert Lewin, in making their first picture for United Artists, *So Ends Our Night*.

The releasing deal with United Artists has been set for a series of pictures. The basic terms provide that United Artists retains a percentage of the gross receipts for the service of selling and distributing the pictures throughout the world. They exercise no authority over the production beyond the understanding that the negative cost is to be not less than an agreed minimum, in order to ensure a minimal quality. Since United Artists has a basic contract with all producers, there is less than the usual amount of debate over terms. Financing has already been provided, a bank loan for a major portion of the negative cost sanctioned by what is known as a "completion bond," a guarantee that the picture will be completed and released, so that the bank loan is automatically retired by the initial receipts. The producers are now in for it: they have to make a picture.

Their first problem is to find a story. Possibilities are laboriously explored. They have read in *Collier's* a serialized novel entitled *Flotsam*, by Erich Maria Remarque. On investigation they find that *Flotsam* has already been purchased by Metro-Goldwyn-Mayer. But they are persuaded to part with *Flotsam* because they have already in work two stories, *The Mortal Storm* and *Escape*, with similar backgrounds.

What made the producers choose *Flotsam* for their first picture? In selecting a story, the producer makes what he considers the best possible compromise between his own and what he estimates to be the public taste. Very often he does not consider his own taste at all. Ideally there is no conflict between his own and the public taste. In this instance there was some question. The producers were aware that so-called anti-Nazi films were commercially risky. Nevertheless, they were themselves attracted rather than repelled by the idea of saying in their own medium something that they felt was worth saying. On the box-office side, the story offered two strong romances, one the tragic devotion of a man and his wife, separated by the Nazi regime, the other the young love of two refugees, unable to marry because they lacked passports and legal papers of any sort. Moreover, there were exciting individual scenes, strong characterizations, "heart interest" and "comedy relief." The chances of success appeared not too slim.

At any rate, the die was cast, and the producers looked about for a scenario writer. They thought Talbot Jennings, who had done the adaptations of *The Good Earth* and *Mutiny on the Bounty*, singularly well-suited to this material. To be sure, Talbot Jennings was at the moment employed by Metro-Goldwyn-Mayer, but he was not bound by contract. *Flotsam* was submitted to him. He liked the story and felt he wanted to write the scenario. He went to work. The methods of collaboration between producers and writers vary according to their personalities and inclinations. In this instance the producers and the writer worked together somewhat as follows. It was decided not to prepare an elaborate treatment in advance of the actual continuity. This decision was made, first because in itself the book constitutes a kind of treatment, and second, because in the common experience of both the producers and the writer, an elaborate treatment prepared in advance is likely to make the writing of the scenario a dull chore, which will be reflected in the script. Instead of a written treatment, therefore, the line of the story was talked out in daily conferences, its general design determined, as many snags as possible anticipated and unravelled. This procedure took some weeks. After that, a discussion in vastly greater detail of the first sequence or episode ensued. Then the writer, without help from anyone, wrote the first episode completely in scenes and dialogue. How many times he rewrites this for himself before presenting it to the producers is his concern, not the producers'. Finally, he presents to the producers his first unrevised draft of sequence one. Suggestions for revisions follow, and a revised first draft is made. Sequence one is then put aside, and sequence two is attacked. In this fashion the preparation of the first draft of the script proceeded, until it was completed in about four months.

During this time commitments were gradually being made for a director and for important members of the cast. John Cromwell was regarded as a fortunate selection to direct *Flotsam*. One could count on his unfailing good taste, his sincere treatment of dramatic and sentimental material, his experience and knowledge of actors and acting. He had, moreover, genuine enthusiasm for the story. Nothing is accomplished in the picture business without enthusiasm. Very often, alas, nothing is accomplished with it. Where it doesn't exist, it must be enkindled, if necessary by the use of a bellows. Mountains are moved by faith—and an adequate supply of steam-shovels. In this instance, everyone connected with the undertaking felt a spontaneous enthusiasm for it. At the time he agreed to direct *Flotsam*, John Cromwell was occupied in directing a picture for another producer. This made it impossible for him to collaborate on the preparation of the first draft of the screenplay. There is, of course, a variety of opinions on the question of a director's relation to the script. There is a school that believes the director should collaborate with the writer and producer from the very beginning. There is another school, now happily almost extinct, which believes the director should be given a shooting script with the preparation of which he has had nothing whatsoever to do. The producers of *Flotsam* felt that the director should come in at the conclusion of the first draft and collaborate on the preparation of the final, revised, shooting script. They felt this for two reasons: first, because to have the director on salary from the inception would involve an expenditure prohibitive for an independent producer; second, because it is good for a director to bring a fresh mind to the first draft. From the debate that follows the script is likely to benefit. John Cromwell started work about two months before actual production began, and collaborated closely with the writer and the producers on the final revisions of the screenplay. One of the major problems in the screenplay is usually length. The first draft of *Flotsam* ran to two hundred and seventy-seven pages. A normal script does not exceed one hundred and fifty. The task of reducing *Flotsam* was a serious one. Actually, the scenario was never squeezed below one hundred and ninety-two pages. This meant a long shooting schedule, and an acutely exacerbated editing problem with the finished picture.

During this time commitments were also made for the principal members of the cast. The book was submitted to Fredric March, who liked it but waited until he could see about a third of the script before agreeing to do the part. Even then he hesitated, because his part did not dominate the story to quite the extent usually expected of the main starring part. Finally, however, his liking for the story prevailed. This was true also of Margaret Sullavan, who felt at first, not without justification, that both male leads were better than the female. But she, too, succumbed to the temptation of the material itself and her sense that the enterprise was worthwhile. With the assurance of two box-office "names," it was possible to consider only performance in the rest of the casting. A big gamble was taken in the romantic juvenile lead opposite Miss Sullavan when the producers cast Glenn Ford. He had appeared hitherto only in B pictures. The producers, however, and John Cromwell were convinced of his talent and potentially starring personality. He was under contract to Columbia Pictures. For giving him this opportunity, the producers exacted options for his future services from Columbia. Presently Frances Dee, Anna Sten and Erich von Stroheim were cast in important roles, and Joseph Cawthorn, Alexander Granach and Leonid Kinskey in comedy parts. Extreme care was exercised in the casting of small parts and bits, unusually difficult in this case since the story ranges over Austria, Czechoslovakia, Switzerland, France and Germany and required more than a hundred speaking parts. Stanley Kramer, assistant to the producers, spent months interviewing prospects and selecting the best possibilities for the consideration of the director and the producers.

With script, director and cast completed, or nearly so, and with a starting date set, the matter of technicians began to assume urgency. About a month in advance of production the art director, William Cameron Menzies, went to work. An experienced and talented artist, responsible for the art direction of

Gone with the Wind, Rebecca and many other notable pictures, William Cameron Menzies is above all an illustrator. For *So Ends Our Night* he drew upwards of one thousand sketches for individual scenes in the script. Photostats were made of these sketches and they were sent to the set to guide the director and cameraman in camera set-ups and compositions. William O. Daniels, a skilful cameraman, was borrowed from Metro-Goldwyn-Mayer, and an entire technical crew assembled. The producers had rented space and facilities at the Universal Studios, where the picture was shot.

In the meantime the "unit manager" had prepared a series of cost estimates leading up to a final budget, and a shooting schedule. A list of the items on a normal picture budget will give perhaps the clearest idea of the complex technical problems involved. The list includes story and continuity, producer, director, production staff, cameraman and camera staff, stars and cast, bits and extras, wardrobe, properties, set construction, set operation, electrical labor, equipment and current, location and transportation, special effects, raw stock, laboratory, studio and sound charges, sound labor, titles and inserts, cutting, music, dubbing, tests, publicity.

During the actual shooting of the production, the director and the producers kept in constant daily consultation, although the producers never interfered with operations on the set except where their advice was called for by the director for the solution of unexpected problems. The producers felt, and this feeling is general throughout the industry, that the director must be an absolute despot on the set. If the producers had any comment to offer, they made it during lunch hour—in order to ruin the director's digestion; or at night—in order to ruin his sleep. Each day producers and director scrutinized the previous day's work in the form of "rushes" or "dailies." The producers, maintaining a certain detachment or perspective, watched closely the consistency of characterization, tempo, stage business, and co-ordination of technical services so that they functioned smoothly and on schedule.

During the ten weeks involved in photographing the picture, the producers collaborated with the cutter in making a rough assemblage of the material as shot, so that by the time the production was closed a first cut was about three-fourths completed. At that time, the director, freed of his other duties, joined the producers and the cutter in a collaborative editing of the picture. A first cut of two hours and forty minutes was reduced to two hours and twenty minutes for the first preview, a tryout before a suburban audience. Further editing and minor retakes were made as a result of the previews until the picture was brought down to two hours and one minute.

In the meantime, Louis Gruenberg, author of the opera *Emperor Jones*, had been engaged to prepare a musical score, an arduous and tantalizing task, because nothing can be considered final until the cutting is definitive, and the composer is, therefore, under the necessity of continually revising his material to fit the new timing.

The final production effort is that of dubbing—the process of mixing dialogue, music and sound effects from many tracks into one composite track. For this tedious task the director and the producers sit in with the sound men as observers and consultants. Then the negative is cut, an answer print is taken off and corrected, and release prints made and shipped to the exchanges.

In the meantime, the producers had been consulting with publicity and advertising men to set the exploitation policy. The title of the picture, at the insistence of the publicity department, had been changed from *Flotsam* to *So Ends Our Night*. The publicity men felt that the great public would not know the meaning of *Flotsam* or how to pronounce it, and might imagine it to be the name of a skin lotion.

The producers had done all that they could and the success of the picture now rested in the lap of the gods. One thing, not as producers but as human beings with hopes and fears for the future, they found encouraging about their picture. They had often seen newsreels of Hitler making a speech to a mob, and had been appalled by the fury and the hatred expressed in his face and voice, had been dismayed by the vicious echo of his hatred in the mob. They wondered whether men are so wicked that perhaps they are not even worth saving. But at previews of

So Ends Our Night they saw the other side of the picture. They saw that audiences are moved more by examples of nobility than by almost anything else. "What's Hecuba to me or I to Hecuba?" Hecuba is happily a great deal to us, and the highest gratification a producer can have—outside of making a profit with his picture—is to observe the extraordinary sympathy of audiences which makes them pity a fictitious character to the point of tears. The element of nobility was strong in this story, especially in the part played by Fredric March. When audiences weep at nobility one finds it possible to hope that men may be moved by something besides hatred, to have faith still in the common humanity of simple people.

This gratification the producers fortunately had at their previews, before the picture was released. Fortunately—because after almost a year of Homeric effort, the picture was at last about to be exhibited, and the critics would have their unhomeric say.

KING VIDOR
(1894-   )

It is generally considered that King Vidor's major "experimental" period ended with *Our Daily Bread* in 1934, and that his later films, whatever their particular merits, were cast in the prevailing mode of Hollywood narrative construction. Yet in this 1941 article Vidor describes his approach to *H. M. Pulham, Esq.* in terms of sequence shots and subjective camera, and certainly extends his claim as one of Hollywood's most consistent innovators. The subjective point-of-view technique employed in this film was not as singleminded as that in Robert Montgomery's *The Lady in the Lake*, for example, but neither was it as extreme or intrusive. The idea was to make the style invisible (see George Sidney's comments) and not to distract the attention of the audience with self-conscious effects. For this same reason Vidor used "the fluid camera" to eliminate the need for excessive close-up inserts and reaction shots. Much has been made of the way Wyler and Welles used the sequence shot in this period for similar ends, but Vidor's contributions have been forgotten. Perhaps his own modesty is at fault here. In his autobiography the discussion of *Pulham* concentrates on his friendship with the novel's author, John P. Marquand, and leaves comparatively little space for the film's "interesting camera ideas." *H. M. Pulham, Esq.* has often been seen as a respite in Vidor's career, a time-marking exercise set between *Northwest Passage* and *An American Romance*. But to Vidor the film was clearly a chance to display yet another facet of Americana, not the bucolic Americana of John Ford or Henry King, but that urban landscape which Vidor charted so graphically in *The Crowd* and *The Fountainhead*, and of which he was perhaps Hollywood's finest interpreter.

BRINGING PULHAM
TO THE SCREEN
KING VIDOR

Transforming J. P. Marquand's *H. M. Pulham, Esq.* to the screen was one of the pleasantest tasks I've ever had. Elizabeth Hill, my scenarist, had been telling me about the great charm and humor of Marquand's previous Pulitzer Prize-winner, *The Late George Apley.* We had been looking for just such a story depicting the true American scene when *H. M. Pulham, Esq.* came to our attention. Here was American life today, told in terms of American humor and romance with a generous sprinkling of our national brand of satire. In addition, the story covered a span of thirty or forty years, and I saw a chance to present a sort of American Cavalcade of the significant events of this century while at the same time telling the human story of an American gentleman.

The book is written in the first person. It was all told from Harry Pulham's viewpoint. This is responsible for much of the deep human psychology of the novel. Here was a challenge, and, if we could accomplish it, a picture with unusual freshness and depth could be attained. Could a motion picture film be told completely in the first person? This would mean that nothing could happen in the entire picture unless it was seen or witnessed or experienced by Pulham. We decided to try it. It means that Robert Young is in every scene of the picture or is in the room when every scene happens. In the case of telephone conversations, no one is shown at the other end of the line. We only hear what Pulham hears. We do not see the other person at any time in any conversation, because this would be letting the audience see something that Harry Pulham didn't see. Also, being in the first person, the book is filled with Pulham's deepest thoughts and it is this deep, honest thinking that paints such a clear, vivid picture and gives such

From *Lion's Roar*, December 1941.

Hedy Lamarr and King Vidor between takes for *H. M. Pulham, Esq.* (1941).

depth to Pulham's character and emotional reactions. Here we were faced with another problem. Has a novelist a wider scope of expression than a motion picture director? If a novelist can put down what a man is thinking when he is alone or with someone else, why can't we do the same? This gave us the idea for the "thinking voice" treatment by which we can show Pulham's innermost thoughts.

The story covers many settings, periods and locations. Another technique that has been developed on this picture is what I choose to call "the fluid camera." Instead of the picture jumping from one static pose to another and having a jarring, startling effect with its suddenly changing backgrounds, I employed in this treatment, because of the story's many localities and settings, a moving camera that has a great tendency to dispense with the constant use of cutting to large close-ups.

Because of the fact that *Pulham* was a widely read book, the casting was quite a problem. We had to be careful not to offend the several million readers and at the same time, we had to be exciting enough in our casting to catch the interest of the people who hadn't read the book.

Robert Young with his performance proves that he is the perfect Pulham. I don't know of anyone who could play and live this part better than he does.

In casting Marvin Myles it was necessary to have a business woman Pulham would remember for twenty years. She is never off his mind. It takes someone as exciting as Hedy Lamarr is to fill this role. She was always my choice.

Although the setting of *Pulham* is laid in Boston, New England and New York, we have been influenced by the atmosphere of the Boston setting, but we have not hung too heavily on this character and not had it predominate the picture, because I like to think that the story is a universal one. I was born and raised in the South, mostly Texas, and I know that there isn't anything in *Pulham* that could not have happened in any part of the United States.

It isn't often in motion pictures that we are able to take such strides in developing new approaches and new techniques and treatments, but I think the close observer will notice in *Pulham* many innovations.

Adapting and directing *Pulham* has been a labor of love. I believe J. P. Marquand has brought forth in a most entertaining manner what I believe to be the true American spirit and American character. *H. M. Pulham, Esq.* should be, if all my hopes come true, the true story of what we all like to believe is the typical American gentleman.

JOHN HUSTON
(1906-   )

In the early 1940's cinematography in Hollywood reached a level unmatched before or since. Recent improvements in lighting, film stock and lens performance gave the cameraman a decided mechanical advantage over earlier years, while schedules were still relatively unhurried and adequate time could be assured to achieve photographic perfection on every set-up, a luxury which came to an end only a few years later. While black-and-white was still the dominant mode, Technicolor had achieved mechanical perfection in the late 30's, and any Technicolor film of this period could expect lavish attention to set and costume design, lighting and laboratory work--another luxury which did not survive the 40's. John Huston had only recently been promoted from the ranks of screenwriters and here is eager to point out the tremendous contributions of the cinematographer, contributions which he finds are especially apt in balancing what he admits to have been an over-literary approach on his own part. Huston's sense of camera style developed early, and his directorial debut, *The Maltese Falcon*, is an important early landmark in *film noir* photography. One also thinks of his pioneering efforts in de-saturated color, *Moulin Rouge*, *Moby Dick* and *Reflections in a Golden Eye*. A year after writing this piece Huston found himself shooting documentaries for the army, and the grisly, matter-of-fact style developed in *The Battle of San Pietro* clearly influenced his post-war Hollywood films, especially *The Treasure of the Sierra Madre* and *The Red Badge of Courage*. Although his later career has suffered an unfortunate series of ups and downs, even in his weakest films Huston develops a sophisticated visual texture not always evident in the work of other ex-screenwriters.

40

PICTURE PARTNERS
JOHN HUSTON

Not so long ago, my concept of cameramen was that they were nice fellows who concentrated their efforts on turning out pretty compositions and making the leading lady look glamorous. To be perfectly frank, I also had an idea that the present system of crediting them as "Director of Photography" was more or less a polite fiction—dressing things up with a new name, and not much else.

But that was before a change from writing scripts to directing them put me out on the set actually to work with these men of the camera. Practical experience very quickly forced me to revise my ideas, and convinced me that the industry's cinematographers are, as a class, perhaps the most invaluable and yet generally underrated men in Hollywood.

My first big surprise came when I discovered that these men are interested in a lot more than just turning out pretty pictures. They do that as a matter of course; it's part of their job. But much more than that, they're storytellers par excellence. Instead of using written or spoken words, they tell their stories with the camera. Often—if you'll only take advantage of their knack of visualizing drama—they can, with a simple, pictorial effect, put over dramatic points upon which writers or directors may have toiled and worried vainly.

Speaking for the moment strictly as a writer, I wish there were some way in which the men and women who write our screenplays could have an opportunity of working more closely with the men who photograph them. As writers, most of us naturally think largely, if not exclusively, in terms of dramatic situations and dialog. Yet we're writing for what is fundamentally a pictorial medium. The situations and dialog are necessary, Heaven knows, but if we lose sight of the basic pictorial appeal of our medium, we're likely to use a lot of words

From *The American Cinematographer*, December 1941. Reprinted by permission.

John Huston directs his father Walter's cameo appearance in *The Maltese Falcon*, John's first film as a director. Humphrey Bogart and Lee Patrick observe from off-camera at right.

to put over a point or situation which could much more easily be gotten across by visual means.

As a writer, I often wondered why so many changes were made in my scripts between the time they left my typewriter and the time they reached the screen. Now I know! Like most of the rest of us, I simply didn't know how to write for the camera: I sometimes wrote things which, when they reached the set, turned out to be impractical cinematically; at other times, and for the same reason, I'd try to put into words things which could more easily be told in pictured action. Even in the course of directing two pictures I've repeatedly seen a story-minded cameraman like Arthur Edeson, A.S.C., with whom I made my first picture *The Maltese Falcon*, or Ernest Haller, A.S.C., with whom I am now making *In This Our Life*, make suggestions which would by-pass a page or so of dialog at a time, putting over the same idea visually in less footage—and far more effectively.

As a director, I've come to value these suggestions from the cameraman very highly. Of course, I'm still pretty young and new at the business of directing pictures, but I can't conceive of any director who really has the interest of his production at heart ever getting so big and experienced that he could ignore the suggestions that come so naturally from his partner at the camera.

And the man at the camera can be just that—a partner to the director: really a co-director taking full responsibility for the visual side of the production, leaving the director free to concentrate on the actors and their work. That title, "Director of Photography" is a lot more than a mere phrase! It's a very specific definition of the invaluable service the cinematographer can offer to a production—if we'll let him.

What do I mean by the "visual" side of the production—? A lot more, I've found, than merely pictorial composition, high or low-key lighting, and the star's appearance! For example, our scripts today concern themselves largely with dialog, with only a sketchy indication of where a scene is laid, and little, if any indication of camera-angles and business. If you shot a picture solely from the indications given in the script, you'd probably end up with a picture that was 85 or 90% long-shots.

The writers, you see, expect the folks on the set to break a scene up into its component individual angles or (as I think the Russians call them) "cutting pieces." And one of the first things I learned when I started directing was that this isn't nearly as easy as it might sound. You've got to figure out how each shot is to be coordinated with all the other shots that will ultimately make up the sequence, even though the individual, intercut shots may be photographed days apart.

Then there are details to remember—such as, in a series of intercut individual shots of two people talking to each other, keeping the figures on the screen approximately the same size; keeping directions of movement straight, so actors don't get apparently crossed up between one scene and the next; even keeping track of the direction in which a player ought to look at another one offstage so as to keep things flowing naturally on the screen.

My experience has been that a director can do a much better job with cast and story if he'll let his director of photography serve as a virtual co-director, taking almost complete charge of these details. And most directors of photography—at least such men as Edeson and Haller—are glad to do so. They admit it makes them work a good deal harder, but they welcome that because it gives them a chance to contribute more constructively to the production—to do their part to make it visually, as well as verbally and dramatically, outstanding.

Here's the way we've worked it in practice so far. Before we start shooting, the cinematographer and I study the script together, in as much detail as possible. We agree on the basic mood and visual treatment generally. Then as shooting progresses, we work together in perfect partnership. At night, the director of photography takes his script home and analyzes the next day's shooting in terms of visual treatment, just as I study things to prepare myself to handle them dramatically. A chap like Haller, for example, will usually break things down into quick sketches to indicate graphically each scene, angle and set-up.

In the morning, before shooting, we'll check these sketches over together, making sure that our concepts are reasonably well in agreement. Then we'll proceed to carry them out on the screen, each dealing with his own part of the job. Of course we sometimes don't quite agree; then, with fellows like Edeson or Haller, we'll talk it over until between us we find just why the scene should or shouldn't be done that way. For example, sometimes I'll listen to the way Ernie wants to deal with a certain scene, and then in my ignorance I'll ask why it can't be done some other way. To that, he may reply with a good, logical reason based on his many years of experience making all kinds of pictures—or we may find we've accidentally hit on something a bit new and useful. In any event, the picture is a lot better for that sort of cooperation.

Frankly, I think the general run of our pictures—"A" productions, anyway—would be immensely benefited if they could have the advantage of the cinematographer's picture-trained brain participating in the final stages of scripting, as well as on the set. Whether you agree with Orson Welles' concept or not, most of us are agreed that *Citizen Kane* was in every way a remarkable achievement in cine-storytelling: and I don't think it is in any way detracting from Welles' acknowledged brilliance as a producer-director to point out that he made full use of the capabilities of Gregg Toland, A.S.C., by having his director of photography work closely with him during the last eight or ten weeks of preparing the production, and then gave him a very free hand in guiding the visual side of the picture during the shooting. Without that, it is very safe to say that *Citizen Kane* would not have been so arrestingly cinematic.

That sort of pre-production cooperation would pay dollars-and-cents dividends, too. I'm sure it would cut down measurably on "protection-shots," set-construction, and the like. I've already learned that if you only give him a chance to make the suggestion soon enough, a skilled cinematographer can show you how to suggest things with the camera, rather than having to build them in expensively literal sets. For example, one of the biggest-appearing scenes in *Kane* was, if you'll analyze it, suggested by simply using a huge fireplace, a massive staircase—and an imaginative camera.

Often, too, in writing or preparing a script, we'll note down this scene or that sequence as "process," and mark it for the attention of the special-effects staff. Actually, it might be more efficient to film that action by straightforward methods—and other scenes we've completely overlooked could be done much more economically as process-shots! The cinematographer's unique grasp of both technique and production methods, if called into consultation earlier, could undoubtedly save us a good many more or less costly mistakes along these lines.

The ideal system, I'd say, would be to have the director, the director of photography and the scenarist work closely together as the script is put into final shape for shooting, sketching out each angle and set-up as they went along, until they finally reached the shooting stage with a script combining words and sketches to make a genuine blueprint of the completed production. In that way, I am sure, we could save on set-construction, save on shooting-time, save on normally over-shot footage and "protection-shots," and turn out a production that was dramatically and visually more coherent, doing it much more easily and surely because of taking the real picture-mind of the cinematographer into full partnership.

ROBERT ROSSEN
(1908-1966)

Born and raised on New York's Lower East Side, Robert Rossen had been associated with the Washington Square Players, the Workers' School and similar left-of-center theatre groups, with whom he served as writer and director. He came to Hollywood under contract to Warner's in 1936, and for the next seven years wrote for them some of the key "socially significant" films of the period, including *Marked Woman, They Won't Forget, Dust Be My Destiny* and *The Roaring Twenties*. During this period he became a member of the Communist Party, and in 1943 he served as chairman of the Hollywood Writers' Mobilization. Rossen spent a year in New York in 1944, rethinking his political beliefs and ultimately deciding to break his ties with the Party, with which he disagreed on mainly procedural grounds. The changing attitudes on screen characterization expressed here mirror in almost transparent fashion his personal political beliefs. Post-war scripts must avoid the down-beat quality of the 30's and instead offer positive and socially constructive moral values, Rossen insists. *A Walk in the Sun* proved a significant reflection of this, but *The Strange Love of Martha Ivers* was certainly as hopeless as any of Rossen's pre-war scripts. In 1947 he directed his first film, *Johnny O'Clock*, followed by *Body and Soul* and *All the King's Men*, films of increasing popular and critical acclaim. At this point Rossen finally ran afoul of the House Un-American Activities Committee, giving testimony which satisfied neither the committee nor his ex-Party associates. He was blacklisted until he returned with a list of names two years later.

NEW CHARACTERS
FOR THE SCREEN
ROBERT ROSSEN

Several weeks ago I had lunch with a friend of mine—a very well known and successful screen writer. He is now an officer in the Army and has for the past year or so done nothing but training and introduction films. This man was known in the industry as the slickest of the slick and the quickest of the quick. His pictures were smooth, breezy, and entertaining—technically, they were beyond reproach. His characterizations were sharp—his dialogue easy on the ear. I can think of no one who could take the familiar and make you like it better than he could. He was the boy who wrote and talked like Forty-seventh Street and Broadway.

For several years there had been a good-natured feud between us—he had always accused me of being what he termed "a socially significant Joe," a writer who was trying to bat his head against a stone wall in a setup forever grooved a certain way.

Now, this man after a year in the Army, leaned over to me and said, "Rossen, you're a dead duck. After this war is over, writers who remain in Hollywood won't have a chance." I asked him what he meant. "It's simple," he said. "You think pictures are going to stay in a groove. Well they're not—they're going to change. If you think an audience is going to accept the kind of pap you screen writers have been dishing out—quick, slick, breezy stuff that's a carbon copy of every other picture ever made—you're crazy. If you think they're going to accept characters as phony as a quarter watch you're even crazier."

I asked him why he had changed his point of view. "I've been dealing with real stuff," he said. "When an actor sweats in one of our pictures, no makeup man sprays it on him—he really

From *New Masses*, January 18, 1944.

Robert Rossen (left) directing Mel Ferrer and Miroslava in *The Brave Bulls* (1951).

sweats. When I have to write a line of dialogue, which in pictures could never get past the gateman, let alone the Hays Office, I write it and the actor says it and the boys who sit in and watch it love it—because it's real and because it's the way they speak and the way they act and the way they think. And so far as phony plot is concerned—well try and think of one to put into a picture of the operation of a tank or how to dig a foxhole."

"That," I said, "is a specialized kind of picture. After the war—"

He interrupted me. "After the war," he said, "these boys and their families are your audiences. Two things have happened to them. The first is that they've been dealing with too much reality to be taken in by what we think is reality. The second is that they've gotten to know more people than they ever knew before, and to know more about them; and what's more important, you can't sell them on the idea that you have to be a special kind of guy to be a hero; you know, the kind of heroes we've always been writing—handsome, tall and cool—special people. They will have seen too many ordinary people become heroes. And very few of them will be handsome, tall, and cool; they'll be all sizes and shapes and they won't be cool at all. They'll be mad and sweaty and dirty. And the gals they meet and know—they'll be different too. They'll have done stretches in war plants, in the Army, in the Navy—for the first time these gals won't be the little woman nobly sacrificing the boy to his career, or vice versa. There'll be a career for both of them and the question of giving up one for the other will be as old-fashioned as Aunt Harriet's hat. And it's these kinds of people that you're going to have to write about in pictures, whether it's comedy, drama, or cartoons—it's the kind of actors that look like these people that are going to pack them in."

He went on: "Take a trip to any Army camp. I've been to nearly all of them, including several overseas, and I've watched the boys and listened to them during and after a picture show-ing. This is what they want and this is what they're going to get—and if writers like *you*," and he pointed an accusing finger at me, "can't give it to them, writers like *me*," and he thumped his chest, "will." With that he got up and left, and I watched him go. This quick, slick, breezy boy, who a year ago had called me "socially significant Joe," and to tell you the truth I began to worry.

I have been writing pictures for almost eight years. In those eight years I've had problems, just as we've all had, but none of them has ever been beyond solution. Now I find myself working on a picture that is, in a sense, the same kind of picture that I've written before. It's about the same people I've written of before, pretty much the same strata of society—people I've lived with most of my life. Specifically, it's a study of a certain section of American life that's been affected most by the im-pact of the war, a home front picture. And yet frankly, I've never had more difficulty in writing anything. I thought when I started this picture that I knew what it was I wanted to say about these people. But when I began to write it, I found that I could never really find the characters and situations that would illustrate it, at least so that an audience of today would believe or identify themselves with it. The story always kept going downhill—it had no finish, no pull in it, no one or nothing to root for. Then I tried all sorts of *technical* approaches, ways of telling the story, to pick it up. None of them worked.

In the past, most of us when we hit a situation like this called the research department and asked them to dig up all the material they could on a particular subject. Now, I think, something new is happening in this industry and will happen more and more. We're beginning to deal with subjects on which there is no research—it's all brand new material. And we're beginning to deal with characters for whom there are no precedents. For example, there were no women in war plants several years ago.

A writer is now forced to go out into the field for this material and the studios are forced to send him if they expect to get any kind of authenticity in their pictures—authenticity that goes beyond mere decoration.

Here is what happened on this picture. I was forced to go out into the field actually to see and talk to the people about whom I was writing. After several weeks of this kind of research, I think I discovered why the story couldn't come off, and the reason for it was that I hadn't recognized the change that had occurred in the characters I had been used to writing.

For instance, a sullen, bewildered little man who rebelled against society. Or a man who had been in the last war and who is convinced that everything is a racket and goes into bootlegging. For instance, the girl who wants nothing in life so much as one last fling, a trip to Havana with the villain, and then to settle down with the man she doesn't love. And, the old philosophical gent who sits on park benches or tenement roofs and spends several reels talking about the futility of life. All of these characters form a pattern. A pattern of despair and defeat.

And it isn't that these characters weren't true and didn't represent reality at a given time. It is that they are no longer true, and that their attitudes are no longer valid, for society has so changed them that they don't behave in the same patterns any more.

The man who used to be sullen and bewildered knows much more about what is going on and he's more and more convinced that he can handle whatever comes his way. He's no longer hopping freight trains or going from jail to jail and being classified as a vagrant. He's too important now. This country needs him. There's a place for him, and he has a sense of his own importance. He has pride now and courage and a belief that he and a lot of other people like him are going to work it out.

The man who's been in the last war is no longer a useless member of society who's forced to go into some sort of racket. The knowledge and skill that he gained are now of some use in this war—he, too, has found a place.

As for the girl, she can afford to pay for her own trip to Havana—if and when she can take it. And as far as the old, philosophical gent is concerned—he's working. The same, I'm sure, is true of people in all classes of society. They have, in a sense, come out of the bewilderment and confusion that beset them and are now taking an affirmative view.

Instead of a pattern of despair I found one of confidence and of hope. Instead of people turning their eyes away from the future they looked at it steadfastly and felt that it belonged to them. I'm not trying to be Pollyannaish about this. I'm not trying to say that all's lightness and sweet—what I'm trying to say is that people have found dignity, they've appraised its worth, and they'll live for it or die for it. And if you think these are words, talk to the waiter who used to bow and scrape; talk to a bus driver; talk to a guy who works in a plant; get a load of a kid of seventeen who's been sent to a forestry camp for juvenile delinquency; watch that kid when they give him a sense of participation in the war—fighting brush fires, picking the crops. Yes, go further, talk to the Okies whom Steinbeck wrote about in *Grapes of Wrath*—the bitter, sullen Okies, the defeated ones. I have. And it's old hat, my friends. They're working in war plants and they haven't got a sense of movin' on any more. They've got a sense of belonging, *wherever* they are, and a powerful sense of knowing that the dark days are over—the hopeless days. And that's what you get wherever you go—a feeling that things are going to be right, a faith, a belief, a hope.

Learning this point of view not only changed my point of view on the characters. That change made me write a different kind of story—that change made me find different situations. What started out to be an exposé story of corrupt, evil forces crushing men and women turned out to be a story of a group of people who were going to win despite any condition. Instead of a negative, downhill story, I found myself with a story that was positive, that raced along, uphill—a story with all the qualities of what we've come to know as good entertainment, a story with a pull, someone to root for. And that's always been a good story, hasn't it? Even the form was a cinch. It could only be told a certain way, the simple way.

I'm not trying to say that this story is going to set the world on fire. That's beside the point. What I'm trying to show is how a point of view on character can change both story and form—why I think this particular point of view is right is because I believe that's the way people are today. And I think the facts, objective facts about the American scene today, justify that belief.

However, I don't think it's enough just to know that people are different. You can read about that in a book. What I think is important for the writer is to understand *why* people are different. And I think that when the writer begins to understand this he has the key to the whole problem, not in terms of politics, but in terms of his own craft, in terms of making himself a better writer. And he must be a better writer because only through this understanding is he able to articulate what people are really thinking and feeling, and if he is able to do this, then he is that much closer to his audience.

I think our greatest difficulty as writers up to now has been to get ourselves to believe that this change has really occurred. We've been so steeped in the cynicism of the last twenty years that we find it hard to think of characters such as the ones I've been talking about in any other terms but people who must be crushed by destructive social forces.

We're still thinking in terms of the last war and not in terms of this war. We're still afraid of being betrayed and that fear goes deep. We've been sick, and this has reflected itself in everything that's been written in the last twenty years. Our stories have been stories of frustration, of defeat—our characters have always gone down to their doom. Our historical approach to stories of America has been the debunking one—all our heroes had feet of clay, and if they didn't they weren't worth writing about.

Well, the average man sees and feels the basic difference between this and the last war, and we can't write him unless we see him and feel and believe with him.

Right here in this town, in Hollywood, I've heard writers say, when Hitler first over-ran France and the low countries, that the machine had finally triumphed and that since Hitler controlled the machines of destruction, the people, even though they wanted to resist, had absolutely no chance, and that they would accept this as a reality and submit to their fate. But the people did resist and the lie was given to this theory by history. They resisted so well that the part that their resistance played is paying off right now in the terms of our coming victory. And out of this resistance a new kind of hero was born. This hero has been around for a long time—he was in China, in Spain, in France, in Yugoslavia, in Russia, in all the countries of the world where free men wouldn't bend their necks. He's a hero, in America, and he's been here for a long time, too. He's all over, waiting for us to write him, and if we are to survive as writers, if we're not to be what my friend calls "dead pigeons," we've got to put this hero on the screen.

NICK GRINDE
(1894-   )

B-pictures were the underside of the rock in Hollywood, but in the years before television no studio was above producing them. Poverty Row operations like Mascot and Monogram existed *only* for the production of Bs (and that related phenomenon, the serial), while even Fox and MGM maintained substantial B-production units. Sometimes the filmmakers involved would be on their way down, others hopefully on the make for better assignments. A number enjoyed long careers as B-picture specialists, and Nick Grinde was one of these. Originally an assistant director at MGM, Nick Grinde began directing Bs for that studio in 1927. When sound arrived he was sent east to direct novelty shorts, then returned to direct features for MGM, Mascot, Universal and others. His many films included *The Bishop Murder Case*, *White Bondage*, *Hitler*, *Dead or Alive* and *Road to Alcatraz*. Like many B-picture specialists, when television arrived he slipped comfortably into production for that medium, feeling right at home with TV-sized budgets and shooting schedules. Grinde's analysis of the B-picture world is remarkably objective, yet laced with the sort of humor apparently necessary for success in the field. Particularly interesting is his plea for a double critical standard for As and Bs, based on the production exigencies he outlines here. It is remarkable how many critics were never able to make this simple adjustment, and throughout their careers dismissed the less pretentious work of many able directors merely because the budgets were not up to standard—hardly the most sophisticated of critical yardsticks.

PICTURES FOR PEANUTS
NICK GRINDE

Over on Stage 6 a million-dollar picture is starting this morning. The call was for nine o'clock. It's ten-thirty already, and with a little well-placed optimism you could say that the epic is beginning to show promise of getting under way. A lot of departments with a whale of a lot of mighty fine technical abilities have been working for weeks towards this very day.

Propmen, grips, gaffers, electricians, boom men, recorders, mixers, cameramen, assistant cameramen, a script clerk overflowing her rose-coloured slacks, a company clerk, an assistant director, his assistant and his assistant are functioning with the occupational movements that will find each one ready when the moment finally comes to record the suspensive scene where Nancy says, "I am tired of wearing other people's clothes. From now on I will wear my own or nothing!"

This confused efficiency, laced, of course, with a fine sense of self-preservation, is going on all unnoticed round, above and in between the associate producer and the director, who already are trying to see who can stay calm the longer. The pattern is familiar to everyone. Too much has been written about the habitat of the colossal picture for anyone to have escaped a willing or unwilling education on the subject.

But over on Stage 3 in this same studio another picture was scheduled to start this morning at eight-thirty. It's ten-thirty over there, too, and they have exactly two hours' work under their belts. There are no press agents or fan-magazine writers hovering around. No newspaper columnists are harvesting their succulent crop. You'd think it said "Contagious" on the door instead of "Quiet, Please! Shooting!"

The difference is that this is just another little picture. A *B* picture, if you please. *B* standing for Bread and Butter, or But-

From *The Penguin Film Review*, no. 1, August 1946. Reprinted by permission of Nick Grinde.

Nick Grinde as he looked while director of Tim McCoy films for M-G-M.

tons, or Bottom Budget. And standing for nearly anything else anyone wants to throw at it. But it's a robust little mongrel and doesn't mind the slurs, because it was weaned on them. If the trade papers give a *B* the nod at all, they usually sum up their comments by saying it will be good for Duals and Nabes, which is why you'll find them on a double bill in the neigh-bourhood theatres.

A *B* picture isn't a big picture that just didn't grow up; it's exactly what it started out to be. It's the twenty-two-dollar suit of the clothing business, it's the hamburger of the butchers' shops, it's a seat in the bleachers. And there's a big market for *all* of them.

Only by perpetual corner cutting can these often quite presentable cheaper pictures be made to show the profit that is so very agreeable to the studios which invested their money in them.

Like the less expensive suit of clothes, the cloth from which they are fabricated is not all wool, the buttonholes are machine made and the buttons themselves are more or less synthetic. But when you are all through, you have a suit or a picture which goes right out into the market with its big brothers and gives pretty good service at that. The trick is to judge them in their class and not by *A* standards.

In the finer pictures, results are all that are aimed at, let the costs fall where they may. The best possible actors are hired to articulate the finest lines the top writers can conjure up. And the best directors mount the stories in convincing and appro-priate settings. Of course, occasionally somebody's aim is a little off, but that's beside the point.

In making a programme picture, all this is different. Cheaper raw materials are used and a more thrifty approach is indicated. No expensive best seller or Broadway play is bought. That's out; it's not even thought about. The whole picture will be made for much less than the cost of such a property. The story used will be an original submitted by one of the free-lance writers who knows just what and whom he is slanting it for. Or it may be a magazine story from one of the pulps or a fif-teen-minute radio programme purchased for its basic idea or twist. These properties are then blown up into script form and length by a writer who either works at the studio already or is brought in for the job. If he gets six weeks' work out of it, he's lucky. If he takes much more, he had better buy bonds with the money, because he won't be back very soon.

There are all kinds of ways of writing a story besides good and poor. It can be written up or written down. It can be costly to produce or slanted on the frugal side. If the cast of characters can't be held down in numbers, it's the wrong story for limited money. And if they can't be kept out of busy places like night clubs, railroad depots and football games, look out for the budget.

Basic emotions can happen in a quiet place as well as at the Stork Club. If John and Peggy are cast in modest circumstances, they can wear their own wardrobe, and a set suitable for their home can be found already standing somewhere in the studio. It's easy when you get the knack of it. Then, instead of taking her to a bustling restaurant for lunch and having some costly busybodies come by and tell them about the murder, they can be discovered coming out of the restaurant and shutting the door on all that expense. A reasonably priced newsboy can sell them a newspaper, so they can read all about the homicide. John's reaction to the bumping-off of his best friend will be of the same fine stuff out here on the sidewalk as it would have been over a crêpe suzette.

John, being who he is, naturally has to catch up with the rat who did it before the police do. There's a matter of a good name and a hunk of money involved. But does John's search take him to crowded bars, well-filled hotel lobbies, busy downtown streets, bus stops and other gregarious rendezvous? Not by two budgets. He interviews a rooming-house proprietor who lives in a little standing set at the edge of town, and who is home alone at the moment. Then he talks to a milkman in front of a brownstone set on the old New York street. The milk wagon really isn't expensive when you consider that it hides a big hole in the front of the house where some gangsters dynamited their way out in the second episode of a serial last week.

When John finally gets into the chase at the end of the picture, does he search the affluent Union League club, or a museum, or the zoo? You guessed it, cousin, the scene is shot in an alley with three cops and some dandy shadows. And if it's done properly, it can be plenty thrilling, even if it is mounted in cut-rate atmosphere.

There are comparatively inexpensive ways of larding a story with a semblance of size and scope just waiting for the resourceful producer. One such fellow is a whiz at using stock shots from newsreels or any other fertile source. Whenever a building is blown up, or a bridge blows down, or a forest burns, or a strike riot breaks out, the chances are that someone is right there making a movie of it. If the stuff is good, this producer will buy a batch, paying for it by the foot, and have a whole story written around it or at least an important sequence. If you have a real forest fire to cut to, you can do wonders with a little cabin, a few trees, a wind machine, sun-dry lycopodium torches, and a batch of smoke pots. And you will have avoided the spending of up to a hundred thousand dollars or more. If you're lucky and things work out right, you can make quite a dent in your picture right here, and you'll probably come out with a climax that will bring a pleasant look from the front office. If you're real careful and have the wind blowing from the same direction as the wind blew in the original film and watch your smoke density, the real and the staged films will cut together like well-hung wallpaper.

Other stock footages that have inspired important sequences are those of train wrecks, rodeos, the rescue of downed aviators, shipwrecks, kidnap manhunts and even baby shows. You may not end up with the story you started out to make, but look at the wallop your detour gave you. And you can always salvage the abandoned sequences in another plot.

One studio struck oil by buying foreign films that had great scenic values and plenty of long shots. These films were bought outright, negatives and all. Then a new story was written around these long shots and American actors hired to play the few reels needed to go with the salvaged scenery. The only demand on the refurbished plot was that the writers had to dream up excuses for their characters to go through the same scenic exteriors in the same groupings and dressed exactly the same as in the original. In that way, all the picturesque entrances and exits could be retained. Shooting the outdoor close-

ups and the interior sets for the new version was a routine matter, quickly done. But the total result was very dressy indeed,
thanks to the Swiss Alps shot by somebody else and bought for
peanuts.

Another sleight-of-hand trick that's used every day in the B-
hives is the so-called montage. That's a series of quick cuts of
film borrowed from earlier pictures. It's the Lend-Lease of the
studios. Whatever the subject, there is always film available
from some other fellow's picture that will add otherwise prohibitive flavour to a sequence.

Say it's a gangster film. Tony and his mob have been ter-
rorising the city for months. You can't shoot a first-class crime
wave on short dough, so you borrow or buy about twenty
pieces of thrilling moments from twenty forgotten pictures. A
fleeing limousine skids into a street-car, a pedestrian is socked
over the head in an alley, a newspaper office is wrecked by
hoodlums, a bomb is thrown into a dry-cleaning truck, a
woman screams, a couple of mugs are slapping a little merchant
into seeing things their way. And so on until we end up on a
really big explosion. All this, garnished with sound effects and
crescendo orchestration, dissolves through to three serious-
looking actors in a standing set. One of the men says, "This
city has got to be cleaned up. Tony and his mob have got to
go." And this is Scene I in the script which will be shot on
Stage 3.

Montages can take care of World War I or II, a cross-country journey, a college education, a rise from poverty to riches
or anything else too expensive in time and money to photograph. Often the determined face of the leading man is super-
imposed over this potpouri to remind you it is he who is having
all these experiences. Of course, he'll never know how he suffered until he sees the preview.

One producer fell in love with a reel of train wheels. Somebody shot too much of a speeding train one day. Probably the
wind on the handcar which was following the engine's underpin-
ning with the camera was so strong that the cameraman couldn't
hear the command to cut. Or something. Anyway, here was

all that lovely footage of train wheels going somewhere.

The producer never really rested right until he found a story where the characters pursued one another from city to city. Every time Joe thought he was being shadowed he got that don't-fence-me-in-look on his face, and they dissolved to a hunk of money-saving train wheels. Then, of course, the detective, who either had to get a clue or end the story right there, got his portion of the wheels, and we knew that he was right after Joe again. So they chased from city to city, using up more and more train wheels, until the picture ended up in a draw between moving drama and galloping wheels.

Stock stuff is not the only thing that is borrowed. Plots are hijacked in broad daylight. The fellows who make the dehydrated films are the most consistent disciples of the biggies. Gold isn't the only thing that's where you find it. If the brand on a cow can be changed with a hot iron, the earmarks of a situation can be camouflaged with a typewriter.

One of the most comforting things about plot lifting is that there are no new plots, and the fellows you raid have no doubt had their own little forays into the published works of even earlier shanghaiers. Plagiarism is a nasty word, but only for amateurs.

Several years ago, a major studio made an all-star picture with a costly scenario wherein a character who was a whaler by trade and went on long trips to sea, as whalers do, was double-crossed during his absences by a landlubber. Things went on like this for a while, until one day the whaler had his leg bitten off by a shark, who got into the picture somehow. Well, the wife wasn't so much of a heel that she could let him down in his hour of need. So she nursed him, but during his convalescence he could see which way the prevailing wind was blowing. All of which made for quite a neat triangle.

Several years later, a producer at the same studio needed a story, but had very little money allowed him with which to get it. He remembered the whale picture, and also realised that it was all paid for. So he told one of his writers how to retread the plot. At the preview of this reclaimed yarn, a lion tamer was being double-crossed by a tightrope walker every time he went in the cage for his act. He suspected it a little, which made him careless, and the lion bit his leg off. Well, the wife wasn't so much of a heel that she could let him down in his hour of need. So she nursed—— See how it's done?

A beautiful set built for one of the more affluent productions has a pull like gravity to the fellow with the short moneybags. He haunts the side lines, drooling while the aristocrats shoot their leisurely schedule. Then he collars the big boss for permission to get his cast in there for just a few hours. The answer is no, of course. It always is at first.

He explains that the way he will shoot it no one will recognize it for the same set. He'll have his director pick new angles and re-dress the foreground. His picture is all action anyway, so it will feel like a different place entirely and it won't conflict a bit with the *A* picture; he'll underwrite that. And what a production lift it will give his otherwise barren little efforts. It will save it! He will even agree to shoot at night while the rightful occupants sleep. He'll be in and out, and they'll never know it.

As soon as he has gained his point, he calls the assistant director from his picture and instructs him to change the schedule to accommodate the plucking of this nocturnal plum. Then he drops in on his writers, who are now busy dreaming up a new script and who have already completely forgotten the one now shooting. He tells them to drop everything for an hour or two and whip up a night's work in this set, which will involve the principals and maybe up to ten or twelve extras, but no more. They point out that there is no conceivable way in which the characters of this yarn could find themselves in such a lavish set. The producer asks them who is paying their salaries, and would they just go down and take a look at the set, and hurry and write something and not be so touchy. There are at least a thousand reasons why the characters could find themselves in that set. All he asks them to think of is one—but by to-morrow night.

Of course, eventually the results of all this nomadic scheming are dumped into the busy lap of the director. It is he who is expected to manipulate these assorted ingredients into a pre-

sentable theatrical offering in what, with practically no under-
statement, might be called no time at all. The *B* director has to
know more tricks than Harry Houdini did, and he has to pull
them out of his hat right now—not after lunch. He has to know
a lot about making pictures and be able to toss that knowledge
at a situation and hope that some of it will stick. He doesn't
have time to do any one thing quite as well as he would like to,
because he can't stop and do just that one thing. He is, for the
moment, a juggler, and must keep his eye on all the Indian
clubs.

The scene to be shot is on the process stage. That, as you
probably know, is where they put scenery from somewhere
else behind you and make you look as though you'd been there
—a handy gadget if there ever was one. The set in front of the
process screen is a Pullman drawing-room. Outside of the
train windows will appear, on command, the retreating countryside of Ohio—Can No. 76, Train Backgrounds; Right to
Left; Please Return to Vault. In the scene will be the leading
man and the leading lady and the Pullman porter, who is to
bring them a telegram. It's a short scene and won't take long to
shoot. Already the assistant from another company is sticking
his nose in to see if shooting is progressing, as his company is
scheduled to use this same process background screen in an hour
from now. Only when his company arrives it will be Times
Square which blossoms behind his heavies and the comic—
Can No. 31, New York Streets; Daytime; Stationary; Please
Return to Vault.

Assistant No. 1 tells Assistant No. 2 that everything will be
on schedule somehow. It always is. The only slight drawback
is the fact that the coloured actor who is to play the part of
the Pullman porter is conspicuously not there yet. Seems he
has been contacted, though, and is even now arranging with a
friend of his to pick him up where his car broke down and
hurry him to the waiting train fragment. While the assistants
are still talking, the director, long since indoctrinated to abhor
a time vacuum, is having the leading man's right hand black-
ened. Then, with the porter's white coat on, it will be his hand
that is photographed knocking on the drawing-room door. In

the hand will be the telegram, and the shot will tell us visually
that a porter has a telegram for the occupants of Room B. The
shot will be even more effective than seeing the porter approach the door in a long shot as it was written, and, of course,
it keeps the company working, which is what those precious
fleeting moments were made for in the first place.

When this shot is finished the leading man will resume his
original identity, and if the overdue Thespian is still not there,
he will be photographed in his individual close-up receiving
the telegram from the supposedly off-screen porter, and will
answer his unspoken questions. By that time the missing actor
will surely have arrived and the necessary three-shot of the
group will be made, and it will all come out just as though it
had been planned to be shot backward in the first place,
whereas the only thing that had been planned for sure was to
shoot, period. One director returned from a three-day location
trip with the full confidence that a New York penthouse
would be awaiting his directorial efforts. His script called for
a refined high-society argument, followed by the blackmailer's
accidental crash through the penthouse window to the street
far below. All of which led quite logically to a big courtroom
scene which was to be the high spot of the picture.

It had been agreed to spread a bit and to spend a respectable
part of the construction money on this particular set and really
make something nice out of it. But in the director's absence it
seems that, just as work was about to start on the building of
the penthouse set, the producer stumbled on a very charming
garden pergola and a bright idea at the same time. The structure was set amid potted foliage and real grass mats, and had
been used for an idyllic love scene in a recent Viennese picture.
Why couldn't the accident happen in the arbour of a pseudo-
Long-Island estate instead of on the rooftop of a downtown
building? A trifling detail, but a thrifty one. The switch was
ordered immediately.

When the director heard about what they had done to him
behind his back, he went into a condensed tantrum. By training and instinct he knew he had to hit his fury fast. He knew
he was entitled to anger, wrath and indignation, and he also

knew that if he took too long about it, he'd have a hard time getting back on schedule. So he pulled out all his emotional stops and inquired why, while they were at it, they hadn't switched him to an igloo or a tepee. How, he demanded, could you plunge a man down to his death from the French window of a garden bower?

So, a couple of minutes later, when he started work, a gun was slipped into the struggle, and when the actors had choked all the dialogue out of each other, the darn thing went off, and everyone except the victim, who was now comfortably off the pay roll, turned up in the courtroom as per plan.

Another corner-chopping expedient is premised on the different rates of pay for bit actors, depending on whether or not they speak. A bell-boy, for instance, who is not playing a part, but who is just in for the day to take someone's bags to the elevator, will get $16.50 if he remains silent. But this is boosted to $25.00 if he articulates so much as a "Yes, sir" or "Thank you, sir." Nine times out of ten it's awkward to keep him silent, but that's how close these budgets are pruned. The actor says, "Take my bags to my room. I'll go up later." The bell-boy nods silently and exits. Eight-fifty saved. Or the lady asks where the phone booths are. The bell-boy points mutely, and the lady says, "Oh, thank you," and the bell-boy wishes he could have said it. It makes the hotel help look mighty surly, to say the least, but the silent bell-boy is here to stay.

One director, who shall be nameless, but whom we'll call Nick, was given a $16.50-bit man who had so much to pantomime that he and everyone else ran out of ideas for suitable gestures. Nods, points, shrugs, smiles and scowls were all tossed to the camera, but there was still more plot and still the order to keep him frugally inaudible. So, like always, something had to be done. He was finally played as a character with laryngitis, and wrote his answers on slips of paper, which were then photographed and cut into the film. The part came out as a nice thrifty novelty.

So by shaving the corners of already clipped corners, by shooting backward and sideways to make budgets and salaries come out even, by re-dressing and doubling the same set three or four times, by shooting only the absolutely necessary footage, by concentrating on speed and novelty and plot pattern rather than on time-consuming characterisations and penetrating emotional studies, you can make a picture that may never get the Academy award, but will, however, have a healthy career and earn money.

Not all *A* pictures are good, any more than all *B* pictures are poor. You can get ptomaine at the classiest hotel and you can get a good steak in a dog wagon. Both kinds of pictures can learn something from the other. To-day, with continuing manpower and raw-material shortages, it wouldn't be a bad idea at all if the super-supers would funnel a bigger percentage of their efforts on to the screen and not on extracurricular waste motions.

By the same token, the quickies, which have brought the efficiency of getting their money's worth down to a microscopic point, could improve their standing in the community if they would apply the same efficient diligence to seeing that their scenario material was a bit more honest. Fast cutting may hide a weak point in the script, but there is a ceiling on fast cutting. Unlike the V-2 bomb, it mustn't go faster than sound—you guess why. So the best thing to do is to tighten up the story points with the same sure hand that whittles the budgets.

A bookkeeper hopped up on a stool in the studio lunchroom next to a director a couple of days after he had finished making a fast detective yarn.

The double-entry fellow said, "Say, your picture came out swell."

The director, being human, rumours to the contrary, was delighted, and said, "Oh, have you seen it? The cutter told me it wouldn't be ready till to-morrow."

The answer was, "No, I haven't seen it. I mean you brought it in a day under schedule and nicely under the budget. Boy, you did a fine job!" Unfortunately, none of this praise comes under the heading of entertainment. When the picture gets to the theatres, its penny-pinching undergarments had best be covered by lace of amusement, or some rude patron of the drama will say, "Your slip is showing."

IRVING PICHEL
(1891-1954)

One of the more obscure directors represented here, Irving Pichel is not mentioned in either Sadoul's *Dictionnaire des Cinéastes* or the *Oxford Companion to Film*. Yet on his death in 1954 he received a lengthy tribute in the formidable *Quarterly of Film, Radio and Television* from such friends as Dudley Nichols and Josef von Sternberg, praising his long career as writer, director, actor and teacher. This is one of Pichel's numerous articles written for the *Hollywood Quarterly* (a forerunner of *QFRTV* and *Film Quarterly*) and is typical of his thoughtful examination of such topics as the relationship between screen acting and directing, the problem of film authorship, and the nature of the cinematographic image. Few Hollywood directors were as analytical as Pichel, yet the surprising perceptions which run through his published articles never seemed very apparent in the films he directed. A graduate of Harvard who had served on the advisory board of the Theatre Guild, Pichel first worked in Hollywood as a writer, then appeared as an actor in generally sinister roles (*The Cheat, The Story of Temple Drake, Dracula's Daughter*). He was co-director on Schoedsack and Cooper's *The Most Dangerous Game* and *She,* and solo director of such films as *They Won't Believe Me, Mr. Peabody and the Mermaid* and *Destination Moon,* films which were never less than competent, but lacked much sense of their director's personality. His identification here of cutting and camera movement as aspects of the same phenomena was generally shared in Hollywood, although few directors bothered to analyze this in the terms Pichel chooses.

SEEING WITH THE CAMERA
IRVING PICHEL

I

It is typical of all forms of spectacle before the motion picture
—the theater, the circus, the sports field—that the spectator remains in a fixed position at a determined distance from the action he sees. The spectator at a football game watches the
movement of the two teams in relation to their respective goal-
posts. The goals remain at fixed distances from him. Only the
players move. The spectator participates in their movement in
so far as he turns his head to follow that movement. His mind
participates in that movement as it estimates the distance of the
moving players from the goal toward which they move.
Knowing the rules of the game, this distance has significance
for him. Assuming that he is concerned with the fortunes of
one of the opposing teams, the lessening distance between the
players and a goal induces excitement which may produce
sympathetic movement on his part. He may jump to his feet,
wave his arms, shout, cheer, or groan.

A newsreel photographer high above the field might photograph a game with so comprehensive a shot that both goals
would be simultaneously visible. For parts of the game, as
when the teams run the length of the field, only such a viewpoint is adequate to convey the significance of the play. However, from this distance the players appear so small that details
of the action cannot be seen, players cannot be identified, and
the ball is invisible. The cameraman, therefore, after a time,
moves closer or changes the lens on his camera. More detail can
now be seen, but his shot includes only half the field. Since the
players are all at that end of the field, approaching one of the
goals, this is a much more satisfactory viewpoint. In moving

Irving Pichel in costume for an extra role during the shooting of his *Miracle of the Bells* (1947).

his camera he has, in effect, moved the spectator. When the newsreel is shown in the theater, the first comprehensive shot will be followed by the closer shot. Though the action will be continuous, the viewpoint of the spectator will change instantaneously. Then, as a player runs with the ball toward the far end of the field, the camera viewpoint will shift again to the more distant position so that the larger sweep of play can be seen and the significant relationship of players to distant goal be realized and measurable.

Changing the position of the camera during action to a closer position without any apparent interruption in the continuous flow of the spectacle was the first technical advance that was to make of motion pictures a new and unique form of visual experience. The fixed relationship between spectator and spectacle was broken down. The action could be brought closer or moved away, or, stated conversely, the spectator could have every sensation of moving closer except that of motility.

It will be noted that this instant change of viewpoint to one more advantageous occurs, in a projected film, not in the action pictured, nor in the actual position of a person watching the film, but in the film itself. This is *movement,* though not action. As the screen play developed, this filmic movement was to take many forms: the abridged movement implied in the cuts from shot to shot—from long shot forward to medium shot, and still nearer to a close shot; the movement of point of view from one character in a group scene to another, and the much greater movements implied in cuts from one locale to another.

The convention which asked an audience to take for granted these instantaneous changes of viewpoint was easy to establish, since, first, it exploited in a larger sense fundamental film characteristics of movement, and, secondly, because it represented not too inaccurately the operation of the spectator's imagination. This structural motion in film objectifies fairly closely the manner in which the eye seeks out of any occurrence or spectacle the most interesting person or action and follows it to the exclusion of other elements presented at the same time. It operates as the mind does when one reads a story, visualizing with the author's account the actions now of one character and now of another, the events now in one place and now in another, the observing of large panoramas and then of minute details. It also objectifies magically, as no other medium can, the wish to be able to come closer, to see more clearly and intimately than life or the earlier forms of theater art have allowed.

Let us return for a moment to our football game. We shall assume that the cameraman is in the closer position, his lens covering only half the field. Through the finder he sees a player start with the ball on a run down the field to the farther goal. He swings his camera, following the runner, exactly as a spectator turns his head to watch the play. Instead of an *instantaneous* move to a viewpoint from which the action can be seen, there is a movement *simultaneous* with the action. The movement, timed with the action, occurs not in the film but in the seeing organ, the eye, the camera.

With the development of screen technique, camera movement has been elaborated. Mounted on wheels, the camera can precede or follow a character. Set on a crane, it can be lifted high above the action. It can recede from a detail to a full shot or, conversely, move from a full shot into a close-up of a single character selected out of the scene. Camera movement, it will be noted, takes place at a much slower tempo than filmic movement and has a different aim. Its rate is related either to that of the spectator's eye, or to that of a moving person or object as the spectator's eye follows that movement in the scene being filmed. Its aim likewise is twofold. It seeks either to imitate the eye movement the spectator would perform if he were present at the scene being photographed, as in most "pan" shots, or it undertakes to convey to the spectator the illusion that he himself shares the movement of the camera.

A person walking has the sense that he approaches a distant landmark which remains rooted at a definite place. The tree grows in one spot although its size and relationship to other objects in that landscape modify as the pedestrian draws nearer. Some part of his own motility transfers itself to the tree. As he draws nearer, the focus of his eye changes, the tilt of his head is greater as he looks toward the tree's top. His approach causes him to bring into play a different set of muscles; to alter his relation to what he sees. He has the sense that, as he shortens the distance between himself and the tree, it is the tree that alters its aspect. He will say, "The tree grew taller" (as he approached), or "The tree loomed larger."

If he approaches a fixed object in a vehicle, an automobile let us say, in which his own physical effort is eliminated, he is likely to attribute the movement not to the vehicle or to himself, but to his surroundings. He will say, "The country flowed by," or "The house drew nearer."

Something equivalent occurs when the camera is moved while photographing action. The moving character or object is centered in the finder and remains virtually stationary on the screen, and the background becomes fluid. Landscape or buildings flow past and, on the assumption that the spectator identifies himself with the moving character, his relationship to the background is in flux while he himself is actually motionless.

In photographing a character in motion, it must be decided

which is more important, the movement or the closeness of the point of view. Obviously, if the camera moves with a moving character, as in dolly shots, movement is negated, since, as has been noted above, the character remains centered on the screen and the background passes by. Comment on this fact will be amplified later in the present discussion (see pages 79-81).

II

Before attempting to make generalizations concerning the use of camera movement it is important to clarify the function of the camera. It is not enough to say that it is the machine by which a screen play is photographed. The chain of instrumentalities which begins with the camera and its negative film and passes through the developing machine and the printing machine, the development of the positive and the projection of the positive print on a screen, is too closely identified with an important human sense to be regarded simply as a mechanism. The camera, by which for brevity we mean the entire mechanism, is an eye. Like the microscope or the telescope or field glasses, it extends the capacity of the human eye. It is an eye that functions in a special way for a special purpose. Whose eye do we conceive the camera to be? And how is it to be used? The answer to the second question will be provided by our answer to the first. Most commonly, since the images photographed by the camera are to be viewed by a spectator, the camera is treated as an extension of the spectator's eye. It sees what the spectator could see if he were himself present at the events photographed. It reports as a newsreel does. It satisfies at each moment the spectator's wish or unconscious need to see now in general and now in particular the places, the people, their faces, their hands, their weapons, their actions toward each other, which compose into an organic dramatic or narrative whole. Through filmic movement it is endowed with selectivity. As a theatergoer with opera glasses will focus them now on one character and now on another, the camera, instantly eliding intervening motion, goes from person to person, from image to image. Exhausting for the moment the interest of one locale and its characters it can go instantaneously to another group in another place to see how they are faring. It may accompany a character in an automobile or an airplane or go under the sea in a submarine. It may walk with sweethearts and overhear their most intimate conversation. It may accompany a criminal to the gallows. If the camera is used as a substitute for or an extension of the spectator's vision, it is limited only by the obligation to maintain at all times feasible human viewpoints.

If the camera is thought of, however, not as a projection of the spectator's viewpoint, but as the narrator's, it may move with greater freedom and latitude. Like the eye of a novelist, the camera then partakes of the character, personality, and approach of the narrator. It has, like a storyteller, omniscience and omnipresence, or, more exactly, the ability to see only what it wants to see and to be only where it needs to be in order to tell its particular fable. It has selectivity, seeing only those instants in the life of various images which add up to a continuity of time, spatial relationships and causative relationships which the natural eye is incapable of seeing. Conversely, it has the ability to avoid seeing everything in the lives of the fable's characters which is not germane to the telling of the fable. In this use of the camera a complete personality is created who, though not appearing before the audience's eyes, is yet real and definite and as highly personalized as the real storyteller, be he writer or director, who employs it. With this concept of the use of the camera the director can achieve personal style as definite as that of a writer. (The term director is here used generically, as the word camera is used generically. By director we mean the individual who creates or the group of individuals who collaborate in the conception, writing, directing, and editing of a film.) The camera will "see" the story as he sees it and will relate it to an audience through his eyes. It will select shots which for that director have acute expressiveness. Shot will be related to shot in a sequence which has special significance to him. If the camera moves, it will move where he wishes to direct the interest and attention of the spectator.

Attempts have been made also to personify the camera more subjectively by conceiving of it as a character of the story, a narrator using the first person; in other words, as the eyes of a participant in the events it describes. Rouben Mamoulian opened his film of *Dr. Jekyll and Mr. Hyde* with a long introductory sequence in which the camera represented the eyes of Dr. Jekyll. However, since the film play was not a story told by Dr. Jekyll, but a story about him, the device had to be abandoned after a few hundred feet.

In a film directed by the writer a few years ago, called *The Great Commandment*, the camera was used in two sequences in the first person, to represent the eyes of Jesus. Since the Nazarene appeared in only two short episodes, of which He was the focus, and since the story dealt not with Him but with a number of characters who encountered Him, the device accomplished two important results unobtainable in any other way. The first and less important was to avoid attempting to represent a Presence which could not be visualized satisfactorily for a large proportion of the spectators, and the second, to enable the camera to see intimately and feel the effect of that Presence on the story's principal characters.

Certain limitations become immediately apparent when the camera is used in this manner as an actual participant. The fact that characters speaking to the character represented by the camera must look directly into the lens means that they look directly from the screen into the eyes of the spectator. Thus the spectator is identified with the character assumed by the camera. In the denouement of Hitchcock's *Spellbound* the camera becomes momentarily the eyes of Dr. Murchison. It follows Ingrid Bergman as she crosses the room to the door and hesitates under the camera in the exact center of the screen. Following her as she crosses, we see Murchison's hand holding the revolver. When the door closes behind her, the hand slowly turns the revolver away from the door, pauses, then turns it directly into the lens and shoots—the spectator. Such a twist may defeat the very aim of the device. Further, scenes must be played without cut in continuous action, and the point of view is unalterably that of an individual, and can be moved or changed only at the pace and within the range of the physical mobility of the individual represented by the camera. It is aware only of what he can see and know. Orson Welles had planned as his first picture in Hollywood the production of Joseph Conrad's *The Heart of Darkness*, to be told in the first person with the camera as the eyewitness and narrator, but the plan was defeated by some such considerations as these.

The camera may be used in another way. It is not conceived of as having a personality of its own, but as being simply an instrument in the hands of the director, capable of highly flexible expressiveness, as a violin is when played upon by a virtuoso. In this sense the camera is not so much an extension of the narrator's eye or mind as it is a wholly new kind of sight instrument, as fabulous as radar and free from most of the limitations that hedge about human sight. The director uses the camera, if this is his concept of its function, quite arbitrarily. It goes where no human eye could possibly go. It moves according to laws, if any, which apply not to the human eye or the human consciousness, but to itself. A number of directors use the camera with this virtuosity, achieving extraordinary effects. One recalls Von Sternberg's use of the camera in *The Scarlet Empress*, or that of Orson Welles in *Citizen Kane*. In the most skillful hands, virtuosity of the camera may enhance dramatic effect and produce a work as uniquely conditioned by the fact that it is transmitted through a camera as a violin concerto is conditioned by the fact that it is transmitted by a violin. The dangers attending this use of the camera are easy to define: it offers a constant temptation to place the camera arbitrarily, on the premise that a striking viewpoint or a striking composition is justification in itself, or that camera movement predicated wholly on the capacities of the machine requires no further motivation. To be sure, the end composition will have meaning which in the eyes of the director seems justification enough for the means employed to arrive at that end.

Such a purely cinematic use of the camera is warranted in semiabstract treatments of nondramatic subjects or moments in dramatic films, as for example, in the photography of musical or dance numbers. The camera movement may have a real or fancied relationship to the music or choreographic pattern, but often enough it simply employs an arbitrarily selected variety of angles and moves with no other object than constantly to refresh the spectator's interest in what he is seeing.

III

In actual directorial practice no compact is made with the spectator concerning the camera's function. He is not asked to recognize the camera either as his eye or the narrator's eye or that of a participant in the action, nor to identify himself with a participant in that action. Commonly, no principle in the use of the camera is constantly adhered to by the director. He uses the camera at one moment as though it were the spectator, at another to score a point of his own as the storyteller, or again, impersonally, as a tool for the achievement of an "effect." He justifies movement of the camera as the pursuit of "fluidity," or adheres to the idea that frequent change of angle gives "life" to the film or that sustained master scenes have a special value. These may all be warrantable generalizations under certain circumstances, but they ignore the fundamental that the camera acts as a living organ rather than as a tool.

For all that, the camera is governed by laws of optics as the eye is also. In function it partakes far more of the biological and psychological aspects of sight than of the purely mechanical physical aspect. Only a few directors exhibit a clear concept of a continuous understanding between themselves and the spectator concerning the function of the camera. Thus it would seem to the writer that John Ford uses the camera as the spectator's eye. He rarely causes the camera to move, thus permitting the spectator to orient himself in a stable world in which the people and not the landscape or the architecture are animate. There is a minimum use of close-ups, and close shots are achieved more often by causing the characters to approach the camera than by moving the camera closer to the characters. Ford holds that camera movement destroys reality, which is his recognition of the fact that the illusion of movement on the spectator's part cannot be supported by his physical experience as he watches the film. This gives to the rare shots in which he does cause the camera to move an uncommon effectiveness and meaning. In *The Grapes of Wrath* one recalls the wobbling progress of the camera through the Okie settlement when momentarily the camera took the point of view of the Joad family as its truck drove into the camp. Or the shot in *How Green Was My Valley* when, for a moment, Ford became the storyteller and moved the camera away from the faces of Mr. and Mrs. Morgan to the street to the left of them to show the two sons leaving home. It is as though he were content to let the spectator see the story as an eyewitness, with occasional comment from the director—comment so infrequent that it gives pith and validity from the very detachment and objectivity with which the rest of the story is told. In Leo McCarey's *The Bells of St. Mary's* the camera is moved not more than half a dozen times—only when it is panned, as the spectator might follow with his eyes a character moving purposively from one part of the scene to another.

There are other directors whose camera technique is more fluid because they employ the camera as a storyteller employs words. The point of view is primarily their own. Although it is shared with the spectator, they seem to say, "Let me show you what I saw." They act as gentle guides leading the spectator from place to place, wittily or poignantly pointing to this or that character. Not infrequently their point of view is revealed with an element of surprise. The camera maintains a credible viewpoint but one somewhat superior to and in advance of the spectator's. It knows, although the spectator does not, where it is going and what it is going to reveal. It has a self-evident sense of plan and foresight. It tells a tale in which not even the accidents are accidental. To illustrate, a picture directed by Lubitsch is told consciously as a tale to amuse or to move the spectator, and the question of the reality or the occurrences shown is secondary. The aesthetic goal is not the illusion of immediacy, but the pleasure of an engaging tale.

IV

A skillful craftsman, regardless of his general philosophy concerning the use of the camera, will be governed by one fundamental consideration—that in every shot the content shall be more important than the manner in which it is transmitted. The story comes first, and every shot deals with characters and what they do. If what they do at a given moment is stated in terms of physical action, the camera will set up space for the action and fixed points of reference. If the physical action is casual and secondary to what the character is saying or thinking, the camera will hold the character in the center of the screen whether he is moving or standing still. If his words or the intention that can be read in his face are important and interesting enough, the movement of the camera as it follows him will go unperceived. If, however, the character is stationary and the camera moves toward or away from him, the movement of the camera is bound to be perceived and must then have meaning in itself, saying, in effect, "Watch this man!" or, "We may now leave this person's thoughts and draw back to a place where we can observe his actions." If this preparation through movement or an act of attention on the spectator's part heightens dramatic effect, it is warranted. If it accomplishes merely mechanical readjustment of viewpoint, it draws attention to itself as movement and diminishes the importance of the content of the scene.

With the exception of pan shots which simulate the turn of the spectator's head, camera movement is of two sorts: either (1) the movement of the camera is motivated by and synchronized with the movement of a character or characters, or (2) the movement of the camera is not synchronized with movement on the screen.

It has already been pointed out that camera movement synchronized with physical movement is justified when it is more important to fix audience attention upon the moving character than upon his movement with relation to other characters or the background. Generally speaking, such movement does not change the initial distance relationship between the spectator and the image on the screen.

In camera movement which is not physically motivated, a proper justification can be found only in the imitation or symbolic reproduction of movements taking place in the imagination either of the storyteller or of the spectator. Such movements may be classified roughly as follows: (1) movement from a longer to a closer angle, (2) movement from a closer angle to a longer one, (3) movement from a scene to a detail, (4) movement from a detail to a scene. If such movements have some correspondence with the emotional participation by the spectator in the action, drawing him closer to characters or retracting him to a fuller scene, directing his attention to an inserted detail or drawing his attention from a detail to the characters to whom the detail relates in some significant way, the movement may be justified. It may be observed, however, that these same alterations of viewpoint can be achieved filmically, that is, through direct cuts, more quickly and usually with less awareness of the move itself. Camera movement used in this fashion decreases the pace at which the film moves. The reduction in tempo may have emotional value in itself, though it should be noted that the primary emotional responses of an audience are to the content of the shot, and the enhancement of these responses through the addition of camera movement is achieved, if at all, at the cost of an arbitrary transferral of motion from the scene to the spectator's eye. Whatever value such movement may have in terms of rhythm or imagination, it must be observed that the effect attained depends not upon an imaginative adjustment of the spectator's point of view, as in the direct cut, but upon an adjustment which inevitably relates itself more closely to the spectator's capacity for physical movement. That is to say, the imaginary journey on which the spectator is taken proceeds at a pace of the body, not of the mind. When this is true, such arbitrary movement defeats the end for which it was planned. The tempi of screen action are set up in the scene itself. Filmic movement can accelerate these tempi; synchronous camera movement can retard or negate them. It is an open question whether camera movement not synchronized to physical movement on the screen or to a normal act of spectator attention adds effect to the screen play. Certainly, if the director doubts whether an effect can be better achieved by moving a camera or by letting it stand, he will let it stand.

FRANK CAPRA
(1897-   )

Like Robert Rossen, Frank Capra felt that post-war Hollywood would be a different place, that the effect of the war on audiences would force a basic alteration in the output of American studios. But while such a transformation did in fact occur, it reflected a change in the filmmakers more than in their audience, especially in such men as Huston, Ford, Wyler and Capra who had had direct experience in wartime documentaries. These directors really did offer audiences more carefully observed characters and more realistically developed situations, but given the first opportunity the audience switched on television instead. Basically the same sort of populist under the skin, both Capra and Rossen misread public attitudes and ennobled movie patrons with the standards and ideals of film artists. Capra's case is perhaps the most extreme. After producing the "Why We Fight" series for the War Department, he returned as a principal in Liberty Films, for whom he made *It's a Wonderful Life*. Unquestionably Capra's masterpiece, the film reflects his deepest feelings about America and its people, unsullied by the requirements of Harry Cohn; its failure with critics and audiences did not damage Capra's reputation as much as his self-confidence. His autobiography describes a growing loss of interest in filmmaking, not resulting from any big-studio pressures, but from this surprising misreading of his audience. A populist out of touch with his public, Capra gradually withdrew from filmmaking and directed only five films over the next fifteen years, years which also saw the withering of the independent producers he describes so hopefully here.

BREAKING HOLLYWOOD'S
"PATTERN OF SAMENESS"
FRANK CAPRA

A change is in the making in Hollywood. It might be termed a revolution, but for the gradual manner in which it is coming about. As things are, however, it's merely a revolutionary change that is coming about so gradually that you, the movie-going public far removed from the scene of action, aren't likely to be fully aware of its force and significance for many months.

As there is no explosion, no violent upheaval, there will be no impact. You'll simply become increasingly aware of what is happening now, after it has happened and the results are in full swing. Perhaps you'll leave your neighborhood theatre one evening and remark to your companion, "Haven't we been seeing an unusual number of good pictures lately, different from the typical Hollywood product? Or am I softening up?"

You'll become aware, for example, that the pattern of sameness is no longer present. The pictures will be different. They will have individuality.

The reason behind this is the growing number of independent motion-picture producers. By way of explanation, there are two groups of motion-picture makers in Hollywood: the major studios, comprising about a half dozen huge organizations, each turning out between thirty and sixty feature films annually, and the independent producers, comprising small units of from one to four film-makers each turning out from one to five pictures a year.

For many years the independent producers have been looked down upon as shoestring operators. Except in a few rare instances, they may have been, for the most part, producers with little more than an idea and a determination to gain a foothold. Before the war there was but a handful of these independent producers. Today there is a growing number of about fifty.

From *The New York Times*, May 5, 1946. Copyright 1946 by the New York Times Company. Reprinted by permission.

Frank Capra shooting *Riding High* at Paramount (1949).

Their ranks have been swelled by producers and directors who have decided to break away, take the gamble, and strike out for themselves.

Most of them are experienced film-makers with records of achievement. They are men who have become aware that the phrase "a typical Hollywood product" has more meaning and significance than just a mere catch phrase. They are men willing to gamble their hard-earned savings to gain independence.

Hollywood has taken great pride for a quarter of a century in being known as "the infant industry." Its spectacular expansion has been a source of gratification to its leaders, and it has preened itself on being listed among the top American industries on each year's commercial calendar. But in the process, it has suffered severe growing pains. Big studios became bigger, and as they became bigger, their number became fewer, until just before the war it had boiled down to a half-dozen major studios. Almost the entire output of Hollywood motion-picture entertainment was flowing from the funnels of this handful of giants.

From a production standpoint, comprising the purely mechanical side of film-making, this was sound. Perfection of setting, of designing and mounting was achieved by Hollywood film-makers beyond anything that could be touched by film-makers in any other country on the globe. In this particular department, the Hollywood product was superior, in a class by itself.

But as the product achieved this physical perfection, some place along the line—as is likely to happen in any machine operation—it lost individuality. It took on an aura of sameness which inspired the phrase "a typical Hollywood product."

It is true that each major studio had as many as a hundred experienced, capable producers, writers and directors. On the face of it, with so much creative talent engaged actively in film-making, it would seem that product would surely have great individuality. With each of these producers or directors selecting stories, picking stars and players, assigning script writers, it should ordinarily follow that the mark of each producer would be evident and apparent in the finished work.

But this was not always the case, in fact, it became the exception. Mass production methods, applied so skillfully to motion pictures to achieve perfection of production, only succeeded in submerging the creative skill of the individual producer and director. As every large industrial organization has to have a head man, on whose shoulders rests the ultimate responsibility, so do each of the major studios have to have a head man, through whom all the product flows.

Had the motion picture been a product which demanded uniformity as its ultimate goal, the results would have been highly satisfactory. But unfortunately it was, and is, a combination of mechanical perfection and creative endeavor. And in applying the mass-production yardstick to both the mechanics and the creative side of film-making, the latter became molded into a pattern.

The efforts and achievements of the individual producers and directors had to meet with the approval of each studio's chief executive. The final product had to be approved by him before it could be released to the public. This head man became the funnel through which all effort, and the results of all effort, of fifty or more individual film-makers flowed.

Producers and directors working under him found that instead of creating as they pleased, letting their own imagination and artistry have full rein, with the public the final judge of the worth and merit of their efforts, they were of necessity obliged to make pictures for the approval of the one man at the top. Thus the creative side of film-making, from the selection of the story, the writers who would put it into script form, the casting of the players, the designing of their costumes and the sets which provided their backgrounds, the direction, the cutting and editing of the final film was tailored (consciously or unconsciously) to the tastes of the studio's head man.

Multiply this situation by a half-dozen studios and you have one potent reason for the "typical Hollywood product." A half dozen head men—a half dozen funnels through which the product flowed—deciding what the public should see, and how the product should be fashioned for 100 million weekly patrons to see.

Curiously enough, this was more the fault of the system than of the head man. This man in practically all instances was a man of tremendous talents, drive and power. The weakness lay in attempting to apply mass-production methods to the creative element as it had been applied to the physical.

There was also another factor which helped to label the product as "typically Hollywood." This could be laid at the doorstep of individuals, although it was, perhaps, an offshoot and an indirect result of the mass production pouring through the few funnels. Hollywood became increasingly self-satisfied, snug, complacent, and these characteristics became evident on the screen. Life as portrayed on the screen became a Holly- wood version of how life should be lived, whether in poverty or luxury, rather than how it was actually being lived.

Hollywood began wrapping itself in a bright, tight little cocoon in which it stirred gently and moved easily in its red plush surroundings. Life, Hollywood version, began to be pre- sented as the real McCoy. We writers, directors and producers began to get ideas not from real life, but from each other's pic- tures. Hollywood was isolating itself with a wall of mirrors.

During the war, films were seen in far-off places, on far-off fighting fronts, and, as a result, through new eyes. And it was there, more than any other place, that the sameness of the product made itself apparent. Because the motion picture com- prised the chief medium for entertainment and relaxation, be- cause there were no outside competing distractions, because the films themselves were looked forward to with such eager- ness and enthusiasm as messages from home, the machine-like treatment of the subject matter made itself glaringly evident.

Many of the men who had been film-makers, producers, di- rectors, scriptwriters, returned from service with a firm resolve to remedy this. Many of the film-makers who had had to re- main at home had the same idea, too, and were branching out for themselves. The result is that these new independent groups of film-makers are on the increase. The film-going public of today has long been familiar with such names as Metro-Gold- wyn-Mayer, Paramount, Twentieth Century-Fox, Warner Brothers, Columbia, RKO, Universal. The film-going public has often heard too the names of such stalwart independent producers as Samuel Goldwyn, David Selznick, Hunt Strom- berg, Walter Wanger, Hal Wallis.

Added to these today are those of Rainbow Productions, formed by Producer-Director Leo McCarey; Preston Sturges, Robert Riskin Productions, Liberty Films, International Pic- tures, formed by William Goetz and Leo Spitz; Frank Ross Productions, Cagney Productions, and many others whose names and trademarks will be familiar in the future.

Each one of these producers and directors has his own particular style of film making, his own individual ideas on sub-ject-matter and material, and the manner in which it should be treated. And each one, on his own and responsible only to him-self, will as an independent producer have the freedom and liberty to carry out these ideas in the manner he feels they should be executed.

So much for the creative side. On the commercial side, the way of the independent has been made smoother, and the fi-nancial incentive enhanced, by the lifting of block booking, a system long established by the major companies. Under this system, the large studio held a distinct advantage, as well as a mighty club, over the exhibitor. Block booking was an "all or nothing" sales policy, under which the exhibitor was obliged to commit himself for a certain portion of a studio's produc-tion, whether the films turned out to be good or bad, in order to assure himself of the handful of top films that studio could be counted upon to produce.

Fortunately for the independent producer, this system has been abolished by Government decree. Pictures must now be sold individually, standing on their own merits. Nor can they be contracted for by the distributor or the producer until the exhibitor has had an opportunity to see the actual production, and bid on it in the open market. Previously, the independent was in the position of hanging on to the tail of a gigantic dis-tribution kite. The major movie studio could take his product or not, just as it wished.

A glance at the growing number of independent producers whose films are being sold and distributed by the sales organi-zations of the major studios, in addition to the regular program of productions which these studios make on their own, indi-cates a significant trend. Today quality spells box office for the independents or the majors.

Undoubtedly there will always be big studios. Their prod-ucts will continue to bear the distinguishing talents of each of the top men who run them. These pictures will have a wide audience and, no doubt, a wide appeal. But we hope they will be divided by the individual creative efforts of the inde-pendents, of which, fortunately, I happen now to be one together with Producer-Directors William Wyler and George Stevens, and production executive Samuel J. Briskin, under the emblem, Liberty Films.

The way of the independents is hard. It is strewn with failures. But the public and the American motion-picture industry will gain by their efforts.

CHUCK JONES
(1912-   )

By the mid-40's the perennial crisis in film animation had developed into outright revolt. A nasty labor dispute at the Disney studio marked the end of animation's innocence, and the concurrent formation of UPA (United Productions of America) signaled a move away from the dominant calendar-art style of Disney and his imitators. Chuck Jones found himself in the middle of this ferment, for while not associated with Disney he was among the most important directors in Leon Schlesinger's animation unit at Warner Brothers, a specialist in Daffy Duck and Bugs Bunny. Jones had worked for various animation studios in the 30's, including those of Walter Lantz and Ub Iwerks, and found a home at Warner's in 1938, joining a staff that would include Tex Avery, Bob Clampett and Frank Tashlin. In 1944, "working nights," he directed the first full-length UPA short, *Hell Bent for Election*, and his concern in this article with the relationship between abstract musical and linear forms indicates the depth of his involvement with the concerns of the early UPA. The various animation studios of the period employed a wide range of styles, from Disney's mock live-action strategies (ersatz tracking shots and analytical montage) to Warner's more fragmentary, nearly expressionist approach. The disgruntled animators who established UPA chose to emphasize the dynamics of the line itself instead of dealing with the rounded, representational forms favored by the other studios. But Jones did not move to UPA; he stayed with Warner's until their cartoon unit closed in 1962, then moved to MGM and finally opened a studio of his own. His recent work has included the theatrical feature *The Phantom Tollbooth* and a series of animated Rudyard Kipling stories for television.

MUSIC AND THE
ANIMATED CARTOON*

CHUCK JONES

The animated cartoon, in its mature form, can be the most facile and elastic form of graphic art. Since the first Cro-Magnon Picasso hacked etchings on his cave wall every artist has longingly sought the ideal medium—one that would contain within its structure color, light, expanse, and movement. The animated cartoon can supply these needs. It knows no bounds in form or scope. It can approach an absolute in technical realism and it can reach the absolute in abstraction. It can bridge the two without taking a deep breath. The technical problems present in live action, when it tends toward the unreal or fantastic, are simply not present to the animator. The transition of Dr. Jekyll to Mr. Hyde is workaday routine to the animator. He can do it and add three pink elephants to the transition. He can do it while stifling a yawn. In fact, he frequently does. A red ant can grow to a golden elephant under his hand, a flying horse recede to a black pearl. He can create thunderstorms, tidal waves, flying carpets, talking hornets, dancing orchids, all with credibility, all with no technical obstructions.

Yet in spite of these potentialities the animated cartoon has been severely restricted in its growth. Its use as an educational device is a comparatively recent development, stimulated by wartime needs. Culturally, the animated cartoon is in the toddling stage, as it is politically. It has made few profound statements about anything. Like all other motion pictures, it is dependent on a wide and highly diversified audience approval—

---

* Author's Note: The title of this article may be misleading, as it implies an easy skill and familiarity with both the animated cartoon *and* music. It is rather an animation cartoonist discussing some of the potentialities of his medium with the musician.

the thing known in some quarters as "box office," and "box office" in terms of animated cartoons is judged almost wholly by the degree of audible audience reaction. The appreciative chuckle, the pleased cluck, does not add up—in animation circles—to good "box office." This has resulted in a wave of reaction throughout the industry against the type of cartoons known as "Rembrandts"; that is, any type of cartoon except those based on the "boff" or belly laugh. One producer asked his artists to use lots of purple in the backgrounds because, as he put it, "purple is a funny color." Well, I think G-flat is a funny note. I mention these instances, not because I am unsympathetic with the producer's viewpoint or wish to suggest that the imperative pressures of the box office can be disregarded, but because I believe that a deeper understanding of the aesthetic and cultural possibilities of the medium can serve to broaden its usage and increase its popularity. My purpose here is the appraisal of one of these possibilities—the function of music in relation to the cartoon.

All cartoons use music as an integral element in their format. Nearly all cartoons use it badly, confining it as they do to the hackneyed, the time-worn, the proverbial. The average cartoon musician was a theater organist during the silent era and so *William Tell* takes quite a beating in the average cartoon. For some reason, many cartoon musicians are more concerned with exact synchronization or "mickey-mousing" than with the originality of their contribution or the variety of their arrangement. To be sure, many of the cartoons as they reach the musician are something less than inspirational, but most of them, even the best, gain less than they should from his contribution. I have seen a good cartoon ruined by a deadly score. If you can visualize *Death and Transfiguration* as a theme to *Peter Rabbit*, you get the idea. Nor is this a diatribe against the practicing musicians in the cartoon field; many are excellent conscientious artists (among them Carl Stalling, Warner Bros.; Scott Bradley, MGM; Frank Churchill, Paul Smith, Larry Morey, and others for the Disney features and shorts), but many tend to underrate the medium and to disregard its musical potentialities.

Here are two examples of what I believe to be the nearly perfect wedding of music and graphics which occurs when the visual and auditory impacts are simultaneous and almost equal. Both examples are from the picture *Fantasia;* both are bits. One consumed about four seconds in the *Toccata and Fugue* sequence. It pictured simply a ponderous, rocklike, coffinlike mass that waddled into a murky background accompanied by a series of deep bass notes. I should not say "accompanied," because this Thing was the music: to my mind there was no separation; the fusion of the auditory and the visual was perfect. The second of my two instances represents, I believe, the happiest, most perfect single sequence ever done in animated cartoons, perhaps in motion pictures: the little mushroom dance from the *Nutcracker Suite.* Here was an instance of almost pure delight; again, an entrancing blend of the eye and the ear in which I found the music itself personified on the screen. There was a personal quality to these sequences, too, that was generally lacking throughout the rest of the film. It may be that if the makers of future *Fantasias* will be less concerned with the pageantry of their project and will search harder for the humanness of the music, we will have better films *and* better box office; for I believe that the mushroom dance has universal appeal, that it will go well in St. Jo and Walla Walla—as well as it will go in Hollywood or New York.

I am not going to attempt a general survey of the use, or misuse, of music in the cartoon of today. It is rather my purpose to suggest certain potentialities.

These potentialities may be classified in six rough categories: (1) Musical Education, (2) Television, (3) Program or Narrative, (4) Regional and Folklore, (5) Satire, (6) Abstract or Absolute.

1) Musical education. This is a wide and exciting field, one in which the cartoonist and musician must band together. Here the simple, strong diagrams of the cartoonist in conjunction with the sound track can do for a classroom of embryo musicians what only individual instruction could do before. I do not mean that we are going to have platoons of Bachs underfoot, but we can have a musically intelligent generation, a

thing that has not been particularly feasible heretofore. But we must be guarded in our use of this new medium, because it will be quite possible to teach a thousand children the simultaneous rudiments of the glockenspiel—a result hardly to be desired. Therefore the musician must be there to direct the artist in what to teach and how to teach it; and he may be sure that the artist will do an exciting and interesting job of presentation. It is important at this time to remember that visual education has a head start on other educational methods in that we have a sympathetic audience to start with. The motion picture is widely known and widely appreciated. It is our responsibility to maintain this attitude, and we have learned valuable lessons during the war in so doing. Education can be fun, it can be attractive, but only if we, as teachers, keep it so.

2) Television. The signature music of today's radio must be bolstered in tomorrow's television by some sort of visual image, something in the nature of MGM's lion, Warners' shield, and so on. Many educational programs will also use the cartoon, as will children's programs, comedy, and musical programs. The opportunities here hardly need elucidation; they are obvious. The points I shall stress in ensuing categories will of course apply to television as well, because the broadcasting of motion pictures will represent an important feature of television.

3) Program or narrative. Here is another wide and tremendously provocative field for the animator and musician to explore together. Here we are free from the prejudice resulting from the visual interpretation of more abstract music.

Peter and the Wolf, *Hänsel and Gretel*, *Don Quixote*, among many others, are exciting possibilities. Richard Strauss' ballet, *Schlagobers* (*Whipped Cream*), about the nightmare of a cream-puff addict, seems to me to offer an enormous amount of fun. And consider two titles of Erik Satie's, *The Dreamy Fish* and *Airs to Make One Run*, parts of which, the composer noted, should be played "on yellow velvet," "dry as a cuckoo," "like a nightingale with a toothache." He must have seen us coming. *Rip Van Winkle*, *The Fire Bird*. The list is endless.

The animated cartoon medium is the logical medium vehicle

for these, because, among all media, it lends the greatest cre-
dence to fantasy. And in this field the greatest delight is measured in the degree of credibility. The magic of the great
juggler, of the trapeze artist, of Charlie McCarthy, of the storyteller, lies in his ability to convince you that the impossible is
quite possible—nay, is logical; is, in fact, as the children say,
"Reely!" The animated cartoon can match, enhance, make
credible the melodic fantasy of the composer. Overlapping
here a little bit, I believe that the educational system will one
day demand a library for its public schools of just such painless
introductions to classic and semiclassic music.

4) Regional and folklore. I believe that the animated cartoon
has immense advantage in the exhibition of regional and national dances, songs, and cultures, because here we can combine the folk art with the folk dance. Straight cinematography
covers this field to a certain extent, but seeing strange people
in unusual costumes, dancing sarabands or tarantellas, gives us
little insight into the thoughts of these people, their dreams, or
their desires. But folk art does. It gives us a rich insight into
the hopes and needs of a people. The pottery, furniture, and
fabrics of any nationality suggest colorful fields for the artist.
The bright blues, yellows, and reds used by the Scandinavian
artisans in the creation of the jaunty figures which decorate
their dish cupboards, ski shirts, and aprons would make a dancing, happy accompaniment to Grieg's *Norwegian Dances* or
Stravinsky's *Norwegian Moods*. No live-action color camera
could do for the West Indies what Covarrubias has done in
painting. I have often thought that the *Habañera,* or even a
group of Calypsos, against his silky greens, murky jungle yellows, and luminescently coppery islanders, would be a striking
experiment. Javanese, Egyptian carvings can be brought to life
to the sounds of their ancient rhythms and instruments.

Mosaics and tapestries have enchanting stories to tell—in fact,
will become understandable to most of us only when they become more human. The run-of-the-mill tapestry contains
about the same degree of credibility to me as a petrified salamander. I can't believe the salamander ever salamandered, and
the tapestry looks about as human as a geological fault. We can

do something about it if we will, and there are several reasons why we should—among them a personal one of my own concerning a seventeenth-century bucolic tapestry called "Apollo and the Muses." The thing is crowded with variously voluptuous and idiotically unconcerned ladies in déshabille, surrounding a handsome rube, dressed in a shirt, with a twenty-five-pound lyre poised lightly in his off hand. His other hand is daintily uplifted, preparatory to a downward strum. He apparently is a past master at his instrument because his head is upturned toward a sort of Stuka angel whose power dive has carried him within about three feet of our hero's face. This little monster is on the point of releasing a very lethal-looking arrow. For three hundred and forty years this scene has remained in a state of suspended animation, and I, for one, would like to unsuspend it—if only to determine whether our friend succeeds in finishing his piece or gets spitted. His girl friends may be unconcerned, but I am not.

5) Satire. Satire, as I use it here, is best exemplified in such cartoons as *The Band Concert* and one we made at Warners called *Rhapsody in Rivets*. I shall consider the latter because I am more familiar with it. Friz Freleng, who made the picture, seemed to have a complete disregard—perhaps contempt—for the pomp, ceremony, and sacred concept of music. *Rhapsody in Rivets* took the second *Hungarian Rhapsody* of Franz Liszt and performed a nice job of first-degree premeditated murder. The visual theme was the construction of a building. The job foreman served as orchestra conductor, using the blueprints as a score. The riveting machines served as instruments. As I describe it, this may sound like the usual cornily gagged cartoon; I assure you that it was not. The music was not used as a background, but as the dictating factor in the actions of the characters. Thus, when the musical pace was *allegro* their actions became quick and lively; if the music moved to *prestissimo* they became frantic in their endeavor to keep up with it. It moved from there to *mysterioso, grave,* or *pianissimo;* in any case, the characters were dragged inexorably with it. It didn't take the audience long to appreciate what was happening. I can tell you they laughed. They split their stitches.

In this field of satire one factor constitutes a limitation of sorts: the piece selected should have a certain amount of familiarity, because this adds anticipatory enjoyment for the audience. Other than this the field is limited only by the imagination of the cartoonist and the satiric ability of the musician. They should "hoke" the number to the nicest degree of subtlety, the cartoonist going the composer one point better in his degree of shading, particularly in pace and arrangement. (Friz Freleng, who displays an unusual mastery of this sort of thing, seems to have a preference for Hungarians; because he later directed a take-off on the immortal *Three Little Pigs*, using as his theme the immortal Brahms *Hungarian Dances*.)

6) Abstract or absolute. Here is the greatest field for controversy because here the composer does not define his intention; he does not tell us what he means, or what ax he is grinding. So we all form our own ideas, and when some lout comes along and presumes to interpret *his* way, we get all stuffy and hot under the collar, and resentful, and start muttering, ". . . where the devil does *he* get off, the big stuffed shirt." Rightfully, too. He has the right to think or say what he wants to, and ours is the right to disagree as vociferously as we will. Dorothy Thompson found *Fantasia* fascistic; she is entitled to that opinion, even though it was a little startling to the artists who made *Fantasia*.

I believe that the best solution to interpretation of abstract music is to go along with it; that is, to be abstract graphically. Audiences may read into your drawings the thing they've been visualizing all the time. I don't mean that you can throw a blob of ultramarine on the screen and hope thereby that the lady in the third row is going to find her dream prince, while the old gentleman in the right rear is mentally gulping flagons of sparkling mead. But there are some generally accepted symbols in art as in music. Just as the low note of a contrabassoon does not conjure in your mind "hummingbird," a single scarlet line does not, in drawing, say "elephant." These are definite things, yet it is possible to find abstract sounds and abstract images that are sympathetic. Here are two abstract shapes.

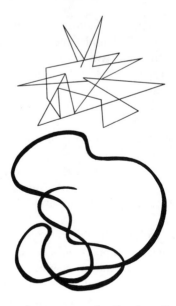

And here are two abstract words: "tackety" and "goloomb." The words become sounds when spoken, but they have no specific meanings. Yet it is simple to match the abstract words and sounds to the abstract shapes. The angular shape is obviously "tackety," and the curved one "goloomb."

Or, and now we are approaching music, take these two figures:

And take the two sounds: "oooooooooooomp" and "pooooooo-oooo-o-."

To go clear into music, which of these is the bassoon, and which is the harp?

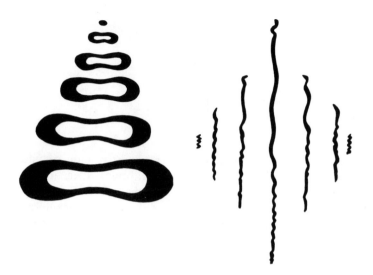

Andante thus becomes:

Abandon:

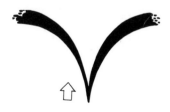

Crescendo could be thus:

Diminuendo so:

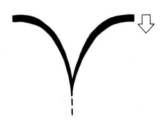

These are static examples of what are mostly static sounds. The art of animation brings them to life, brings them fluidity and power; endows them, in short, with the qualities of music. The field of graphic symbols is a great but highly unexplored field. It will, I believe, prove an important one to the musician, and to any audience that is interested in satisfying the visual appetite, side by side with the auditory appetite.

An article of this kind can only be sketchy. We are dealing with a relatively new but immensely versatile and horizonless medium. The ideas suggested in this paper serve merely to suggest, or outline, a few possibilities from *one* viewpoint. Any imaginative person can easily elaborate on it. My sincere hope is that such people in the motion picture industry will see fit to do so. Only one serious danger confronts the animator: an underevaluation of his medium. If the motion picture producer, writer, or musician believes the end purpose of the animated cartoon to be the cartoon short of today, then it must follow that the end purpose of easel painting is the comic strip. The animated cartoon as an artistic, educational, and entertainment medium is in its infancy. Its maturity depends on you.

WILLIAM WYLER
(1902-   )

Born in Alsace, William Wyler came to the United States
after the First World War on the invitation of his uncle,
Carl Laemmle, founder and president of the Universal Film
Manufacturing Company. He began in the New York office taking home twenty dollars a week but soon was out
at the studio, eventually working up to assistant director,
and in 1925 to director of two-reel westerns. Wyler rapidly
advanced to the direction of feature-length westerns and
finally the ultimate rank at Universal, non-western features.
By the time sound arrived, he was one of the studio's
top directors, and was awarded such plums as the sophisticated John Barrymore vehicle, *Counsellor-at-Law*. In
1935 he broke with Universal and eventually went under
contract to Sam Goldwyn, directing *Dead End*, *Wuthering
Heights*, *The Little Foxes* and (after wartime service) *The
Best Years of Our Lives*. Wyler's reputation as one of the
screen's most exacting craftsmen is well detailed in this production history, particularly so in the account of pre-production work, script development and casting given here.
Note also his explanation of the use of deep-focus photography, published the year before André Bazin's seminal
essay "William Wyler, ou le janseniste de la mise en scène"
first analyzed the importance of Wyler's innovations. The
director's acknowledgment of the contributions of Sherwood, Toland, Mandell, Friedhofer and his other collaborators is typically generous, and only makes more strange the
complete omission of the name of Sam Goldwyn, producer
of the film.

NO MAGIC WAND
WILLIAM WYLER

The director in Hollywood is a man who is continually on a spot. He gets on the set at nine in the morning, really quite early for serious thinking, and looks around at a hundred or more people who are all staring at him, waiting for him to give "the word." Sometimes he hasn't got it. Sometimes he feels like the European director of some years back who, unable to make a decision about the scene he was shooting, pounded his head on the floor of the stage and cried, "Will it ever come to me?!"

I know, because this sort of thing happens to me all the time. Eventually, "it" comes to you, and you're off the spot until the next problem, which comes along in the form of a property man who wants an okay on a pocket comb (to be used next week), or a producer who thinks there is a conspiracy to bankrupt him by making too many takes. This process of getting along with people, making decisions, thinking up things for people to do, and saying "yes" or "no" is a recognized and socially acceptable form of making a living, and in some quarters even considered "art."

A great deal of serious writing has been done about it, too. You'd think it would be of some help to you in solving your problems; however most of this writing pertains to D. W. Griffith, the silent film, the German film, the documentary film, the Soviet film, Charlie Chaplin's *Shoulder Arms* or the "transition" to sound, with occasional references to Rene Clair and the tradition of French comedy.

As yet, as far as I know, there is no recognizable aesthetic for our contemporary fiction film, the kind people are going to see nowadays. The people who make pictures, and face problems, have to solve them on their own hook, without any connection or communication with other minds on the creative level. I

From *The Screen Writer*, February 1947. Reprinted by permission of the Writers' Guild of America.

Frederic March and Myrna Loy listen to William Wyler's instructions for the next take of *The Best Years of Our Lives* (1946).

should like to point out that the field is open for a great deal of serious work. However, I am not the man to attempt it. I feel ill-equipped to undertake any more than a kind of personal testament which may throw light on how one man approaches these problems from day to day, getting on and off spots as gracefully(?) as he can.

It may be of some interest as "source material" for me to recount briefly the steps by which one film was made in the year 1946, with reference to some of the problems faced along the way. Because the events connected with filming *The Best Years of Our Lives* are still fresh in my mind, and because in many ways, that picture is most representative of my own particular way of directing, I'd like to discuss how we made it.

The emphasis on the personal is deliberate, for I feel that in films, as in any other art form, no general rules which must be followed can apply. Each man or woman making films must evolve his own personal style; I do not believe great films can be made on a factory-conveyor belt basis, untouched by human hands, as it were. I have always tried to direct my own pictures out of my own feelings, and out of my own approach to life. I have tried to make them "by hand," and it has been hard work, work which has left me drained of energy for months after the completion of each film.

In the case of *The Best Years*, I should like to make the point that the picture came out of its period, and was the result of the social forces at work when the war ended. In a sense the picture was written by events and imposed a responsibility upon us to be true to these events and refrain from distorting them for our own ends.

In 1945, when it became apparent that the war would end soon, and for the first time in years we would think about getting men out of uniform instead of into it, serious work on the problem was being done by the American Veterans Committee, a new Veterans organization of World War II. They enunciated the principle that the veteran could not be isolated from the main body of the nation, for his problems were also national problems. The slogan "Citizens first, veterans second" expressed this well, and the head of the American Veterans Committee expressed the belief that if the veteran came home to a working family relationship, and to a job, and a place to live, there would be no veterans' "problem."

While these concepts were being enunciated, MacKinlay Kantor, well-known novelist, had been engaged by the studio to prepare an original screen treatment on the veterans. Because Mr. Kantor had been overseas as a correspondent, and had flown missions with the 8th Air Force, he knew both sides of the coin—civilian and veteran—and felt the importance of presenting the story fairly. The result of his work was a novel in blank verse, *Glory for Me*.

This book, in manuscript form, was presented to me as one of several properties owned by the studio to which I was committed for one more film under a pre-war contract. I knew of no subject which was as important to me, for I was just about to become a civilian myself.

Glory for Me was a story of three men who came back to their home town, which Kantor chose to call Boone City. One man, Captain Fred Derry, an 8th Air Force Bombardier, had been a soda jerk in civilian life, and had lived on the wrong side of the tracks with his weak, drink-destroyed father and crude, insensitive step-mother. He had married a girl while training in Texas, and had only a few days of marriage before being shipped overseas. His first night home, he finds her making love to another man (ironically an ex-Marine), and gives her enough money to get a divorce.

Al Stephenson, the second veteran, had been an infantry sergeant. His first night home, memories of combat come back to contrast with the soft and easy life he will lead with his wife, grown daughter and adolescent son. He has a sense of guilt in accepting the luxuries of a home and family, when he thinks of his friends who are not coming back. Stephenson had been a banker before the war, and has no problem in making a living. His problem becomes that of working in a bank and reconciling the sharp business practice he sees with the social conscience he developed during the war.

The third veteran, Homer, Machinist's Mate second class, a nineteen year old kid, had become a spastic through combat injuries. Unable to coordinate his movements, awkward, even grotesque, he finds homecoming sheer misery because his people don't understand him. His situation is aggravated by his love for the girl next door, his high school sweetheart, Wilma, and his fear that she will go through with marriage only through pity for him. Through drink, Homer finds he can coordinate his jerky movements a little better, and is on the verge of becoming an alcoholic.

The problems established, Kantor proceeds to solve them by having Fred fall in love with Peggy Stephenson, almost rob her father's bank when he finds himself unable to get a job, eventually go into partnership with the man who owned the drug store in which he used to work before the war.

Al Stephenson makes a GI loan to an ex-SeaBee named Novak, which brings down the wrath of the bank president about his ears. His fight with the bank cannot be resolved since Al sees men in terms of human beings, rather than in terms of dollars and cents. Al resigns from the bank, and goes into partnership with Novak to "grow things."

Homer drinks more heavily, fights with his parents, tries to shoot himself, but bungles that because of his spasticity. Eventually the strength of Wilma's love becomes apparent to him, and their story ends on a note of hope, with Wilma studying medical texts in an effort to understand and help him.

I have gone into the details of MacKinlay Kantor's plot for *Glory for Me* because they must be understood in any technical discussion of how we made *The Best Years of Our Lives*. Besides, the story is always the central problem in any film I have directed. A director can take a poorly written script, and perhaps he can present it a bit better than the writing indicated. But he cannot take a bad story and make a good story out of it by some magical process of direction. I hold a brief for the screen writer, who has only too often been underestimated in his contribution to motion pictures. But it is just as true that a good script is no guarantee of a good picture, as many writers have discovered to their sorrow.

Mack Kantor's book provided the basis for most of what we subsequently put on film. Some things, however, had to be changed, and the story re-told in screen terms. For example, the book was written in 1945, and we were making a picture for release in 1947, which meant we had to make certain changes to keep the picture from being a period piece. The alterations we made are in no way a reflection on Mack Kantor, whose original creative impulse got us started.

Robert E. Sherwood agreed to write the screenplay, and he began work in November 1945.

As almost everyone knows, Sherwood won the Pulitzer Prize for drama three times, had a fine war record as an infantry soldier in the first World War, was the brilliant head of the Office of War Information's Overseas Division, and friend and aide to Franklin Delano Roosevelt during all of World War II. I got out of the Army in November 1945, and had some preliminary discussions with Bob in New York. However it was not until December, when he came to Hollywood, that we really began our intensive work on the screenplay.

I had as my assistant on the production of the picture Lester Koenig, a talented young writer who had written and helped me make both *Memphis Belle* and *Thunderbolt* for the Army Air Forces. Les was also keenly aware of the central problem as a result of his experience as a GI and in his own readjustment to civilian life, which added considerably to the value of his contribution to the picture during the four months of our intimate working relations with Sherwood.

The first, and major deviation from the book was in the character of Homer, the spastic sailor. The deviation came about in this way: I had seen a training film made by the Army Pictorial Service, called *Diary of a Sergeant*. In very simple, moving terms, it told the true story of Harold Russell, a sergeant in the paratroopers who lost both hands when a dynamite charge exploded prematurely during maneuvers in North Carolina. The picture showed how Russell was outfitted with new devices which enabled him to do most of the things anybody else does. How he rose above physical limitations seemed to be a great object lesson. He had a wonderful face which expressed strength, courage and great faith in the future.

Bob Sherwood was keen on the idea of changing the character of Homer, and did his rewriting only after meeting Harold Russell, and getting a really intensive understanding of the boy and his problems. Incidentally, it may be of interest to note that we wanted Russell himself to play the part, rather than an actor. No matter how good a performance an actor gave of a man without hands, an audience could reassure itself by saying, "It's only a movie." With Russell playing Homer, no such reassurance was possible.

The second major deviation from the original novel came in the story of Fred Derry and his wife, Marie. Instead of having him discover her infidelity the first night, Sherwood decided to avoid a meeting between them, and allow a love story to start between Fred and Al Stephenson's daughter, Peggy. Marie would be kept alive throughout the story, not merely as the third side of the conventional triangle, but as a symbol of a way of life diametrically opposed to the way of life represented by Peggy.

In a sense, the love story is an allegory, although an implied one—for first of all, characters have to be real human beings who exist independently of an author's symbolic use of them. Marie, the wife, stands for the kind of a fellow Fred Derry was, prior to his going into the Air Forces. Ignorant, insular, and selfish, such people have no insight or concern for the problems of the nation, or of the world. They are concerned only with their own problems, which are summed up in the simple quest for "a good time." These were the people who patronized black markets during the war, never gave blood to the Red Cross, bought no War Bonds, and did no war work. Yet they considered themselves "100% Americans." On the other hand, Peggy, Al Stephenson's daughter, is knowing, aware of the larger world about her, interested in problems beyond her own. She knew what the war was about, and participated in it by becoming a nurse's aide in a local hospital. It is she who understands that the conflict in Fred Derry is the conflict between an old way of life in America, and a newer, healthier way of life born out of the experience and sacrifice of the people who fought the war.

It may appear that I am digressing from my theme—which is "direction," to discuss something which appears to be in the writer's province; however it cannot be stressed too often that the director's job should not begin only after the script has been written. There is no definite dividing line where writing ends and directing starts. They must overlap.

In resolving the stories of the characters, Bob Sherwood faced some problems which we discussed together. We had to be honest in ending the three stories, for we felt the picture would be seen by millions of veterans. We could not indicate any solution to a problem which would work only for a character in a movie. Sherwood felt, for example, that it wasn't a fair solution to let Al Stephenson quit his job at the bank and go into something else where he could avoid "problems," because millions of other veterans would have no such easy alternative to a job they did not like. Most men would have to stick with the job and try to change it for the better. So we left Stephenson still working at the bank, having thrown down the gauntlet to the bank president, and announced his intention of fighting for a more liberal loan policy toward veterans.

Homer's story demanded a particular resolution in terms of a man who had no hands. We wanted to have a scene in which Homer tells Wilma the reason he has been avoiding her is not that he doesn't love her, but that he doesn't feel it fair to her to marry her. "You don't know, Wilma," he says, "You don't know what it would be like to live with me, to have to face this every day—every night." Wilma replies, "I can only find out by trying, and if it turns out that I haven't courage enough, we'll soon know it." This was intended to lead to a scene in Homer's bedroom in which, in order to prove his point, he demonstrates his difficulty in undressing, removes his hooks, and explains how helpless he is once they are off.

This scene affords a good example of how writer and director can function together, for I had to decide whether or not I could do such a scene on the screen. There were delicate problems in bringing a boy and girl to a bedroom at night, with the boy getting into his pyjama top, revealing his leather harness which enabled him to work his hooks, and finally, taking the harness off.

After discussions with Bob, we solved the problems, and felt we could play the scene without the slightest suggestion of indelicacy, and without presenting Homer's hooks in a shocking or horrifying manner. As a matter of fact, we felt we could do quite the opposite, and make it a moving and tender love scene. Wilma meets the test squarely, makes Homer see that she doesn't mind the hooks, and what she feels for him is not pity, but love.

The Fred Derry story also required a new ending. After establishing so strongly that Fred couldn't get a good job because he had no training for anything except the trade of a bombardier, Sherwood didn't feel it was fair to have him fall into a soft job, almost by accident. Instead we wanted to say to

millions of men like Fred Derry, that if they were being realistic, they could expect no special favors because they were
veterans, and they would not get good jobs unless they were
qualified to hold them. Therefore it was up to Fred to pick a
trade or profession, and learn it, as thoroughly as he learned the
trade of a bombardier.

When Fred Derry decides to leave town in defeat, unable to
get a job, no longer married to Marie, and at odds with Peggy,
whom he loves, he goes to the airport to hitch a ride on an
army plane. While he waits, he wanders around among endless rows of junked combat fighters and bombers. In long
moving shots, made on location at the Army scrap-heap for
obsolete planes at Ontario, California, we followed Fred Derry
as he moved thru the gigantic graveyard. At once the parallel
was apparent: for four years Fred was trained, disciplined, and
formed into a precise human instrument for destruction. Now
his work is done, and he too has been thrown to the junk pile.

At this point, we wanted to have Fred Derry re-live one of
his war experiences, and as a consequence have him realize that
in order to win his personal battles as a civilian, it was necessary to apply the same courage and strength of character that
he and twelve million others applied to win the war.

This was the climax of Fred's story; unlike most movie stories, it had to be resolved in terms of a basic change in attitude,
which is always difficult to handle in such an objective medium. "You'll have to do something cinematic here," Bob told
me. "I know just what we want to say, but it isn't to be said in
words—it must be said with the camera, and that's your business." He was right. In such instances the author has a right to
expect the director to do some "directing."

After we had Fred Derry crawl into an abandoned B-17, the
problem was to make clear what was going through his mind.
There were several ways.

Finally we hit on what I feel is a good dramatization of the
whole situation, and yet very simple and direct. We did nothing in the interior of the B-17 except show Fred Derry seated
and staring out through the dusty plexiglass. Then we went to
a long exterior shot of the plane, in which we could see the en-

gine nacelles, stripped of engines and propellers. We panned from nacelle to nacelle, as though there really were engines in them, and the engines were starting up for take-off. Then we made another long shot, on a dolly, and also head on. We started moving our dolly in toward the nose of the B-17, through which we could see Fred Derry seated at the bombardier's post. This shot moved in, from a low angle, and as it moved in, it created the illusion of the plane coming toward the camera, as if for a take-off. To these shots we planned to add sound effects of engines starting, and then let the musical score suggest flight. We then cut inside to a shot of Fred's back, and as we moved in, we saw his hand reach for the bomb release. We continued moving until we reached an effective close-up of Fred, framed against the plexiglass nose of the bomber.

What made this scene give the audience the feeling that Fred was re-living a specific combat experience was a scene immediately preceding which was designed for the purpose. This was a scene in Fred Derry's home, in which his father was reading aloud from a citation for the Distinguished Flying Cross. The citation gave us not only a capsule form of exposition, but allowed us to make a sharp and ironic comment on Fred's reward for his war record being discouragement and hopelessness, and defeat as a civilian.

The reading of the citation tells the audience the story of Fred's determination and courage, and the audience remembers it subsequently while Fred sits in the nose of the wrecked B-17.

As a result of re-living this experience, Fred decides to take a job as a laborer, which isn't well paid, but which may lead to a future in the building business. And so his story is resolved, not by letting him have a good job, but by a change in his attitude to a realistic appraisal of himself in relation to the time in which he lives.

It is readily apparent that this is not a story of plot, but a picture of some people, who were real people, facing real problems. It was important for all of the people connected with the making of the picture to understand this. Consequently, I had many long talks with Gregg Toland about the photography weeks before we started shooting. Gregg had to make certain basic decisions about how he could best transfer our scenes to the screen, and finally we decided to try for as much simple realism as possible. We had a clear cut understanding that we would avoid glamour closeups, and soft, diffused backgrounds. No men in the cast would wear make up, and the make up on the women would be kept to a minimum so that we could really see our people, and feel their skin textures.

Since Gregg intended to carry his focus to the extreme background of each set, detail in set designing, construction, and dressing became very important. But carrying focus is not merely a stunt; it is to me a terribly useful technique. In *The Best Years of Our Lives*, the sharp and crisp photography, filled with good contrast and texture, is one of the key factors in establishing a mood of realism. Gregg Toland's remarkable facility for handling background and foreground action has enabled me over a period of six pictures he has photographed to develop a better technique of staging my scenes. For example, I can have action and reaction in the same shot, without having to cut back and forth from individual cuts of the characters. This makes for smooth continuity, an almost effortless flow of the scene, for much more interesting composition in each shot, and lets the spectator look from one to the other character at his own will, do his own cutting.

In playing each scene, I have tried to work it out in such a way that generally I shoot into sets the long way, which means I can get the fullest use of each set. I suppose I have certain habits, like most directors who have been at it for any length of time, and without really being conscious of doing so, arrange the scene so that the characters are close together, and can all be included in shots which are close enough so that the expressions on their faces can be clearly seen. But this kind of elementary technical approach to the staging of a scene does not intrigue me. I have never been as interested in the externals of presenting a scene as I have been in the inner workings of the people the scene is about. I am not minimizing the importance of correct use of the camera, or staging of the action.

I mean that they are important only as they help the audience understand what the characters are thinking, feeling, saying or doing. For me, the most trying, and yet the most rewarding work on the set is with the cast.

I have no consciously formulated theories of acting; I cannot teach anyone how to act. However, what I try to do is help the actor or actress understand clearly what the scene is about. I believe if the actor or actress really understands the scene, and understands the inner motivations of the character, that half the battle for a good performance is won.

I have found most actors extremely cooperative, and lacking in the kind of "temperament" that makes for trouble on the set. In the past, I have had a reputation of being tough on actors, and on occasion there have been violent arguments, and unpleasant situations. In most cases I have insisted on doing the scene my way. I have not wanted to be arbitrary, but I feel that the director is held responsible for what gets on the screen, and therefore he must have final say on the set. In filming *The Best Years of Our Lives*, I had the most pleasant associations with its stars Myrna Loy, Fredric March, Dana Andrews and Teresa Wright. In general my method of working was to set one day aside for rehearsal before going into a major sequence. We would spend the morning sitting around a table, reading the script, much as it is done in early stages of a theater rehearsal. After reading and discussing the scenes until we felt we understood them, I would stage each scene, usually letting the actors work in the way which seemed most comfortable to them. In this way we could tell how the scenes played, the actors would have a chance to study them in the way we intended doing them, and Gregg Toland would have a chance to observe what would be required of him in the photography.

On the set, before shooting, I rehearse the scene as a whole, and each time we go through it, I try to make suggestions for improving it. I very rarely give actual "readings" of lines, but rather try to show the actor where he was missing some shade of meaning the writer had intended. Sometimes the actor shows me where my concept could be improved. I try not to hurry, or give the cast a feeling that I am impatient with them. This is not merely diplomacy. It is a recognition that it is not easy to play a scene well, and that a director cannot hope to go through a brief rehearsal, shoot a take, and let it go at that. I try to be patient because I recognize that film-making is a long, slow, detailed process, which requires patience. I have been called a perfectionist, but that hasn't usually been intended as a compliment. I do make a great many takes, when necessary, but there is always a reason. I consider it a loss when something which might have been in the scene doesn't come across. To anyone who looks at the scene, it appears to be fine. But I know how much better it could have been, had we worked just a little harder to make a point. And I have long ago decided that whatever extra trouble was necessary to make a scene right, or better, was worth it. Often, toward the end of a day, when people wanted to get home to their wives and children, I could sense a resentment toward me on the set. I knew I was not making myself popular by working until seven or seven-thirty. I knew that a lot of dinner plans (including my own) were being upset. But I also knew that if I kept working on the scene it would be a better scene.

The people might hate me on the set, but when they went to see the picture in a theater, if it was a good picture, I knew they would be proud to have worked on it, and perhaps they might forgive me for being difficult. But I also knew that no matter how nice I was on the set, if the picture laid an egg in the theater, nobody who worked on it, and no critic who reviewed it would say, "The picture stinks, but Wyler is a nice fellow to work with." If I have to choose between personal popularity, or the popularity of my pictures, I have to choose the picture every time.

During the shooting, which began April 15th and ended August 9th, 1946, I worked very closely with Daniel Mandell, one of the really fine film editors. Danny has put most of my pictures together, and knows as much about the subject as anybody you could name. Our company met at 8:30 every morning to see the film we'd shot the day before. Danny sat next to me, and I would pick the takes to be used, and briefly discuss the way I intended the scene to be cut. Then, during the course of the day, Danny would come on the set and we would talk over specific problems. Occasionally, every few weeks, I would devote an evening to running the assembled film with Danny, and making suggestions to him. By working this way I was able to avoid making mistakes on the set, for I had a feeling of the picture as a whole. The day after we finished the long four month shooting schedule, Danny had a first rough cut ready to show. It ran just a few minutes under three hours, and very few changes had to be made in it.

It was after this amazingly fast job of editing was completed that I had several discussions with Hugo Friedhofer, the composer who was hired to write the music. I find that this consultation is very necessary, even with the best of musicians, because the director must make sure that the composer sees each scene as he sees it. Since the director shot the picture, he is best qualified to be the final authority on his own dramatic intent. While my decisions as to which scenes will have music is subject to change, I try to be quite certain the composer and I are in agreement as to the meaning the music should have in relation to each sequence.

At the start of this article, I referred to the lack of communication among people on the creative level in Hollywood. We are going to try to remedy that situation at Liberty Films where Frank Capra and George Stevens and I hope to benefit from an exchange of views. Each of us will be in absolute control of his own picture, but each of us will welcome the criticism and advice of the others, as well as of Sam Briskin, our executive producer.

There is another aspect of the Liberty Films set-up which seems important to me. All four of us have served in the armed forces, and we have a staff of younger executives and writers who have seen overseas military service. All of us at Liberty Films have participated in the major experience of our time, and while I cannot prove it, I believe it will have a healthy effect on our work. I know that I most certainly could not have directed *The Best Years of Our Lives* as I did without the knowledge of the people and the background which came out of my own Army career. But aside from specific knowledge and experience of war and fighting men, I think that all of us have learned something and gained a more realistic view of the world. Frank Capra has told me that he feels this strongly, and I know George Stevens is not the same man for having seen the corpses of Dachau.

Hollywood seems a long way from the world at times. Yet it does not have to be. Unfortunately, at the moment, the motion picture in Hollywood is divorced from the main currents of our time. It does not reflect the world in which we live. It often has very little meaning for audiences at home, and even less for audiences abroad. It is time that we in Hollywood realized the world doesn't revolve about us.

In Europe, I believe great prospects for films are in sight. I have met some of the film-makers of France and England who approach their work with a simplicity and directness which eludes many of us in Hollywood. The European motion picture people have gone through the war in a very real sense, and I think they are closer to what is going on in the world than we are. The competition from Europe will force us to meet the challenge.

JEAN RENOIR
(1894-   )

During the Second World War Hollywood played host to a wide range of emigrés, men and women who joined the already existing expatriate colony (Lang, Lubitsch, Dietrich et al.) in creating a unique group of 40's films, not quite Hollywood standard, but hardly typically European either. The most notable of the wartime emigrés was undoubtedly Jean Renoir, whose *La Grande Illusion* had been a great success in America in 1938-39. This American reputation enabled him to find work much more easily than Max Ophuls, and to avoid the B-picture budgets that plagued Douglas Sirk. In films like *Swamp Water*, *The Southerner* and *Woman on the Beach* Renoir successfully transferred the spirit of his most intimate 30's films to an American landscape not so far removed from that of his earlier *Toni*. His final Hollywood film, *Woman on the Beach*, had only recently opened when he published this article in defense of Chaplin's *Monsieur Verdoux*. Many critics have drawn parallels between Chaplin and Renoir, and it is interesting to note that those Chaplinesque characteristics which Renoir chooses to single out—integrity, sharp observation of humanity, avoidance of "phony bathetic goodness"—are those which mark his own films as well. Renoir's defense of Chaplin is as clearly a defense of Renoir, and of all those in the cinema who value personal expression over collective authorship (Renoir had by this time forgotten *La Vie Est à Nous*, apparently). But neither man would do much future work in Hollywood: *Limelight* would be Chaplin's swan song, while Renoir soon left to continue his career in Europe.

CHAPLIN AMONG THE IMMORTALS
JEAN RENOIR

"Man is interested in only one thing: man."
PASCAL

Last night, I had a strange dream. I was sitting at my dining-room table carving a leg-of-mutton. I went at it in the French manner, which is to slice it in length. In that way, you get a great variety of cuts. Those who like it well done are served first. You wait till you get closer to the bone, for those who prefer it rarer. My guests had been lost in a sort of fog, but as I asked each one how he liked his meat, they suddenly came into a very sharp focus, and I recognized them as people I admire and like. The couples of *The Best Years of Our Lives* were right there at my table, smiling amiably at me. I served them, and they ate with robust appetite. Next to them were the priest and the pregnant woman of *Open City*, a bit more reserved but no less cordial. At the end of the table, the loving pair of *Brief Encounter* were holding hands. This abandon was proof that they felt themselves among friends, and I was gratified by it. As I was about to proceed to the beautiful courtesan of *Children of Paradise*, the doorbell rang.

I went to open the door and found myself facing a gentleman of distinguished appearance. Offhand, he reminded me vaguely of someone I knew well, a little old tramp who had made the whole world laugh. But I quickly understood that the resemblance was merely physical. Even under the rich fur coat of a goldmine owner, the other one had remained a bit of a guttersnipe. It was obvious that he would never completely get rid of his lowdown ways. Whereas this one, on the other hand, was most certainly the scion of a "good family." His parents

From *The Screen Writer*, June 1947. Reprinted by permission of the Writers' Guild of America.

Jean Renoir rehearsing Joan Bennett and Robert Ryan in a scene from *Woman on the Beach* (1947), his last American film.

had taught him proper table manners, and when and how to kiss a lady's hand. He had breeding. And all of his person gave off that impression of suppressed passions, of hidden secrets, which is the earmark of the bourgeoisie in our old Western civilizations.

I introduced myself. With exquisite politeness which bespoke his old provincial background and his prep-school education, he told me his name was Verdoux. Then he placed his hat and cane on a chair, flicked a speck of dust from his jacket, adjusted his cuffs, and headed for the diningroom. Immediately, the others edged closer together to make room for him. They seemed happy to see him. Obviously, they were all members of the same social world.

After dinner, we went outdoors. But word of the presence of my famous guests had spread, and the street was crowded with people. When we walked down the porch steps, the public enthusiasm burst out. Everyone wanted to shake their hands, there was a terrific crush, the autograph-seekers were at work.

Suddenly, a very dry lady, wearing an aggressive little hat, recognized Monsieur Verdoux and pointed a finger at him. And, strangely, the enthusiasm turned into fury. They rushed at him, raising their fists. I tried to understand, and kept asking the same question over and over again: "What did he do? What did he do? . . ." But I could not hear the answers, for everyone was speaking at once and the caning the poor man was taking made a deafening racket. So deafening, in fact, that I awoke with a start and had to close my window, which a sudden stormy wind was violently banging back and forth.

I don't believe that the people who attacked Chaplin so sharply over his latest film did so for personal or political reasons. In America we haven't yet reached that stage. I think rather that the trouble is their panic terror before total change, before a particularly long step forward in the evolution of an artist.

This is not the first time such a thing has happened, nor will it be the last. Molière was a victim of the same kind of misunderstanding. And the Hollywood commentators who have been unable to recognize the qualities of *Monsieur Verdoux* are in very good company, indeed. Molière's detractors had names no less important than La Bruyère, Fénelon, Vauvenargues, Sherer. They said he wrote badly. They criticized him for his barbarism, his jargon, his artificial phrasing, his improper usage, his incorrect wording, his mountains of metaphors, his boring repetitions, his inorganic style. "Molière," said Sherer, "is as bad a writer as one can be."

This animosity on the part of certain self-appointed intellectuals is not the only point of resemblance between the careers of Molière and Chaplin.

In his early stages, the former achieved great success by simply following the traditions of the Italian Comedy. His characters bore the familiar names and costumes, their predicaments were those to which the public was accustomed. Only, beneath Sganarelle's makeup and behind Scapin's somersaults, the author injected a rarer element, a little human truth. But on the surface, there was not too much of an apparent change. When the action slowed down, a solid laying-on with a stick was always good for a laugh. The sentimental side was taken care of with formulae no different, except for the author's masterful touch, from those used elsewhere in the same period: a noble young gentleman falls in love with a scullerymaid and his family will have none of her. But, in the end, it all works out. It is revealed that the ingénue was really a well-born maiden who, as a baby, had been carried off by pirates.

Chaplin, to begin with, simply followed the traditions of the then most popular form in the world, English farce. His feet foul him up on the stairs and his hands get entangled in fly-paper. The sentimental side in his films is represented by babies left on doorsteps, streetgirls mistreated by life, or other carry-overs from the good old mellers. In spite of that, he never falls into the worst vulgarity of our time, phony bathetic goodness. And beneath his character's flour-face, as well as behind the fake beards of his companions, we rapidly discern real men of flesh and blood. As he grows, like Molière, he introduces into the conventional framework, which he has made his very own through the vigor of his talent, the elements of a sharper and sharper observation of humanity, of a more and more bitter social satire. Nevertheless, since the appearances remain the same, no one is shocked, no one protests.

One day, Molière decided to give up the form which had brought him his success, and he wrote *The School for Wives*. Accusations were heaped upon him. He was called a mountebank. People became irritated with him because he was director, actor and writer all at the same time.

One day, Chaplin wrote *Monsieur Verdoux*. He turned his back on the outward forms to which he had accustomed his public. There was a great hue and cry of indignation, he was dragged through the mud.

After *The School for Wives*, instead of giving in, Molière went on hitting harder and harder. His next play was *Tartuffe*, which impaled phony religion and bigotry.

What will Chaplin's next film be?

I think it is unnecessary to explain why I like the Chaplin of the old school, since everyone seems to share that taste. It is even probable that some of the attackers of his present film must have written glowing tributes to *The Gold Rush* or *The Kid*. I would like, however, to present a few of the reasons which, to me, made the showing of *Monsieur Verdoux* a pure delight.

Like everybody else, I have my own ideas about what is conventionally called Art. I firmly believe that since the end of the period in which the great cathedrals were built, since the all-pervading faith which was to bring forth our modern world is no longer present to give artists the strength to lose themselves in an immense paean to the glory of God, there can be quality to human expression only if it is individual. Even in cases of collaboration, the work is valuable only insofar as the personality of each of the authors remains perceptible to the audience. Now, in this film, that presence is, to me, as clear as that of a painter in his canvas or of a composer in his symphony.

Moreover, every man matures, his knowledge of life increases, and his creations must develop at the same time he does. If we do not admit these truths in our profession, we might as well admit right now that it is an industry no different than the rest, and that we make films like efficiency experts supervise the production of iceboxes or shaving cream. And let's stop priding ourselves on being artists, and claiming that we're carrying forward the grand old traditions.

It is agreed, some will say, that Chaplin has created a highly personal work, and we admit that he has undergone a natural artistic transformation. We only feel that he has done all this in a wrong direction. And they add that the greatest crime of *Monsieur Verdoux* was the killing-off of the beloved little vagabond who had been such a charmer. His creator should not only have kept him alive but depended on him in his search for a new form of expression. I cannot share this opinion.

In giving up the rundown shoes, the old derby hat and willowy cane of the raggedy little guy whose pathetic hangdog look used to melt our hearts, Chaplin has gone deliberately into a world that is more dangerous, because it is closer to the one we live in. His new character, with neatly-pressed trousers, impeccably-knotted tie, well-dressed and no longer able to appeal to our pity, does not belong in those good old situations, outlined in strong broad strokes, where the rich trample the poor in so obvious a manner that even the most childish audience can immediately grasp the moral of the story. Before, we could imagine that the adventures of the little tramp took place in some world that belonged exclusively to the movies, that they were a sort of fairy tale.

With *Monsieur Verdoux*, such misapprehension is no longer possible. This one really takes place in our time, and the problems faced on the screen are really our own. By thus giving up a formula which afforded him full security, and undertaking squarely the critique of the society in which he himself lives, a dangerous job if ever there was one, the author raises our craft to the level of the great classical expressions of the human mind, and strengthens our hope of being able to look upon it more and more as an art.

Let me add a purely personal note here: Having given up the powerful weapon which was the defenselessness of his old character, Chaplin had to look for another to be used by his latest creation. The weapon he chose is one that appeals particularly to the Frenchman in me, steeped as he is in the 18th Century: paradoxical logic.

I understand perfectly the misgivings of certain conformist minds before this method which seems to belong to a bygone aristocratic era. I hope they will forgive a devoted reader of the works of Diderot, Voltaire and Beaumarchais for the pleasure he found in *Monsieur Verdoux*.

Moreover, even when it is not thus spiced with paradoxical logic, genius often has something shocking about it, something subversive, some of the characteristics of a Cassandra. That is because it has better vision than ordinary mortals, and the commonsensical truths that it sees still strike the rest of us as something akin to madness.

Another reason for liking *Monsieur Verdoux:* I love to be amused at the movies, and this film made me laugh until my tears flowed like wine.

I believe I see growing up about me a certain taste for collective accomplishments, the anonymousness of which is a tribute to the adoration of new deities. Let me mention at random some of these false idols: public opinion polls, organization, technics. These are but the saints of a dangerous god that some are trying to substitute for the God of our childhood. This new divinity is called Scientific Progress. Like any self-respecting God, he tries to attract us with his miracles. For how else can one describe electricity, anaesthesia or atomic fission? But I am very leery of this newcomer. I am afraid that, in exchange for the refrigerators and the television sets that he will distribute so generously, he may try to deprive us of a part of our spiritual heritage.

In other times, every object was a work of art, in that it was a reflection of the one who made it. The humblest early American sideboard is the creation of one given woodworker, and not of any other. This personal touch was present in everything, in houses, in clothes, in food.

When I was young, in my village in Burgundy, when we drank a glass of wine, we could say: That comes from the Terre à Pot vineyard up over the hill behind the little pine wood, or from the Sarment Fountain, or from some other specific spot. Some bottles left on your tongue the silex taste of their vines, others were like velvet and you knew they came from a lush green valley with plenty of moisture. Closing your eyes, you could see a certain greyish hill, with its twisted little oaks and the imprints of the boars' feet which had been found there last fall after the harvest. And later the young girls bending under the weight of their baskets full of luscious grapes. Especially, you recalled the wrinkled face of the vintner who had devoted his life to the culture of that difficult soil.

All the manifestations of life took on a profound meaning, because men had left their mark upon them. You felt that you were in the center of an immense prayer sent heavenward by all of the workers, with their plows, their hammers, their needles, or even simply their brains. Today we live in a desert of anonymity. The wines are blended. The nickel-plated tubing in my bathroom, the harwood of my floor, the fence around my garden, all bring to mind for me only the uniform purr of the machines that turned them out.

There are still a few places where we can seek a refuge. A painter can still speak to us of himself in his canvases, as a chef can in his culinary creations. That is probably why we are ready to pay fortunes for a good picture or for a good meal. And then there is also this film craft of ours, which will remain one of the great expressions of human personality if we are able to retain our artisans' spirit, which fortunately is still very much alive. That spirit is Chaplin's, down to the tips of his toenails. One feels it in a certain decent way he has of going into a scene, in the almost peasant-like thriftiness of his sets, in his wariness of technique for technique's sake, in his respect for the personalities of actors, and in that internal richness which makes us feel that each character just has too much to say.

Monsieur Verdoux will some day go into history along with the creations of artists who have contributed to the building of our civilization. He will have his place alongside the pottery of Urbino and the paintings of the French Impressionists, between a tale by Mark Twain and a minuet by Lulli. And during that time, the films which are so highly endowed with money, with technique and with publicity, the ones that enchant his detractors, will find their way God knows where, let us say into oblivion, along with the expensive mahogany chairs mass-produced in the beautiful nickel-plated factories.

(Mr. Renoir wrote this article in French and translated it into English with the assistance of Mr. Harold Salemson.)

GEORGE SEATON
(1911-   )

As the 40's wore on, more and more screenwriters were hungrily eyeing the director's chair, eager for a chance at the power, prestige and salary that the title afforded. The journal of the Screen Writers' Guild (now the Writers' Guild of America) published this article by George Seaton as a sort of outline for upwardly mobile screenwriters, a guide to becoming a "genuine film author" by achieving writer-director status. That phrase "film author" had been coined by Joseph L. Mankiewicz in an earlier article which had caused considerable comment. Mankiewicz postulated a "film author" who was totally responsible for what happened on screen due to his dual writer-director capacity. Such claims prefigured in a surprising fashion the claims of the later *politique des auteurs*, with the key difference being an *insistence* on the director's control of the writing (not a surprising theory to be generated by a group of writers, after all). George Seaton had functioned as a writer in Hollywood since 1933, working on such scripts as *A Day at the Races, Song of Bernadette* and *Miracle on 34th Street* (for which he won the Academy Award for best screenplay the year this article appeared). In 1943 he directed his own screenplay of *Diamond Horseshoe*, and afterwards he continued to function mainly as a director of his own material. This later work included *The Country Girl, The Proud and the Profane* and *Teacher's Pet*, but his greatest success came in 1969 as writer-director of *Airport*, cornerstone of a whole cycle of 70's disaster epics.

ONE TRACK MIND ON A
TWO WAY TICKET

GEORGE SEATON

On April 28th I received a telegram from the Editorial Board
of *The Screen Writer* asking me to contribute a few hundred
words to a symposium on how newer writers could become
genuine film authors under present conditions.

On April 29th I set down, under several neatly numbered
paragraphs, about four hundred words of counsel.

On April 30th I read it over and threw it in the waste basket.
I realized that in giving advice one must necessarily run the
risk of seeming patronizing, but I never knew how much brevity increased that risk. I hope that now, having been permitted
to go into the subject a little more fully, I will not be found
guilty of looking down from any lofty heights—for, although
Mr. Mankiewicz placed me in some rather fast company and
named me as one who has learned his trade thoroughly, I certainly do not consider myself, even after fifteen years, a genuine film author. I only hope that after another fifteen I might
be able to sit through one of my pictures without wincing too
many times. However, directing my own screen plays for the
past four years has taught me a lot—not only about direction
but more importantly about screenwriting. It is solely from a
standpoint of experience, then, that I venture a few opinions.

As for Mr. Mankiewicz' critique—I liked it. I have always believed that far too many of us know far too little about the medium. But more than appreciating what it said, I like what it
did. With the exception of the opening salvos on A.A.A., I
have never seen an article in our magazine cause so healthy a
controversy. Seminars and symposiums were held under the
sponsorship of the Guild; every studio commissary became a
debating platform; and the traditional battlefield, Schwab's
soda fountain, got its best workout. I was impressed by the sin-

From *The Screen Writer*, September 1947. Reprinted by permission of
the Writers' Guild of America.

cerity of the comments and suggestions that poured in, for, although they both blasted and praised, they all had one thing in common—an honest desire to improve the lot of the writer in Hollywood.

This piece is written in the same spirit for screen writers who respect their craft. So if you are a novelist who is a little contemptuous of the medium, using Hollywood merely as a comfortable motel on your travels between one book and another, this piece will be of little interest. If you are a playwright who is here "to knock out a quick screenplay and pick up a few bucks" while your producer tries to find some picture name for your new show, you'll find glancing at a casting directory much more profitable. Or if you are one who looks upon motion pictures as nothing more than the bastard offspring of the theater and a 2A Brownie and considers a script just a hundred and twenty pages of "gimmicks," "twists," "formulas," "weenies," "heart," "routines," "boffs," "yaks," "toppers," "bleeders" and "chases"—please go home.

If, on the other hand, you agree as I do with Sheridan Gibney that "screenwriting is a new form of dramatic art," and are willing to give it the respect and effort that such a definition commands, then maybe what I have to suggest might be of value. Not that I recommend what follows as the only solution, nor do I claim that by heeding my advice you will become a Dudley Nichols overnight. I merely state that it helped me and, all other things being equal, it might help you.

To my way of thinking there are two ways of acquiring that technical facility, that awareness of the medium, which help to make a competent writer a genuine film author. The first method is by the process of osmosis: a gradual absorption of knowledge from any number of sources—discussions with directors and competent producers, working with experienced collaborators, seeing countless pictures, studying bales of scripts, trial and error, etc. The second is by watching pictures being shot. Having tried the "osmosis" school for ten years, I heartily recommend the second method, not because those ten years were without activity and reward (as a matter of fact I think I received as many credits and as much employment as most), but because that period was without satisfaction. It was filled with insecurity and fear—fear, I imagine, that someone was going to discover what I knew all along—that I didn't know what the hell I was doing.

I was able to hold my own in conferences and salt my conversation with phrases like "Mat shots," "Dolly back," "Zoom in" and "Traveling inserts," but it didn't help. I felt like one of those Benchley Americans in Paris. I knew just enough of the language to get around and impress other Americans but I felt that the French were laughing at me. I had picked up a few key words but I hadn't bothered (or been given the opportunity) to learn those all-important irregular verbs. So, deciding to go back and cram, I took up residence on a set. Believe me, in three months I learned more than I had in the preceding ten years.

The first suggestion, then, is watch a picture being shot. If it happens to be one of your own scripts, so much the better—if not, any script will do provided you've studied it sufficiently. Now by watching shooting I don't mean dropping in on the set for a few minutes on your way back from the commissary. I mean sitting behind the camera all day every day. (Okay—we might as well stop right here and settle the question of "How do I get on a set?")

I know that some of the studios won't allow you to observe production. But let's be honest—why should they allow it? Why should they pay you while you learn something you were supposed to have known when you took the assignment in the first place? You shouldn't expect it any more than you should be expected to pay a secretary while she takes a course in typing. The answer then, though simple to give and difficult to follow, is—go off salary. I have never heard of any studio that closed a set to a writer if the writer was willing to visit it without being paid for the privilege. I realize that giving up six to twelve weeks of employment or the chance of it, is not without sacrifice—but I'm sure that before you learned the technique of writing a short story, a play or a novel, you went a lot longer without remuneration. And if we agree that screenwriting is a new dramatic art form, then achieving a greater knowledge of it becomes well worth the time, sacrifice and effort.

An author who chooses to write for motion pictures is very much like a general medical practitioner who decides to become a specialist. To accomplish it the doctor gives up his practice, takes a residency at a hospital, and studies his specialty for a couple of years. To a lesser degree the would-be screenwriter must study in the same way, and the place to do it is on the set. Although there will be no salary coming in, the period of observation will not be without compensation. What you will learn will make you a better screenwriter and consequently place you in a position to demand more money.

What will you learn on a set? The same things a playwright learns during an out-of-town tryout. No matter how beautiful the script sounded when you read it to your wife you'll discover, by seeing it on its feet, that it has many shortcomings. The countless rehearsals and takes will magnify the little faults you thought unimportant. Scenes will be overlong and static. At first you'll blame it on the actors, the director or anybody else who happens to be handy. But after a time, if you're able to look at the whole thing objectively, you'll have to admit that when you wrote the script you did not concern yourself with the possibilities of the camera. You depended too much on dialogue to score your points. You'll discover you're both showing and telling and consequently the scenes appear obvious and overwritten. Gradually you'll begin to think in terms of the camera—you'll visualize scenes not as framed by a proscenium arch or the margins of a printed page but as seen through the "finder"—that little black box that tells you exactly what you're going to get on the screen. If your values are not in the finder you're a dead duck and no amount of brilliantly written stage direction will help you. If you learn nothing else, your time will not be wasted because, all other things being equal, the ability to use the camera as a collaborator is the primary difference between a good screen craftsman and a bad one. But you *will* learn more—dozens of things which you never thought essential but which will prove invaluable when you tackle your next script.

After the picture is shot sit in with the film editor. Most of them whom I have met are only too anxious to answer questions and help in any way possible. Here again you will be reminded of the importance of the camera. When you see all of the film put together you'll notice that many lines of dialogue—yes, even entire scenes—are unnecessary. When you wrote the script you fought for them—the story, you felt, would never get across without them. Even on the set you were against cutting too drastically. Now you find, with some expert use of a couple of close-ups and reactions, that a three-page scene can be told in a dozen lines and with no values lost. It might even be more subtle and have better tempo than when you first conceived it. A good cutter is as much an artist as you are—don't avoid him.

My only other suggestion is one which no one else has deemed important enough to mention. Maybe I'm overestimating its value but since it has been of tremendous help to me, here it is: while preparing a script consult one of the studio's art directors. He will show you how you can get the maximum of production with the minimum of construction and probably make your scenes photographically more interesting. Economy of construction, as well as economy of words, is a writer's problem and the art director will help you achieve it. I mention this for your self-protection. If you disregard the number and size of your sets you'll discover that the production will be cut down later anyway, and most likely without any consideration for the import of the scenes. Furthermore, by working closely with an art director you're not so apt to go to the preview and find your professor-hero living in a twelve room penthouse. If he's consulted at an early stage and sees what you're trying to achieve you'll get a much more realistic production. Lastly, you will know what your sets will look like and consequently will be able to devise pieces of business that will heighten and make for less static scenes.

There will be many who will argue that the above suggestions are not sound, principally because they contend that a writer is a story-teller, no more, no less, and his mind should not be cluttered with a lot of technical mumbo-jumbo. They maintain that that is the director's province and we should keep out of it. I might agree if this business were run differently. If a writer and a director were assigned simultaneously and worked together, each contributing his particular talents in a collaborative effort, that would be one thing. But I was asked: "How can newer writers become genuine film authors under present conditions"—and that is quite another. Aside from a few teams in the tradition of Capra-Riskin and Ruggles-Binyon, *present conditions* means that a writer finishes a script one week and a director starts shooting the next. More often than not the two never meet. Under such an arrangement it behooves the writer to become more than a story-teller. Because a hundred and twenty pages of story, no matter how beautifully told, is not a shooting script, and a director with budgets and schedules staring him in the face has no alternative but to make changes as he goes along. Since this method of operation has proved at least financially successful I have little hope that it will be altered. The change must come then in the writer's concept of screenwriting.

The phrase "present conditions" also implies another glaring fault. The studios cry for "fresh" writing talent, men and women with "new ideas." These walking panaceas are brought out from New York by the dozens. Most of them, quite honestly, admit they know nothing about writing for motion pictures. The answer is always the same: "Don't worry about that. What we want is your great feel for character and your sparkling dialogue." Somehow this "feel" and "sparkle" seldom face a camera because most of the time the scripts never turn out the way the producer dreamed they would. Could it be that the studios have been crying and searching for the wrong thing all the time? I think so. I think what they've really been praying for are genuine film authors. Men and women who not only feel and sparkle but who know the medium and are able to get it on the screen.

Although "present conditions" is a brick wall in many ways, it also offers an opportunity. Two studios have thrown open their stages to writers who want to learn. At 20th Century-Fox,

Darryl F. Zanuck has promised that any writer who wishes to observe production may do so. The only conditions are that you do not expect remuneration and are not on an assignment at any other studio. You will not be herded from stage to stage like visitors. You may pick your director and, if agreeable with him, will be allowed to remain on his set for the entire production. Every effort will be made to help you achieve a greater understanding and knowledge of the medium. At R-K-O, Dore Schary makes the same offer. All you have to do is call the Guild office and arrangements will be made. Any takers?

FRITZ LANG
(1890-1976)

Originally trained as an architect, Fritz Lang turned instead to motion picture directing, and in the years after the First World War created such forbidding masterworks as *Die Nibelungen, Metropolis* and *M*. He left Germany with the advent of the Nazis, and after directing a version of *Liliom* in Paris signed a contract with MGM, arriving in 1934. MGM in the mid-30's was a petty tyranny which may very well have reminded Lang of his last days in the German studios; out of many proposed projects only one film resulted, but this was the incisive and inflammatory *Fury*. Lang left that studio and spent the remainder of his American career working for a wide range of other studios and independent producers, reaching his peak success in the 40's and early 50's with such *film noir* thrillers as *Ministry of Fear, Scarlet Street* and *The Big Heat*. Lang's complaints about censorship restrictions were shared by many filmmakers, but few were willing to attack directly the power of the Breen Office and the Legion of Decency; indeed, as the 50's approached, Hollywood was about to enter the most circumscribed years in its history. (The direct cause of this article—the New York State ban on *Scarlet Street*—was eventually solved by making several cuts, particularly in the number of times an ice-pick is driven into Joan Bennett.) For Lang it was not just the concept of censorship which offended, but the idea of power inevitably abused, and the further necessity to "watch the watchers"—themes not unrelated to those of his own best work.

THE FREEDOM OF THE SCREEN
FRITZ LANG

Some twenty years ago I made a film. It was called *Frau im Mond (The Girl in the Moon)* and it purported to show the flight of a great rocket through space, its landing on the moon and the subsequent adventures of the crew in that first exploration of the moon's surface. It was a film which portrayed man's daring in the face of the unknown. That film was withdrawn from circulation by the Nazis, and the models of my space-ship were confiscated by the Gestapo. Of the technical experts who helped me, Willy Ley fled from Germany to become a rocket expert in the United States, but Professor Oberth remained and used those models in developing the infamous V2 bombs. The results of censorship are not always so spectacular.

I do not believe in censorship. There are times, during wars for example, when it seems essential, but at best it is a necessary evil. Attempts by majority or minority alike to impose a pattern of thought on the great body of the people lead only to general ignorance and misunderstanding and to a disaster in which all are involved, both the would-be instructors and the misinstructed public. Free discussion, the cut and thrust of argument and the wide circulation of information are the very life-blood of a democracy. We must constantly guard against handing over these freedoms and privileges to the care of others. No group can do our thinking for us. In the words of Lord Acton, all power corrupts and absolute power corrupts absolutely.

It seems obvious that mature and properly educated citizens should be subjected to the widest possible variety of experience and opinion. It is only by the presentation of new ideas that our civilization can move forward. Yet by its very nature censorship rejects the unfamiliar. Censors play safe. In the name of

From *Theatre Arts*, December 1947.

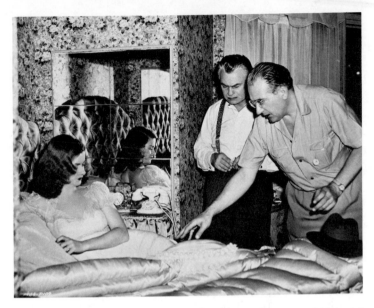

Fritz Lang acts out a murder scene for Joan Bennett and Edward G. Robinson during production of *Scarlet Street* (1945).

law and order and of morals they reject new ideas as subversive. There is in all of us, to a varying degree, a certain antipathy to change which springs from the deepest instinct of all—that of self-preservation. This is especially true of older people, who, conservative and liberal alike, become hardened in beliefs implanted during their earlier impressionable years. As Michael Blankfort said in one of his novels, "Reform is always the dream of the young and the nightmare of the old." The way of real security and progress lies neither in the blind acceptance nor in the undiscriminating rejection of new ideas; they must be scrutinized, tested and, if found of value, adopted. The censors would deny us the right to examine what is new.

Censorship, whether of books, of plays or of motion pictures, is never effective in combating social ills, except in a negative sense. It can, to a limited extent and for a short time, prevent the spread of ideas or suggestions which might evoke a dangerous or unhealthy response among the immature, illiterate or irresponsible. However, people do not encounter such ideas in literature, theatre and film alone; they are constantly exposed to them in the normal course of life. To pretend that such ideas do not exist and to deny them an honest treatment in the arts is to treat the public as children. But perhaps this is the idea of censorship: to keep the public in a state of immaturity so that it can be the more easily influenced and imposed upon.

Censorship never cured a social evil. Crime is forbidden (censored!), but it does not vanish from the life of our nation. Nor can disease or poverty be eliminated by looking the other way. Such evils originate in social and economic conditions; the idea that people are poor just because they are lazy or that they commit crimes simply through weakness of character is as outmoded as the doctrine of original sin from which it stems. The way to abolish crime is not to hush up its existence but to examine its sources and, having laid them bare, to eliminate them. This has been the immemorial function of dramatic art, which has its very being in the situations arising out of conflict between character and character, character and environment. Drama is convincing only when the motives of the action are thoroughly understood and demonstrated. Let us look for motives, then, and in tracing them we shall throw light on the pressing problem of our time and society. If the film producer is allowed not less but more freedom, he will be in a position to spotlight the causes of crime and to prepare the way for reform and progress.

With the alleged intent of protecting the public from obscenity, censors frequently throw a veil around the frank treatment of sexual relations; too often they only succeed in ridiculing sex by reducing it to an affair of adolescent necking and petting. At the present moment, sexual questions are presented more frankly and forthrightly to children at school than to adult cinema audiences. In the classroom, at any rate, it is recognized that sex is concerned with more than double entendres; it is an essential element in the healthy life of a nation. The danger, as always, lies not in telling the truth but in telling half-truths.

It is sometimes maintained that motion pictures, as a form of entertainment, should avoid the sterner issues of life. Yet when that happened in Hollywood, to quote the critic Otis Ferguson, "Gag men rushed in and flooded the public with plays on words and plays on situations which were no more than the sly echo of the jaded laughter of burlesque." True recreative entertainment can never flourish in a vacuum; the art of Dostoievsky, Zola, Dickens, Shaw and a hundred others proves the precise opposite. Films must draw strength from life, for only by modeling themselves on the ever-shifting patterns and conflicts of society can they continue to interest, to stimulate and, by dramatizing society's problems, to indicate solutions.

It is the contention of those who favor censorship that the mass of people is not mature, that it is not sufficiently educated politically, socially or sexually to escape the harmful influence of books, drama, etc., which have been shaped with some ulterior motive—political or simply pornographic and mercenary. It is sheer hypocrisy to suppose that people at large are any less mature than those who govern them—than those persons in particular who, without any mandate from the public, find their way to censorship boards. The imposition by a minority of a censorship of ideas is a very different matter from the popular enactment by a majority of laws against obscenity, and it may be pointed out that indecency and pornography are forbidden in motion pictures under the same laws that govern cartoons, books, stage shows and magazines. Where taste or morality is violated, the police have power to step in, and the public is amply protected by the courts.

There is one section of the community especially susceptible to the influence of the motion picture, namely, children and adolescents, and their position requires separate examination. Children are so imaginative, so open to suggestion and unequipped to assess the underlying significance of much of what they see that the supporters of censorship are only too ready to take up the cudgels in their behalf, obscuring the issue by a wholesale use of such terms as "poisoning the minds of the young." Investigations carried out by psychologists and social workers have shown that the proponents of censorship over-emphasize the possible dangers to which children are subject at ordinary film showings. The evidence goes to prove that children absorb from pictures what they have learned already from their environment. The investigations show further that the most harmful effect of films is not in those aspects currently subject to censorship but in implanting the idea of a dream world, where the rewards come without corresponding effort, and in thus maladjusting children to the struggles of real life. References to sex tend to bore rather than to excite young children, and it is only at the adolescent stage that the sexual element becomes important.

In some foreign countries, England, for example, a solution has been sought by dividing films into categories suitable and unsuitable for children. One of the objections to such a scheme is that children reach maturity at very different ages and that to fix a definite age, such as sixteen years, seems most arbitrary. Control by the parents, in itself a kind of censorship, affords sufficient protection. The crux of the problem is to raise the educational and social standards of the parents, so that the children may grow up in enlightened homes. I can see only disastrous results if we should actually succeed in raising a generation unfamiliar with the realities of life, misled by false, Pollyanna films and books into believing that life is a bed of roses, where all people are good, trustworthy human beings, or else come to a bad end in the last reel!

The word censor is a Roman one, but there was censorship before Roman times, and Socrates had fallen its victim before the Roman Senate appointed two censors to watch manners and morals and to punish those who offended them. In those days, as now, no appeal was possible; the power of the censors was absolute. An old Latin watchword rings down the centuries as a warning to us of today: *Quis custodiet ipsos custodes* —who shall watch those who have been set to watch us? The answer is that we of a later generation have watched them. We have watched them gag Milton; we have watched them while they denounced Copernicus and jailed Galileo; we have watched all the bigots from Savonarola down to Hitler while they defaced and mutilated and made bonfires of the books. The stench of those fires lingers in our nostrils.

I do not believe in censorship. All history speaks against it, all good feeling informs against it. As an American and a working creator of films I take a special and personal interest in the development of film censorship in the United States. Given the imperfect state of the world it would be foolish to pretend that we are confronted by a uniformly rational and educated audience or that filmmakers are always creative artists. After the 1914 war, and perhaps through the shortsighted efforts of its own publicists, an impression was created that life in Hollywood was a single unbroken drunken orgy and that such behavior was mirrored in its films. A storm of protest raged up and down the country and was activated by innumerable protests, bans and resolutions framed by women's clubs, youth movements, church organizations, veterans' associations and the United States Senate. In the face of a spectacular drop in receipts and the prospect of a crippling Federal censorship, the leaders of the industry banded together and engaged Will H. Hays to take charge of public relations. As part of his program of reform he instituted and began the administration of the Production Code, a form of self-censorship which, with various revisions, has governed the industry since; and as a direct result the various clubs and institutions were prevailed upon to drop their demands for official censorship. The crisis had been averted.

Now that the heat of the conflict has died down, it may be observed that such outcries do not always arise because the ordinary citizen is offended. They are as apt to start with the objections of a clamorous and narrow-minded minority—just those people, in fact, who are so ready to band themselves into censorship boards. It is possible that the self-imposed discipline of the industry is essential at the present time to meet the complex demands of our society, but even this regulation should remain flexible and sensitive to changes in public understanding and taste. In due course it should prove feasible for the Johnston-Breen office, successors to the old Hays office, to relinquish the censorship of films which it now applies, in effect if not in name, through denying, to films not awarded a certificate, access to theatres controlled by companies subscribing to the Code. Then the Office can continue to advise producers as to the likely reactions of audiences at home and abroad, leaving the film-makers free to decide for themselves what they shall or shall not discuss.

There can be no justification for the rigid and compulsory censorship, above and beyond the Production Code, which is today exercised by certain state and local authorities. Such censorship reaches far beyond the areas over which such boards have assumed jurisdiction, for the film companies, in their natural desire to reach the largest possible audience, bear in mind the tendencies of local censors when planning their productions. The exclusion of a film from, say, the state of New York entails serious financial loss. My own picture, *Scarlet Street*, was originally banned in New York State, Milwaukee and Memphis and, in each case, the ban was removed only after prolonged representation, though elsewhere in the country the picture was shown quite freely.

There are in America today some 56,000,000 moviegoers, and what those millions see or do not see is subject to the whims and prejudices of the seven state film censorship boards in Kansas, Maryland, Massachusetts, New York, Ohio, Pennsylvania and Virginia, and some sixty-four city censors. The political powers of the south, for instance, by insisting on a certain limited film presentation of the Negro people in their own area have imposed this picture of the Negro on the United States as a whole. The position has now been reached where the film companies, pressed by the southern politicians on one hand and criticized on the other for their inadequate presentation of the American Negro, are deliberately avoiding any inclusion of Negroes in their pictures. The film companies could not possibly afford to release separate versions to tell different stories to the varying sections of the population.

Censorship is an unwarranted intrusion on the civil liberties of a great nation. A people which, through years of effort and opposition to demagogues great and small, has won the right to frame its own destiny is treated as if it were a collection of minors or wards of the state, to be protected, guided and deceived. By what decree are the descendants of those who left Europe to escape religious or political persecution, or of those others who struck at an English domination two centuries ago, now to be told what they may think and what they may not? In an age of prefabrication honest opinion is one thing which no people, least of all the Americans, can afford to have delivered to them packaged, tested, approved and sealed. In the field of the cinema such misguided efforts can only prevent the free operation of the one legitimate censorship—the censorship applied by the public. That censorship, as every producer knows, the public exercises to the full when it registers its reactions at the box-office.

FRED ZINNEMANN
(1907-   )

Today *The Search* is a nearly forgotten exercise, seldom revived and barely even discussed in histories of 40's cinema (the only extended study of the period, that of Higham and Greenberg, fails to even mention it in passing). Yet despite its all-too-apparent sentimentality, this well-intentioned fusion of American documentary and Italian neo-realism deserves a second look today. At a time when Hollywood films were once more leaving the studios and going out into the streets, Fred Zinneman made this one film which actually incorporated that world as a key dramatic element, and not mere window dressing. Zinnemann's first important credit, as a collaborator with the Siodmak brothers, Edgar Ulmer and Billy Wilder on *Menschen am Sonntag* (1929), predicted such a mingling of fictive and documentary elements. So did his work with Paul Strand on *The Wave* (1934-37) which he refers to here. In *The Search* Zinnemann's feeling for the dramatic character of a locale and its people does in fact recall such films as *Open City* and *Shoe Shine*. But if Zinnemann ultimately fails where Rossellini and De Sica succeed, that reason too is at least hinted at here: to "soften the truth" is the kiss of death in such an enterprise. Nine years as director of Pete Smith specialties and inexpensive program features at MGM had taken their toll on Zinnemann, and if *The Search* is ultimately less affecting than *The Wave* the blame might very well be laid to the imposition of Hollywood movie stars and an all-too-neatly developed storyline. Yes, *The Search* does follow the neo-realists out into the real world, but it manages to drag all the sentimental encumbrances of the film studios along with it.

DIFFERENT PERSPECTIVE
FRED ZINNEMANN

Critics of *The Search*, the film which depicts the plight of Europe's war orphans, were kind enough to credit its makers with pioneering a different point of perspective from which a screen story can be conceived.

It is, of course, understood that there is nothing essentially new or revolutionary in this approach. It was used with great success by many European film makers—the real pioneers of this approach—such as Rossellini in *Open City*, De Sica in *Shoe Shine* and Lindtberg in *The Last Chance*. It is new only insofar as its application to an American film, destined for the regular American market, is concerned.

Stated in its simplest terms this approach consists of using the raw material of contemporary history in order to make a dramatic document. The important element in such an undertaking is, of course, the fact that the story and its details must be conceived on the spot; second, that the inner truth of the subject matter is of such paramount importance that it must not be sacrificed to ulterior considerations such as star names and conventional treatment.

Our primary concern was *not* to attempt an artistic achievement, but to dramatize contemporary history for the large American audience and to make them understand in emotional terms what the world outside looks like today. We felt that if we could contribute even a small amount to such an understanding, all our efforts would be not in vain.

All of us realized, of course, that it would be necessary to soften the truth to a certain extent, because to show things as they really were would have meant—at least in our sincere opinion—that the American audience would have lost any de-

From *Sight and Sound*, Fall 1948. Reprinted by permission of *Sight and Sound* and Fred Zinnemann.

sire to face it, used as they have been through the years to seeing a sentimentalized world.

Before the start of the enterprise, we—i.e. Mr. Arthur Loew,
Mr. Lazar Wechsler and myself—unanimously agreed that the
picture was primarily destined for the American market and
that it must reach as many people as possible for the reasons
stated above, besides the very obvious reason of box office. We
were interested in a general acceptance of the film both as a
method of educating the large American public to a vital modern problem and also as a money maker. In this sense, *The
Search* was a test case, and from recent reports, it appears that
the test has been passed successfully.

While it is not too difficult for films in Europe to be extremely successful on their own merit regardless of important
box office names, this has been almost impossible up to now in
the United States. The American public has been consistently
"sold" on looking primarily for star names and personalities.
Therefore it is difficult indeed to expect them to go to see a
film only because of its inherent value. As everyone knows,
some of the great pictures of our time—such as *Open City*, *To
Live in Peace*, etc.—are patronized in the United States by a
comparatively restricted public.

It was producer Lazar Wechsler who first conceived the idea
of making *The Search*. He was familiar with the plight of Europe's "unaccompanied" children. Various people, among them
Leopold Lindtberg, the director of *The Last Chance* and *Marie
Louise*, and Therese Bonney, the well-known reporter and
photographer, who had authored a great book of photographs
on Europe's children, approached him regarding the idea and
urged him to develop it.

On a visit to America in 1945, Wechsler became impressed
with two things: the innate generosity of Americans and their
lack of comprehension of the extent of suffering abroad. He
realized, too, that this lack of comprehension had made Europe
suspicious of American generosity. He was keenly aware that
a motion picture, correctly done, could serve to interpret this
problem internationally.

My choice as director for *The Search* came about for a number of reasons. *The Seventh Cross*, with Spencer Tracy, which I had directed, had been quite popular in Europe. Very often, American films dealing with a European locale are severely criticized when shown in Europe, because of an apparent lack of authenticity: we were gratified that *The Seventh Cross* was an exception.

The fact that I speak German was undoubtedly a persuading factor. But I think that my work on *The Wave*, Mexican-made and one of the first successful "documentaries" was a more important case in point.

Mr. Wechsler, Mr. Richard Schweizer, the writer, and I fully agreed on the method to be followed in writing the scenario. We felt that the main thing was to get as much of the elements of the story as possible from first-hand observation; from seeing and studying the locale and talking to a maximum number of people who had been directly involved in the period of history we wanted to portray—veteran UNRRA employees who had been in Germany since the liberation, adult DP's and "unaccompanied" children. (The term "unaccompanied" in UNRRA parlance means children who have lost their parents and families and who have no one in the world to look after them.)

It is heartening, at this juncture, to remember that films like *The Search* are marketable to the public and *can* make money. The picture's box-office record bears out our contention. The Los Angeles showing of the film, for instance, was a near record. Its run of eight weeks at the Four Star Theatre has been bettered by very few films.

It is even more heartening to remember that this type of motion picture need not bring in grosses of four or five million dollars in order to be profitable. There seems to be a close connection between authenticity and economy; the realistic story can be told without help of large studios, expensive stars and elaborate wardrobes.

This approach is not limited in its application. The entire world is—potentially—a stage, and the motion picture is at its best when it provides a kind of common human language.

My future plans are predicated on the idea that this approach may be used successfully, everywhere. As my next picture, I plan to do a story on Palestine. This film will take no sides. Also, I should like to do an American date-line film story of the essential subject matter of *The Search*, presenting the "unaccompanied" children of the United States, those psychological orphans and displaced young people whose maladjustments have created a tremendous national problem of juvenile delinquency.

We will continue to think of the word "box-office" in its larger meaning, as an index of public acceptance. In the beginning, we may have to make certain compromises to bring about this acceptance, for we will always primarily aim at the general American audience. We hope, however, to keep on developing and improving the quality of such films as rapidly as possible.

LEWIS MILESTONE
(1895-   )

"As a creative artist it ought to be my business to create. Yet today I must concern myself with more than the aesthetic principles of film making." Lewis Milestone found that in 1949 the additional concerns of any filmmaker had expanded to include First Amendment rights, congressional committees, atom secret leaks and "the political beliefs of the chief hairdresser." Many in Hollywood were running scared in 1949, shaken by the impact of the first HUAC investigations two years earlier. Milestone is quite right here in attributing to the political atmosphere a great deal of Hollywood's artistic indirection. The great films of the period might be escapist romances (*Letter from an Unknown Woman*) or classical thrillers (*Strangers on a Train*) but few films of a directly political nature were produced. Even a film like Rossen's *All the King's Men* deals more with the abuses of one man than with the deficiencies of any political system, a distinct retreat from the posture of many pre-war films. After a strong post-war start with *A Walk in the Sun* and *The Strange Love of Martha Ivers* (both from Robert Rossen scripts), Milestone's career was also sidetracked into ennui, and while some of this might be attributed to the political climate, his own artistic limitations seem just as much to blame. On the practical side his suggestions for streamlining Hollywood's production policies are well taken, and again we see the resentment of the producer system (see the Milestone article in the first volume of this anthology) and the insistence on better scripting and pre-production work, demands shared by most directors and writers. But Milestone was hardly given a chance to see them work, as he directed relatively little in 50's Hollywood.

FIRST AID FOR A SICK GIANT
LEWIS MILESTONE

No pictures with "messages." No pictures that cost more than a million and a half. Nobody goes to the movies. Business is bad. In all Hollywood only 370 actors under studio long-term contracts, compared to a normal 1,200. Out of a total of some 1,800 writers who have worked on scripts during the last three years fewer than 250 are employed, and of these only about 50 are under long-term contract. One-third of all unemployment-insurance applicants in the Hollywood area are studio workers. A long list of directors, a Hollywood *Who's Who*, unemployed. RKO dumping 150 finished screen plays on the writers' market for sale to other studios. A domestic gross of two and a half million dollars is a smashing success, compared with a wartime gross of seven or eight million. The average picture is lucky to bring back a million and a half. The foreign market is practically nonexistent. This is the picture of Hollywood which confronts those who work in the industry. And there has not been a single suggestion for a cure that makes sense.

Public apathy, in my opinion, is the result of Hollywood's own inept propaganda which characterizes current output as cheaply made, inferior, message-less and third-rate. And I quote no less a source than the *Hollywood Reporter*, industry spokesman. Publisher W. R. Wilkerson, in his daily column, "Tradeviews," writes:

> In all other big industries, when the going gets tough, that's the time the organizations put on their greatest selling splash. . . . Not so our business. When ticket sales fall off a bit, whether through bad product or a general decline in the traffic at our box office, our companies add to this condition by playing dead, yelling murder, and, through their activities (or lack of them) further accentuate the situation in the eyes of the public, causing less ticket sales.
>
> At this moment ALL of our customers have been sold the

From *The New Republic*, January 31, 1949. Reprinted by permission.

Lewis Milestone, Sam Goldwyn, James Wong Howe, and Aaron Copland during production of their Eastern Front melodrama, *North Star* (1943).

idea that the motion picture industry is in great economic trouble. The depression that's now hit us is a self-made depression, inflicted by our company heads who became frightened into hysteria at the loss of foreign revenues and the slackening of business at our domestic windows. . . . Our companies have discontinued every effort to inspire our former customers to buy tickets.

. . . Our company heads, hysterical in their fight for "greater economy," have cut the very ingredients that did most of the selling to the people who buy our shows. . . . Our product is no worse than it has ever been; our entertainment is just as good for our customers, but these customers have been sold by our inactivity to stay away. And they are.

Wilkerson's tradeview editorials, although no monuments of journalistic literature, do faithfully mirror the producers' state of mind. People are staying away from pictures because th industry has nurtured the popular notion that Hollywood is making fewer but shoddier pictures, a notion sped on its way by the industry's trade press, by Hollywood's radio tattlers and daily columnists. Widespread information about studio shutdowns and layoffs, cutbacks and economy drives have all been assurances of cinematic inferiority. There is no necessary relationship, it should be emphasized, between limited output and increased quality; Hollywood is making about half the films it made five years ago, but it does not follow that these four hundred features are being made with greater care and excellence. For the men responsible for what Wilkerson calls "greater economy hysteria" are also responsible for Hollywood's output.

Public apathy and indifference, in my opinion, are directly attributable to two elements: Hollywood's well-publicized home-cooked depression; and the content of almost all of Hollywood's current product.

In the somewhat happier days of Hollywood's past, the creative artist—director, writer, actor, art director—worked to the best of his ability at making pictures. We were not remotely concerned with the First Amendment, risk insurance, the political beliefs of the chief hair-dresser, atomic secret leaks or New Jersey congressmen. We thought that the successful box-office picture was invariably the result of complete coöperation among all the crafts, guilds, unions and the front office. We made some good pictures, and we made some bad ones. We made errors of judgment and mistakes in execution. We were chiefly concerned with evolving a formula for the production of entertaining and intelligent box-office winners. In these interesting and stimulating debates we generally agreed that there was no rule for success, and that the risk of success or failure would always be present, for no one in the business could gauge the indeterminates of changing taste, varying public moods, fads and favorites of the moment.

At this moment, disputations about the relative merits of the original screen story v. the published novel, of the star system v. the qualified unknown, or any of the other craft questions which occupied our time, seem academic. Today the question is not what kind of entertainment shall we make; the question is: Under existing conditions can we make pictures at all?

If Hollywood wants to recapture its public, then it needs a forceful, positive public-relations campaign to overcome the popular conception that it has lost its skill in making good pictures; and to hold this recaptured audience the industry will have to do something about the blandness of its output. A fear psychosis pervades the town, engendered by recent witch hunts on the national, state and community level. Producers are asking for and getting pictures without ideas. In the frantic effort to offend no one, to alienate no group, to create no misgivings in congressional minds, studios are, for the most part, obediently concentrating on vapidity. The public, let it be noted, did not ask that pictures be sterilized of ideas; the notion was self-imposed. The "think pictures," as the New York *Times* has characterized them, are gone; and so are the audiences.

Producers are also saying that "quality production" is impossible because of prohibitive costs, and since there is less risk in a 14-day, $600,000 feature, why bother with quality? The bankers are saying if a $2 million "A" grosses $2 million today, let's make a $150,000 stinker that grosses $160,000. The usual explanation is that story costs, stars' salaries and labor bills have conspired to make motion-picture production unprofitable. This is a canard which has been given the widest hearing and credence in Hollywood, and very little analysis.

If producers are sincerely eager to make quality films, and if they feel that costs are keeping them from "A" production, let them consider cutting costs in the following spheres without sacrificing quality, without union-breaking, without shutdowns and layoffs:

In story preparation. Rarely is the director given time to prepare his script properly. Intelligent preparation means that the director, working with the writer, will solve story problems *before* production.

In pre-production rehearsal. This means that the cast, the director and key members of the crew develop the story action in rehearsal time instead of walking into the story cold.

In the purchase of basic stories. Studios pay too little attention to the original story vehicle. Although elementary, it is not always understood that a Broadway hit or a book-club selection is not an automatic guarantee of box-office success.

In front-office feather-bedding. The producer system—in which one man supervises the production of a number of films during the year—was created out of economic necessity. The producer was supposed to supervise the picture before production, thereby eliminating the director's need for pre-production preparation. His salary was to be prorated among all of the films he was supposed to produce. But the producer has become more than a businessman; he has developed an esthetic sense, and sometimes he takes as long as two years to develop a single feature. What began as an expedient time and money saver has now become an economic millstone, and in some instances twelve producers on one lot turn out an aggregate of three pictures a year.

In selection of backgrounds. There is some, but not much, imagination in the selection of story setting and backgrounds. Authentic locales are often better and less expensive than studio sets.

In the establishment of effective story departments. For mysterious reasons, when economy drives begin studios cut these departments first, firing story analysts and readers in the blind haste to save money. Story-department heads, men trained to know screen and literary values, are rarely given adequate standing or authority. The story department ought to be the all-important base of any studio operation.

As a creative artist it ought to be my business to create. Yet, today I must concern myself with more than the esthetic principles of film making. I want to make pictures. I want others to make pictures. Lots of pictures. I think Hollywood is at its best when it is most active. We know for sure that the paucity of feature production today has been no guarantee of greater care and more quality. As a director I must, therefore, not only be concerned with craft and art problems; I must have a vital interest in the climate in which I work. I must do what I can to combat Hollywood's manufactured hysteria. We are still making a few good pictures, and we should give these films our encouragement. And above all, I think we ought to get away from the seventy-minute soporifics and get back to making films with content, substance and meaning.

ALFRED HITCHCOCK
(1899-   )

In 1949 Alfred Hitchcock was on the brink of the most successful phase of a long and successful career. *Rear Window*, *Vertigo* and *Psycho* were only three of the masterworks to come, but it should be remembered that at the time this article was written Hitchcock's reputation was at low ebb. He had returned to Britain to film *Under Capricorn*, and while there delivered this paper to a meeting of film technicians, supposedly outlining his approach to a new production. Supposedly, since this oddity is at once very typical of the Hitchcock image created by post-*auteur* criticism, and yet utterly unlike that image. Here is the director known around the world for the intricacy of his pre-production work. Every camera movement, every angle must be written into the script well in advance of shooting; there must be nothing left to chance "when the time comes" on the set itself. On the other hand, this Hitchcock also declares that "the making of a picture is nothing but the telling of a story," and that "techniques, beauty, the virtuosity of the camera, everything must be sacrificed or compromised when it gets in the way of the story itself." Hitchcock must have been keenly aware that his previous film, *Rope*, had been denounced as a stunt, ten reels of ten-minute takes which seem determined to impress their style over the flimsy content of Patrick Hamilton's play. So is he recanting here, or merely letting his wry sense of humor get the best of him? Hitchcock's public statements are often as tricky as his films, and always as carefully considered: the clever Hitchcock-watcher seldom accepts obvious interpretations.

PRODUCTION METHODS COMPARED
ALFRED HITCHCOCK

The filming of each picture is a problem in itself. The solution to such a problem is an individual thing, not the application of a mass solution to all problems.

Something I do today makes me feel that the methods I used yesterday are out of date, and yet tomorrow I may be faced with a problem which I can best solve by using yesterday's methods. That is why I try to make my first rule of direction—flexibility.

Next, I try to make it a rule that nothing should be permitted to interfere with the story. The making of a picture is nothing but the telling of a story, and the story—it goes without saying—must be a good one. I don't try to put onto the screen what is called "a slice of life" because people can get all the slices of life they want out on the pavement in front of the cinemas and they don't have to pay for them.

On the other hand, total fantasy is no good either—I'm speaking only for myself remember—because people want to connect themselves with what they see on the screen.

Those are all the restrictions I would place on the story. It must be believable, and yet not ordinary. It must be dramatic, and yet lifelike. Drama, someone once said, is life with the dull spots removed.

Now, having got our story—what next? Obviously we must develop our characters and develop the plot. All right, let's say that's been done. It may be putting a year's work in a few words, but let's say it. Are we ready to go on the floor? No, because our picture is going to need editing and cutting, and the time for this work is right now. The cuts should be made in the script itself, before a camera turns, and not in the film after the cameras have stopped turning.

From *The American Cinematographer*, May 1949. Reprinted by permission.

Hitchcockian humor. The director "pretended to cut his own throat instead of the cake" at a birthday party thrown for him during production of *Shadow of a Doubt* (1942). Or so says the original studio caption.

More important, if we shoot each scene as a separate entity out of sequence, the director is forced to concentrate on each scene as a scene. There is then a danger that one such scene may be given too great a prominence in direction and acting, and its relation with the remaining scenes is out of balance, or, again, that it hasn't been given sufficient value and when the scene becomes a part of the whole, the film is lacking in something.

You are all familiar with the "extra shots" that have to be made after the regular schedule is completed. That is because, in the shooting of the scenes, story points were missed. The extra, expository shots are generally identified by an audience for what they are—artificial devices to cover what had been overlooked in the preparation of the film.

Now, how can this be avoided? I think it can best be avoided if a shooting script is edited before shooting starts. In this way, nothing extra is shot, and, most important, story points will be made naturally, within the action itself.

Let me give an example of what I mean. Let's suppose that our story calls for two scenes in a certain street, one a view of a parade going by, and the other—several days later in our plot—being an intimate conversation between two people walking along the pavement. We shoot the scenes on different days, the parade a long shot, and the conversation a close-up. Now, after we've finished our scenes, we discover that the locale of the conversation is not quite clear to the audience. We must now shoot another long shot of that street which we will tack onto the front of the conversation merely to identify the street.

That "identifying long shot," in this case, is an unnecessary one. Because it's not really needed, it's awkward. If we'd seen to it that the script had been given expert editing before the film went on the floor, we would have found some way to identify the street within the structure of the conversation itself. Or, better still, since the parade scene is a long shot, we could have tried, at least, to combine the two. In this way, the parade would serve a dual purpose, its plot purpose, and its expository one.

Another example: if we do not edit before we shoot, we may be faced, in the cutting room, with one of the nastiest of all editorial problems—the unexplained lapse of time. Our characters speak on Monday, and then speak again on the following Monday. That a week has gone by may be essential to our plot, but we may have failed to make it clear in the sequences we have shot. There was a time—long since past—when we would simply have photographed the words "One Week Later" in transparency and caused them to appear on the screen in mid-air during the second scene.

The lapse of time can easily be indicated by the simple method of shooting one scene as a day scene and the next as a night scene, or one scene with leaves on the trees and the next one with snow on the ground. These are obvious examples, but they serve to illustrate what I mean by editing before production commences.

I try never to go to the floor until I have a complete shooting script, and I have no doubt everyone else tries to do the same thing. But, for one reason or another, we often have to start with what is really an incomplete script.

The most glaring omission in the conventional script, I believe, is Camera Movement. "Jane embraces Henry," the script may read. But where is the camera while the two have their fun? This omission is of very great importance. Of course, the director may decide how he is going to film the embrace "when the time comes," as the story conference idiom has it. I think the time is before shooting. And here we come face to face once again with the fact that the tendency today is to shoot scenes and sequences and not to shoot pictures. The embrace can be shot from the front, from either side, or from above. If we are really going to be arty about the thing, it can be filmed from behind. But when we make that concession we are speaking only of the embrace by itself, and not as part of a sequence which is, itself, part of a picture which ought to be a dramatic whole. The angle from which that embrace is to be shot ought to flow logically from the preceding shot, and it ought to be so designed that it will fit smoothly into whatever follows it, and so on. Actually, if all the shooting is planned and incorporated into the script, we will never think about shooting the embrace, but merely about shooting a picture of which the embrace is a part.

I've taken a long time to get around to telling you that I favor shooting pictures in sequence. After all, the film is seen in sequence by an audience and, of course, the nearer a director gets to an audience's point of view, the more easily he will be able to satisfy an audience.

A picture maker need not try to please everyone, of course. It is important to me, before anything else is done on a picture, to decide just what audience I'm aiming at, and then to keep my eye on that target from that moment on. But it is obviously uneconomic to shoot for a small audience, and a motion picture costing some hundreds of thousands of dollars, which has taken the efforts of one hundred or perhaps two hundred men, has no more business directing its appeal toward people with a special knowledge of film-making than exclusively towards, say, Seventh Day Adventists, or Atomic Research scientists, or Chicago meat-packers.

Now what of the actual techniques of picture making? I happen to have a liking, for instance, for a roving camera because I believe, as do so many other directors, that a moving picture should really move. And I have definite ideas about the use of cuts and fadeouts which, improperly handled, can remind the audience of the unreality of our medium and take them away from the plot. But those are personal prejudices of mine. I do not try to bend the plot to fit technique; I adapt technique to the plot. And that's the important thing. A particular camera angle may give a cameraman—or even a director—a particular satisfying effect. The question is, dramatically, is it the best way of telling whatever part of the story it's trying to tell? If not, out it goes.

The motion picture is not an arena for a display of techniques. It is, rather, a method of telling a story in which techniques, beauty, the virtuosity of the camera, everything must be sacrificed or compromised when it gets in the way of the story itself.

An audience is never going to think to itself: "what magnificent work with the boom" or "that dolly is very nicely handled"; they are interested in what the characters on the screen are doing, and it's a director's job to keep the audience interested in that. Technique that calls itself to the audience's attention is poor technique. The mark of good technique is that it is unnoticed.

Even within a single picture, techniques should vary, even though the over-all method of handling the story, the style, must remain constant. It is, for instance, obvious that audience concentration is higher at the beginning of a picture than at the end. The act of sitting in one place must eventually induce a certain lassitude. In order that that lassitude should not be translated into boredom or impatience, it is often necessary to speed up things a little towards the end, particularly towards the end of a long picture.

This means more action and less talk, or, if talk is essential, speeches ought to be short, and a little louder and more force-ful than they would be if the same scene were played earlier in the picture. Putting it bluntly, it's sometimes necessary to ham things up a bit. This rule was recognized very early in the picture business, and the old-timers used to say: "when in doubt, get louder and faster." They were putting it a bit crudely, but perhaps the rule still applies.

It takes a certain amount of tact, of course, to induce a good actor to over-act and this is another argument in favor of shooting pictures more or less in sequence, because, once you have edged an actor into over-acting, it is, sadly enough, en-tirely impossible to edge him back again.

Direction, of course, is a matter of decisions. If it were pos-sible to lay down a hard and fast rule that would cover all the decisions, all directors would be out of work. I shudder to think of *that*, but fortunately, it's impossible.

The important thing is that the director makes his decisions when the need for them arises, and operates with as few rules as possible. The fewer rules you have, the fewer times you'll have to experience the unhappiness of breaking them.

CLARENCE BROWN
(1891-   )

Clarence Brown was perhaps the most successful inhabitant
of the MGM film factory, a capable and enterprising director who could satisfy the requirements of Louis B. Mayer
without compromising his own highly personal standards.
Originally an assistant to the director Maurice Tourneur,
Brown had won a small reputation for himself in the mid-
20's as director of films like *The Goose Woman* and *The
Eagle,* and in 1926 signed a contract with MGM. With the
single exception of *The Rains Came* (Fox, 1939) he stayed
at Culver City throughout his career, directing the brightest stars in the MGM firmament—Garbo, Tracy, Gable,
Rooney and many, many others. Garbo was of course his
special property, and he directed nearly all her key films,
including *Flesh and the Devil, A Woman of Affairs, Anna
Christie* and *Anna Karenina.* But Brown was also Metro's
master of Americana, and only Vidor could approach the
feeling for rural landscape behind *The Yearling* or *Intruder
in the Dust.* Brown was a product of the most producer-
infested studio in Hollywood, and if his analysis of the
actual duties of a producer echoes Albert Lewin, it stands
in sharp contrast to the plaints of Welles and Milestone
(Brown had by this time achieved producer status himself).
The director-vs-producer confrontation would seem to
come down to a matter of personality on the director's
part: how flexible is he? What ability does he have to get
along with the other studio workers and make use of the
studio facilities at his disposal? Like so many of the others
in this book, Brown sees the necessity of one man's being in
charge of any film, but unlike the others Brown sees that
man as the producer.

THE PRODUCER MUST BE BOSS
CLARENCE BROWN

Few creative undertakings require such complex technical activity and effort as that which goes into making a motion picture. The *administrative* requirements are more extensive than those of any other story-telling medium. And the technological processes require an astonishing range of talents and skills. The functional correlation of these talents at the peak of shooting activity in a busy studio is almost comparable to that of operating a battleship in combat.

There is a widely held misconception, nurtured by gag-writers and cartoonists, that picture-making is a fantastically profligate business in which enormous amounts of money are squandered on the whims and unpredictable impulses of producers with fat cigars and directors with berets.

It is true that the nature of picture-making permits and sometimes encourages unnecessary extravagances. This was especially true in the past. But movies are nevertheless an investment for profit, and the movie-maker who doesn't get a profit out of his expenditures is on his way out.

There was a period when it was supposed to be a mark of superiority on the part of the director to waste production money. If he wasted enough he was considered a genius. That was a long time ago. Nowadays directors pride themselves on being able to bring their pictures in on budget, on achieving a maximum of effect with a minimum of money.

Pictures are very carefully planned now. There is very little of that business of "shooting off the cuff," so widely practised in the early days.

It has been fashionable in some quarters to refer belittlingly to Hollywood as a "factory." In a sense, it is.

From *Films in Review*, February 1951. Reprinted with the permission of Films in Review, National Board of Review of Motion Pictures, Inc., 210 E. 68th St., N.Y., N.Y. 10021.

There must be a production department to oversee all the setting up, and to schedule the shooting on all pictures on the lot so that the proper stages, players, etc., are available at the right times. In other words, so that the various companies are not forever getting in each other's way. Merely forestalling such confusion is frequently very involved.

Good pictures don't spring full-blown from some writer's or producer's mind. Their creation is a process, elaborate and involved. Starting with the paymaster and on up or down, a studio *has* to be factory-like to be efficient. The way to get excellent camera work, for instance, is to have a set-up in which the photographers are well-trained and experienced, have the finest of equipment and facilities, and able and ample assistance. And that is the way comparable things are done in a factory.

The idea that efficiency and creative achievement are incompatible is absurd. The reverse is true. The more the physical and technological processes are organized, the freer and the more effective are the creative processes. Great movie-makers have overcome technical deficiencies, obstacles and delays, and have turned out fine pictures despite them. But never because of them.

The privilege of being able to pick up a phone and order any service or object and of being absolutely certain that it will be delivered with factory-like efficiency, precision, and dispatch, is an actual *spur* to make a better picture.

The operations involved in making a motion picture are so varied and widespread that one central authority is an absolute necessity. This central authority must be the producer. He is in charge of an army of workers, artisans, and creative artists of many different kinds. And he must see that the key places, in the technical and the creative departments, are assigned to the best candidates. The old saw that a good executive's main responsibility is seeing that capable people are selected is as true of movie-making as of any other business.

Because of countless cartoons and radio gags, a certain section of the public has evolved a conception of a motion picture producer that is a caricature: he is a portly, gross, illiterate despot given to thick cigars, swimming pool siestas, and a fabulous profligacy with money. He is a martinet with subordinates, a rascal in his professional dealings, and a cad in his relations with screen-struck girls. He is dismally incompetent in everything except flagrant opportunism. He orders his lieutenants to put Shakespeare under a writing contract. He lures gifted playwrights and novelists to Hollywood with his tarnished gold and then flogs the inspiration, not to mention the daylights, out of them.

All of which is on the level of comic Valentines of the Landlord, the Old Maid, and the Suffragette.

There is another more widespread attitude, almost as misleading, which is expressed in the question: "Yes, but what does a producer *do?*"

What does a producer do indeed!

At the present time producership is in a state of transition. It used to be that the functions of the producer and the director tended to fuse into one office, and were the prime example of how movie-making operations can telescope. But the present tendency seems to be toward a separation of the functions of the producer and the director.

In one sense, the creative activities involved in making a motion picture flourish better when a number of minds are involved in the single creative effort. There are definite reasons for this. They arise from mechanical and technical requirements.

It is a situation peculiar to the cinema. One dynamic creative mind conceives and executes a novel, and any intrusion of another personality or influence, makes the novel the poorer. Nobel Prize Winner William Faulkner's *Intruder in the Dust*, for example, is a monument to the one mind that created it. Such purity and singleness of conception and form are possible only when the work is the product of one artist. (I happened to have the genuine pleasure of making the picture based on this book. That Mr. Faulkner was well pleased with it has been one of the most gratifying rewards I have received in some 35 years of making movies.)

Fine as it was as a novel, *Intruder in the Dust* could not have been transformed for the screen, even in its purely creative story essence, by one person. I am not here considering the actors, the set designers, the thousand and one artisans whose joint technical efforts result in a movie. I am talking about the artists who work only with the story.

The screen constitutes a medium unlike any other. It partakes a little of the novel, a little of the play, a little of every other story-telling medium ever devised, including ancient archaeological pictographs and their modern counterpart, the comic strips. Yet what it has borrowed it has had to adapt; what it has been able to use it has had to transform into new narrative techniques.

In the early days specialization in the various fields that contribute to movie-making was intense, and probably because of this the separation of creative functions became too wide.

When we grant that a movie doesn't emerge from one mind, we run into the question of just how many cooks it takes to spoil a movie broth.

There is no pat answer to this question. Each picture has its own equations, different from those in all other pictures. The past experiences of the creative artists concerned are unlike. There are numerous other influences and considerations.

Looking back at Hollywood's products, good and bad, over the years, I can justly lay many a cinematic sin on the doorstoop of the separation of the creative functions and of the division of command.

From the almost primitive—but, within the frame of their time, magnificent—pictures of such giants as D. W. Griffith and my personal mentor, Maurice Tourneur, most of the *great* pictures have been the work of a single, dynamic, dominating mind.

Take casting. Our casting departments are indispensable. They work miracles in delivering to the producer the player needed for any type of role. Their resources and recourses are remarkable. If at the close of a day's shooting, you change your script and suddenly order Casting to dig up 11 one-legged Tibetan yak-herders, believe me, come the following dawn, you'll have 11 one-legged Tibetan yak-herders.

The casting department relieves the producer and/or director of endless tedium. It fulfills its function well. Yet, consider how many poor pictures would have been much better if the producer had been permitted, or able, to select each key member of his cast.

In Hollywood's history there have been times and situations in which the studio administrative set-up, or personality conflicts between executives, or sheer indifference on the part of the producer, has let this final casting authority slip entirely out of the hands of the real picture-maker, i.e., of the producer.

Probably the most perfect set-up is one in which the producer has absolute authority on all final decisions, but reaches them after conferences, and in agreement, with his director and other associates.

GEORGE SIDNEY
(1911-   )

Best remembered today for his direction of such classic
musicals as *Anchors Aweigh, The Harvey Girls* and *Show
Boat,* George Sidney arrived at MGM in 1932 as a director
of tests, short subjects and second-unit material. His work
included Our Gang comedies and Pete Smith specialties,
and when two of his films won short subject Oscars in 1940
and 1941 MGM promoted him to feature director. His
career prospered well into the 60's with such light but stylish musicals and biographies as *The Eddie Duchin Story,
Jeanne Eagels, Pal Joey* and *Bye, Bye Birdie.* Sidney's best
films have a definite sense of movement and visual grace, a
quality apparent not only in his musicals but in such costume pictures as *The Three Musketeers* and *Scaramouche*
(a film which contains one of the screen's most brilliant
dueling sequences). The craftsmanship evident in these
films is in the best tradition of Hollywood narrative construction: seamless editing, unobtrusive camera movements, a general "invisibility" of the filmmaker's hand. Sidney's essay here is not only a tribute to this invisible style,
but a frontal assault on those directors who violate its principles in pursuit of "fads" and "symbols." Note that Sidney
is not suggesting the superiority of styleless films, but instead attacking those films that substitute mere style for
substance. His definition (and the standard Hollywood
definition) of an overly-styled film may not be that of contemporary critics and audiences, but it did serve as the main
"theoretical" grounding of Hollywood style throughout
the long years of big-studio affluence.

THE DIRECTOR'S ART

GEORGE SIDNEY

It is an ironical axiom of motion picture direction that the more knowing, the more adroit, and the more finished a director is, the less conscious nine out of ten people will be of his achievement. And conversely, the more his audiences are aware of his work and his personality, the poorer the picture will usually be.

By contemporary standards very little, if any, "intrusive" direction is really good direction. Whenever I see a scene in which the director seems to be saying "look at this clever presentation," or "look at this novel camera trick," I write it off as inferior story-telling.

The acid test of any directorial or camera innovation is whether it makes the point, creates the intended emotional response, furthers the story, or whether it merely calls attention to itself.

The art in directing lies in drawing an audience into a story so gracefully and so completely that the audience quickly loses its objectivity. The audience should never be reminded that the director is a very clever man and is manipulating its emotions. Just as it shouldn't be conscious that actors are acting.

The degree to which people become absorbed in a motion picture, and become subjectively involved in a kind of emotional third dimension, is the measure of a picture's success.

In the past directors have developed fads and gone in for such shenanigans as injecting their own personal "symbols" into each picture. One always had a Shetland pony in his films; another always opened a picture with a shot of a ladder; a third included lace panties or cactus plants in each of his pic-

From *Films in Review*, June-July 1951. Reprinted with the permission of Films in Review, National Board of Review of Motion Pictures, Inc., 210 E. 68th St., N.Y., N.Y. 10021.

tures; a fourth insisted on including one-eyed landlords. Others liked to identify themselves by using particular kinds of sets. If they "specialized" in elaborate or ornate scenes, then they insisted that each new picture have more elaborate sets and more razzle-dazzle than the last. With the inevitable result that their sets became preposterous to the eye and foreign to the story.

Another directorial fad was to chase after such "realism" as close-ups of runny noses and plumbing.

There is a difference between fads and innovations. After all, such standard camera techniques as the close-up, the running-shot and the lap-dissolve were once innovations—inspired innovations. They survive because they project a story and its characterizations more convincingly.

The incomparable D. W. Griffith used a spectacular running-shot when he had his camera move with Miss Gish in her climactic flight across the ice in *Way Down East*. I have never forgotten it. Its impact on me (I was a child) was staggering. And so was its impact on the adults of that day.

Overcoming or circumventing technical obstacles or difficulties doesn't by itself result in greatness on the screen. In fact, some scenes that are the simplest to shoot, and the least involved technically, are the most memorable. Such a scene was that brief, poignant moment on the deck of an ocean liner in *Cavalcade* when honeymooners, planning their future, walked away from in front of a life preserver and revealed the name of the ship—the doomed *Titanic*.

Another scene beautiful in its simplicity was at the end of *All Quiet on the Western Front*. The camera showed Lew Ayres' hand grasping for the single wild flower blooming in No Man's Land. And another: the shot in John Ford's *Stagecoach* in which the camera roved languidly and lovingly over the idyllic scenery of Monument Valley until it picked up the ambushing Indians.[1]

Of course it is always easy to look back on mistakes. Second-guessing, we call it in Hollywood. But there was a period, some

[1] Sidney's memory of these sequences was not entirely accurate.—R. K.

fifteen or twenty years ago, when the most outlandishly involved shots were turning up on the screen. I don't question the
artistic integrity or the intent of the men who devised and
executed them. Nevertheless, it became a sort of a contest.
Directors vied with each other to top all previous records for
sustained boom shots—for example. Cameras moved across
rooftops, they rose vertically up the sides of skyscrapers for
40 floors, they followed characters through labyrinths of
rooms and down into cellars and out onto the street. They
probably caused comment at trade previews and awed critics.
But essentially they were intrusive and diversionary and sometimes downright silly.

Directors are sometimes said to have a "touch." Sometimes
they do, and it is actually a personal style. But usually it is an
affectation—labored and self-conscious. I have seen revivals of
silent pictures in which camera tricks and effects were dragged
by the beard into stories to which they added absolutely nothing. For instance, there was the period of soft focus photography, in which the actors' faces drifted hazily through pictures
like disembodied wraiths. There was an orgy of pallid, out-of-
focus, foggy close-ups which revealed very little of the star's
face and did nothing for the story. I recently saw a private
showing of a couple of old Mae Murray vehicles in which the
lovely Miss Murray was little more than an amorphous and
miasmic haze, pierced here and there by the glitter of spangles.
It was too bad for her that the diffusion style prevailed when
her career was at its height.

There was also a low-key photography period in which,
immediately following the title and credits, the screen was
plunged into Stygian darkness, pierced here and there by moving blobs of gray.

The screen is a living organism and thirty years from now
our pictures will probably look pretty heavy-handed. However, Hollywood's best efforts have been devoted for some
time now to screen story-telling in its most effective form—
sans whimsical, self-conscious camera angles; directorial cart-
wheels; or intrusive tricks from any source. It is not likely that

professional movie-makers will again stray into these old fads. Hence it is very likely that as you watch a movie you will not in future realize how much the director and the camera man steer your eyes to just what they want you to see. It is their job, and their art, to prevent you from realizing it.

LASLO BENEDEK
(1907-   )

Born in Budapest and educated in Vienna, Laslo Benedek first entered films as a cameraman for the German UFA and Terra studios, then worked as a cutter for Joseph Pasternak, who was producing films in Europe for Universal. He worked for a while in Paris and London, then came to Hollywood in 1937 as a director of montage sequences for MGM. Benedek functioned fairly anonymously during the war as a writer and associate producer, but in 1948 MGM gave him the chance to direct his first film, *The Kissing Bandit*. The dozen films directed by Benedek since then are generally unremarkable, but they do display a considerable range of subject matter, all the way from *The Wild One* to *Namu, the Killer Whale*. Benedek seems to have been more at home with television than with film, and has directed numerous episodes of such series as *Perry Mason*, *Naked City*, *The Untouchables* and *The Outer Limits*. With the obvious exception of *The Wild One*, *Death of a Salesman* is Benedek's best-known work, one of several well-meaning attempts to transfer the work of Arthur Miller to the screen. To date Miller's writings have successfully resisted all these efforts, and it is difficult to decide if the fault lies in the material, the adaptors, or both. The high-strung theatricality which can make Miller's plays notable experiences on stage seems to collapse into hothouse melodramatics on screen. Somehow the eye of the camera is less interested in Willy Loman's famous whipped cheese than in what sort of cornflakes he eats for breakfast.

DIRECTING *DEATH OF A SALESMAN* FOR THE SCREEN

LASLO BENEDEK

The task of faithfully transforming a successful play into a motion picture offers a rare challenge. This is especially true when the play involved is *Death of a Salesman* which established Arthur Miller as one of the nation's foremost dramatists, and won every theatre award including the Pulitzer Prize, the Drama Critics' Circle Award, the Donaldson Award, the Theater Club's Gold Medal, the Antoinette Perry Award, and the Front Page Award. In addition, it was translated into twenty-six languages.

One can imagine, then, the somewhat mixed feelings of a motion picture director assigned to bring such a play to the screen. From the outset, there was fundamental agreement between Stanley Kramer, the producer, Stanley Roberts, the screenwriter, and myself; here was a great piece of dramatic literature, with something very important to say, and it was our determination to bring it to the screen with complete honesty and integrity.

As far as its form was concerned, we felt we were faced with an interesting challenge. In order to bring his unusual mixture of reality and fantasy to the stage, Miller had borrowed certain motion picture techniques, such as the flashback and the dissolve, and used them most effectively. We now had the opportunity not only to expand the use of these techniques but to employ the full scope of the screen medium in the telling of a story that was so extraordinarily cinematic by its own nature.

As a former cameraman and film editor, I was tempted to go overboard in camera tricks and techniques. I remember, for example, some early conferences with Frank Planer, our cinematographer, in which we discussed the possibility of filming the fantasy sequences through gauze, to emphasize their unre-

From *Theatre Arts*, February 1952. Reprinted by permission of Laslo Benedek.

ality, or the use of special lenses to set them apart from the real sequences. The better our ideas became technically, the more we realized that we were on the wrong track. This was Willy Loman's story and it had to be seen through his eyes. The very point was that to him the fantasies were exactly as real as reality. To express this dramatic point visually, there had to be no difference in the presentation of past and present, reality and fantasy. I abandoned all ideas of technical hi-jinx. In devising our time-transitions and visualizations of memories, I kept reminding myself: "Don't fancy it up!"

Similarly, we decided that while the people and places in the fantasy sequences would change according to Willy's memory of them, Willy himself would not change. In playing the role without any make-up or wardrobe changes, Fredric March achieved these transitions in time and place entirely through the power of his performance, with a sensitivity and depth that make his performance deeply moving.

While the stage presentation of *Salesman* had been highly stylized, the picture uses real sets, furnishings and props. This decision was made without any theoretical discussion on our part, as to the merits of the two styles, but simply out of the natural requirements of the film medium. I believe the resultant reality adds to the impact of the picture. At the same time, I was anxious to keep the elements of this reality only as a background and not let them intrude upon the essential human drama. In trying to strike this balance, I found myself faced with questions I was not always ready to answer. When a breakfast scene was to be shot, the prop man wanted to know, with the thoroughness characteristic of good Hollywood craftsmen, what Willy Loman would eat in the morning: cereal or ham and eggs? While I did finally settle this one, I refused stubbornly on the other famous question: what merchandise did Willy carry in his sample cases? Just as in the play, the picture will leave this unanswered.

Transforming the play into a screen drama inevitably demanded certain changes. They were of different types and degrees. Many scenes were kept entirely intact, as far as their structure and dialogue were concerned, the only change was in method of staging. There's the scene, for instance, early in the play, where Willy denounces the encroaching city: "They boxed us in here, bricks and windows, windows and bricks." Here the camera, with its selectivity, was able to concentrate on whatever was dramatically essential at the moment: Willy and Linda close together, when his outburst and her reaction to it was important—the brick walls pressing against his bedroom window when this dismal view had to be emphasized, and the moment of Willy's realization of how far he had lost himself in his memories, his face filling the screen, his eyes alone betraying his unspoken terror. Here, in effect, the camera became a partner in telling the story.

In some cases, we retained the general structure of a scene, but went beyond its original presentation. In the first fantasy, for example, Willy leaves the kitchen of today as his mind wanders back to an afternoon some sixteen years before. Through the kitchen window, he sees his sons, now back in high school age, polishing the family car. In the stage production, the car had to be kept offstage and was only talked about. We felt that if one could accept and believe that Willy's imagination could conjure up his sons, as of years ago, in flesh and blood, then, in psychological and dramatic truth, his imagination would also made the little old Chevy, the symbol of his great nostalgia, appear in its material reality. Thus, we made the little car the background for his scene with his young sons.

In still another approach, we occasionally altered the play's structure to place a scene in an entirely different setting. A fantasy with Willy's dead brother, Ben, had been played in the office of Willy's employer, who had just fired him. Having added reality to the office, however, where it had been only suggested on the stage, we felt that this fantasy would not be believable under the altered circumstances. Following closely the actual continuity of the play, wherein Willy has to go from this office to Charley's to borrow money from him, we made this fantasy come upon Willy during his trip on the subway. It seemed to me that this made dramatic use of the almost universal experience of day-dreaming during a trip on the subway or a train.

Curiously enough, this change led—I believe—to a strengthening of the second part of this same fantasy. During this subway trip, when Willy is forced to borrow money from Charley, his life-long rival, he recalls another trip on the subway, long ago—at that time to Ebbets Field where his son Biff was to be the football hero of the day, and he, Willy, was proudly lording it over Charley. The dramatic irony of this juxtaposition seemed to add to the poignancy of Miller's beautiful scene.

All these changes cited, just as the entire approach to the whole production, were the result of the most thorough preparation I've ever enjoyed in the making of a picture. In addition to the genuinely cooperative effort on the part of Stanley Kramer, Stanley Roberts, Frank Planer and myself, a great contribution was made by the production design of Rudolph Sternad.

I had always felt that one of the most important steps in the making of a picture was that certain indefinable process in which the director visualizes his scenes in terms of camera and movement, even before the first foot of film is shot. By necessity, as long as this process is confined to the imagination, it remains a vague one. Working closely with Sternad, these ideas received their first test of reality in his series of sketches, executed with great knowledge of sets, camera, lighting, and all the intricate problems of movie making, not to mention those of the shooting schedule. But far beyond that, out of these remarkable sketches and, mostly, out of a detailed discussion of them, constantly new and more exciting ideas were born. These, then, received their final test during an exacting two weeks of full-scale rehearsals, involving the whole cast and the key members of the technical crew.

It was this method of production, with its thorough preparation and attention to detail before the rushed tenseness of the actual shooting period, that enabled us to shoot a picture as dramatic and technically as complicated as *Death of a Salesman* in the unusually short time of 26 days. In reality, the 26 days were the culmination of many months of intensive work and equalled, therefore, a schedule of several times that length.

We took a great play, we approached it with respect and love, and we believe that we have turned out a true and honest motion picture.

RICHARD BROOKS
(1912-   )

The temptation to film successful novels and plays is apparently irresistible, and has carried with it a running debate on just how such adaptations should be carried out. Laslo Benedek argues for a certain organic expansion of stage plays, with an insistence on maintaining the integrity of a text judged worth filming in the first place. But Richard Brooks finds wholesale recasting into film terms a necessity for even the finest literary works (including his own) if they are to be at all successful in motion picture terms. His major example here is the adaptation of his novel *The Brick Foxhole* into Dore Schary's *Crossfire*, and he details with apparent equanimity how entire sections were lopped off to fit the requirements of the screen. But there was a major controversy at the time over the filming of *Crossfire* that involved not a condensation of material, but the transmutation of the central character from a homosexual to a Jew. Brooks is not completely honest when he claims that critical reaction to this change was "almost all favorable." And his assertion that the alteration made no change in the point of the film is also on shaky ground—especially in terms of 1948 society. Brooks directed his first film, *Crisis*, in 1950, and many of his most important projects have been dramatic or literary adaptations (usually scripted by himself). The most notable of these have included *The Brothers Karamazov*, *Elmer Gantry*, *Lord Jim* and *In Cold Blood*, and to each of these Brooks applied his theory that "a good novel . . . cannot be made into a good picture *without* changes." In nearly all instances the fate of the finished film rested directly on the success of the "changes" which Brooks subjected it to.

A NOVEL ISN'T A MOVIE
RICHARD BROOKS

Paul Gallico is said to have said on seeing a movie made from one of his stories, that he had only one regret. He had entertained at dinner the writer who adapted the story and hadn't poisoned him.

But anguished cries from authors that the snow-white bodies of their brain children have been sacrificed on the altar of Hollywood's lust for gold, have a hollow ring in the ears of anyone who is familiar with both media, with both the novel and the screen.

Those who are familiar only with the novel have the idea that story-stuff is spun out of the author's own substance, as a spider spins a web, and thus can never harmlessly be touched by another. Or that an author and his work are forever linked by a bond equal to the one between mother and child. And that this author-story relationship is unaffected by any other consideration whatsoever—such as the fact that the author gladly accepted a fistful of Hollywood moola in exchange for the picture rights to his story.

Well, I don't think it is *really* so terrible for Mr. Gallico or any other non-screen writer when their creations, in their transformations to the screen, take on a different, or even an alien, hue.

The novel and the screen are very different story-telling media. Short of putting the book in front of a camera and filming the text direct, page for page, any novel must necessarily undergo critical changes. Indeed, one hallmark of a good novel is the fact that it cannot be made into a good picture *without* changes. And it is equally true that a novel filmed scene for scene will not be a good movie. Nor would a good film make

From *Films in Review*, February 1952. Reprinted with the permission of Films in Review, National Board of Review of Motion Pictures, Inc., 210 E. 68th St., N.Y., N.Y. 10021.

Peter O'Toole with Richard Brooks during the shooting of one of Brooks's most important literary adaptations, *Lord Jim* (1965).

a good novel if it were literally and painstakingly transformed to the written word.

The author who says "you've got to make a good movie out of my novel and you cannot change it in the process" is double-talking. There is no answer for such a man. His idea contains two mutually exclusive conditions.

He can demand—though he has no legal right to do so—that Hollywood *either* make a good movie of his story, *or* film it as is, unchanged.

It is simple enough: a movie has to be a good movie *first*. It has to be a good adaptation of a novel, story, play, or what-not, *second*. Any compromise of these principles means the conscientious movie-maker has forsaken his prime obligation.

One of the most common complaints is that screen-writers —or directors, or producers—oversimplify everything, especially motivation and the delineation of character. It is said, for example, that the evolution of such complicated characters as the lush in *The Lost Weekend* and the psychotic professional assassin in *This Gun For Hire*, was hurried over with a brief cut-back or two, and a couple of lines of expository dialogue.

It is difficult for authors who have never written for, or made, or studied, pictures, to realize how precious screen time is, and how swiftly things can be gotten over to an audience that is looking at *moving* pictures.

The audience must be acquainted with the central characters, the mood, locale, and the main story line or problem, within from two to five minutes of the start of the film.

There have been several pictures in which all this was stated by the time the titles and credits were completed. Impossible? No. In Nunnally Johnson's *Along Came Jones* the titles and credits were unreeled before a violent background in which a masked bandit, identified only by the initials M. J., was shown in a series of train and stagecoach holdups. As the last credit faded Gary Cooper leisurely rode into a Western town sitting on a saddle on which were the initials M. J. The audience knew immediately, and certainly after the first two lines of dialogue, that Cooper was a good-natured, shy, inept, trouble-shunning cowhand whose initials were the same as the bandit's. The first person he sees in the town is the girl, and their first scene together establishes the problems that will involve them both. Within possibly a minute after the titles, Johnson was into his story.

And don't tell me *Along Came Jones* was a formula picture. It was one of the most unformulated—and best—Westerns I ever saw. Proof of how little it stuck to formula is the fact that its hero was clumsy, slow with a gun, always came off worst in his encounters with the heavies, and stayed that way, too. There was no final triumph in which the lamb suddenly became a roaring lion.

Of course movie audiences form impressions of character from the actor or actress who plays the part. This goes for bit players as well as stars. As soon as audiences see Cooper's face, for instance, they assume that the character he portrays will resemble other Gary Cooper roles. If the new role *is* similar to his preceding ones, it requires little delineation on the screen to tell an audience that he is slow-tempered, absolutely honest, shy, and so forth. A novelist might spend five or ten thousand words describing what the camera conveys in the flash of a face.

The better novelists now and then get a lot over with just a little exposition, too. Off-hand, I submit as an example Robert M. Coates' excellent novel, *Wisteria Cottage*. Despite this somewhat dubious title, it happens to be one of the finest studies of a psychopath I have ever read. It presents what must be one of the most authentic and completely valid portraits of a nut this side of Kafka, and I recommend it heartily. Yet its "motivation," and its exposition of what makes the murderer tick, is confined to one short paragraph well over in the book.

Another point which must not be ignored is that consciously or unconsciously many novelists are influenced by the screen. I offer as examples, again off-hand, two quite different books that became movies: Dashiell Hammett's *The Thin Man* and John Steinbeck's masterful *Of Mice and Men*. These novels, as very few stories ever have, straddle both screen and fiction story-telling. As you read you practically see scenes opening and fading on the screen, and in a way that doesn't detract from their literary value.

But this doesn't invalidate the contention that 99 per cent of the novels that are adapted have to be greatly changed in order to become good screen.

The good old device of identifying a character with certain gestures, or turns of speech, and repeating them, is common to both screen and novel. But there is a difference. The novelist may repeat them twenty or thirty times to get an effect the screen gets by repeating a gimmick gesture or phrase once or twice.

The novel demands a leisurely and thorough development, and the screen, just as inexorably, demands deft, effective, *quick* delineation—of the same things.

Perhaps my own experience will not be taken amiss.

I spent my spare time during three years in the Marine Corps writing a novel called *The Brick Foxhole*, which can be said to have been a successful book of its season. It was acquired by RKO and brought to the screen as *Crossfire*, which I considered a good picture, as did nearly all the critics.

The movie-makers who transformed it to film, notably Dore Schary, made some rather extensive changes. They would have been inept or incompetent not to. I thought the changes were not only justifiable, but mandatory.

The most obvious and easily identified change was that which switched the murder victim from a homosexual who became the target for a sort of military mob violence, to a Jew who became the target for military mob violence. The change was commented on by many reviewers with varying reactions, almost all favorable.

It can serve as an excellent laboratory case of a story change, for while it switched the symbol of the victim from a homosexual to a Jew, *it did not in any way alter the basic story*.

The basic story was the violence, not the victim. *The Brick Foxhole* was not a novel about a homosexual, and *Crossfire* was not a picture about a Jew. Both were the story of unthinking passion, of vicious, hysterical, violent compulsion toward brutality, which is sometimes engendered by the militarization of civilians, and which is sometimes unleashed for trivial reasons on any handy victim.

Schary talked to me a number of times before RKO bought the novel, and frequently during the year that passed before the actual writing of the screenplay began. I worked closely and constantly with Schary and with John Paxton, one of the finest screen writers, in transferring the novel to the screen. I was consulted on every point, and where there were differences, my opinions were solicited, heard, and considered.

On almost all points, however, we saw eye-to-eye. I did not wince when, at one conference early in the project, we threw out the first third of my book. What I had considered good novel was not good screen. The screen story began well along in the novel story, and its telling was obviously improved by the surgery. I might note parenthetically that if I were writing the novel over I would handle it today just the way I did the first time.

From the beginning we were faced with one big, inescapable, basic problem. It had nothing to do with whether the victim was a homosexual, patently a subject unsuitable for the screen, or whether he was a Jew. It hovered in the background of all the story conferences, and was: how far dare we go in pointing up and identifying the violence as the direct result of the bad phases of military life. Soldiers are civilians who have been taught how to kill. National defense requires that military personnel become familiar with violence. And we were still in the shadow of war.

We personified this spirit of violence in the sergeant. Our full solution of the problem was too complex for analysis here. If you saw the picture you know.

Another change was stepping up the end. We did this by chopping off the final section of the book, but retaining the device used in the novel for identifying the murderer, and having the identification immediately after the action peak of the story.

We changed very few of the characters, although we dropped many. Frequently it is necessary to condense several similar characters in a novel into one for the screen. We did not have to resort to this.

While I was stationed at Camp Pendleton in 1944 another Marine came up to me, said he had read *The Brick Foxhole*, thought it a good novel, and was sure it could be made into a good picture. He even said he'd like to play the central role. His name was Bob Ryan, and play it he did.

WILLIAM DIETERLE
(1893-1972)

Dieterle was one of the most successful, if not the most celebrated, of the many Europeans in Hollywood, and his balanced discussion of American studio operations gives us a clue to his longevity. In fact, this article is mainly retrospective, since by 1952 the flow of Europeans to Hollywood of which he writes had long since slowed to a trickle. More up to date might have been a discussion of the return to Europe, at least as a location, by such directors as Wilder (*A Foreign Affair*) and Hitchcock (*Under Capricorn*). Dieterle himself returned in 1956 as producer and director of *Magic Fire*, an eccentric biography of Richard Wagner, and a film which demonstrated at least one of the benefits of the Hollywood studio system. Dieterle's 30's biographies of Pasteur, Zola and Juarez were reverent creations of the Warner Brothers studio, guided with a sure dramatic sense by producers like Hal Wallis. *Magic Fire*, on the other hand, seems almost a parody of the Warners films, a non-stop parade of "biopic" clichés that no self-respecting Hollywood producer would ever have tolerated. It could be argued that Dieterle was always at his best when most plainly under the heel of the studio system, either as a director of fast-paced (and faster-produced) program pictures for Warner Brothers (*Fog Over Frisco*) or as Selznick's hired hand on elaborate productions like *Portrait of Jennie*. Hollywood was the perfect home for Dieterle, a director who needed the guidance and support which only that system could provide, and who lacked the temperament to bang his head uselessly against its strictures and regulations.

EUROPEANS IN HOLLYWOOD
WILLIAM DIETERLE

Some scholars, critics and motion picture fans like to regard the European films of the early twenties as representing the highest standard of motion picture production. Films such as *Atonement of Gosta Berling, Variety, Un Carnet de Bal,* and *Potemkin* were generally hailed as masterpieces, and their directors soon were lured to Hollywood by attractive Hollywood offers. But in the new environment much of their genius seemed to flounder. Their pictures reflected little of the spirit of their European work and many returned disappointed to their native countries; among them, Maurice Stiller, Victor Sjostrom, Sergei Eisenstein, Julien Duvivier, René Clair and Ewald Dupont.

Inevitably their failure produced recrimination, charges of temperament from the American side of the Atlantic, the cry of lack of appreciation from the European shore. Regardless of the viewpoint with which one concurs, the Hollywood misadventures of such original film creators has resulted in a great loss to motion pictures and by no means parenthetically, to themselves.

The convenient explanation blames Hollywood entirely, using all the stereotyped arguments of gross commercialism, stupidly in high places, "the system" *per se.* An attitude of objectiveness places the analyst in the uncomfortable position of seeming to straddle the issue. However, the fact remains that there are two sides to the issue when it is stripped of the emotionalism that invariably tinges controversy about the arts.

I am not a "squirmer" nor a "straddler" but as a director who has worked happily and individualistically in European studios and enthusiastically within the framework of the Hollywood system I am capable of seeing good in both methods. Each has

From *Sight and Sound,* July-September 1952. Reprinted by permission.

William Dieterle (right) directing a "fluoroscope" shot of Merle Oberon (underneath apparatus at left) for *This Love of Ours* (1945).

merit, each occupies a valid position in the international motion picture scheme, each deserves respect.

Hollywood frequently has been accused of nursing a mass inferiority complex induced by its emphasis on quantity rather than quality films, a condition that invites patronizing. Too little note is taken of Hollywood's gigantic accomplishment in transforming the "flickers" of early days into a world-scale people's entertainment, inexpensive diversion for the masses. With its exciting star personalities, vast publicity machinery, flare for colourful showmanship and superior technical resources, Hollywood has spread the influence of film to the four corners of the globe, creating a huge industrial structure manifested in the thousands of theatres across the hemispheres where thirty years ago there were none. Hollywood alone, among the production centres, supplies the major portion of the flow that keeps the doors of these theatres open. Actually, sporadic native production is indebted to Hollywood for its means of reaching the public, the theatre.

With the global expansion of American films there necessarily has grown the "system of Hollywood production," a more polite description than mechanization. The shipping date, the day a picture is scheduled to go into release, has become the supreme arbiter of creative effort; the budget and shooting schedule, its allies. Experts to carry out the "system" have been born in the form of the front office, producers and associate producers.

To the foreign director making his first picture in Hollywood this industrial approach to an art form is alien to his previous experience. He is baffled by the hugeness of the studios, the amazing efficiency, the rigidity with which the budget and shooting schedule are controlled, the cool atmosphere of impersonality. He discovers he is only one of many directors, and like them, responsible to a producer who holds the power to change the script, often to veto the director's interpretation, choose players and who assumes final control of the editing. This contrasts dramatically with the European tradition where the director's authority is unquestioned and his creative freedom permits him to make his own schedule on a flexible budget.

Overwhelming is the one word description of his reaction to the Hays office with its code of morals and manners. It exists nowhere else, and acceptance of its restrictions is a matter of conditioning. Hardly a Hollywood director exists who, at one time or another, has not dreamed of tearing the code to shreds. For purposes of expediency we accept the system of self regulation as the most effective device for combatting state and local censorship in America.

This acquiescence to localism contains an important clue to the psychology behind Hollywood's mode of mass production. It is international in scope and just as the individual film must be acceptable morally in varied geographical points, it must also be acceptable as entertainment. The European director, accustomed to making pictures for his own country, sometimes fails to grasp this fundamental point. He seems incapable of visualizing the larger audience for whom he "is playing."

With restrictions descending upon him from every side the European director naturally becomes frustrated. Automatically, he undertakes the hopeless challenge of "changing things." He questions "the system" and fumes helplessly when he discovers he cannot completely mould it to his own concept of individualistic film making. The frustrations he creates in his own mind are as much responsible for his inability to do his best work as the conditions imposed by Hollywood. His failure, if he takes it seriously (and who doesn't?) becomes an excuse for Hollywood to bear another tongue-lashing. Hasty retreat to home territory follows; everyone is sorry, everyone is bitter.

It would require the wisdom of Solomon to set down infallible rules by which an acceptable compromise between the two systems might be reached, and my own observations, culled from twenty years in Hollywood, hardly fall into this category. However my experience has been that by persistence in my work, by accepting and making the best of assignments as they have come, I have occasionally enjoyed the pleasure of pure creative expression. *Zola, Pasteur, Juarez, All That Money Can Buy* and *Boots Malone* are a few cases in point.

If, in the intimacy of my drawing room, I rail against the Hollywood system of mass production, I confess considerable respect for it during working hours at the studio. In its pursuit of efficiency, quicker, more economical ways of making movies, Hollywood has developed the backlot as its unique and considerable contribution to the celluloid art. Here are the real geniuses, technical craftsmen unsurpassed in ability and constantly on the alert to improve their skills. They provide a bulwark the director enjoys nowhere else in the world.

In Europe the director is faced constantly with the problem of training new workers because too few pictures are made to sustain a crew for any length of time. It is impossible for the technical workers to attain the high degree of talent and co-ordination that in Hollywood is accepted as commonplace.

As for the restrictions on imaginative film creation by the speed-up process, production control and censorship, they are not insurmountable barriers to artistic integrity. Time and experience can hurdle them more effectively than snarling and gnashing of teeth. Surely the works of Ernst Lubitsch form their own testimony of his quiet, whimsical way of forging his own imprint on Hollywood. Lubitsch possessed the subtlety to dazzle the censors into seeing one thing, believing another. His was compromise on the most intelligent level—beating the "opposition" at its own game.

I think the European director should come to Hollywood in a frame of mind to take the best from Hollywood and give his best, ignoring, even when it hurts, the pettty irritations imposed by the impersonal handling of pictures. Eventually, if he gains a reputation as co-operative and craftsmanlike, he may be allowed fuller freedom of expression. And it isn't altogether a hit or miss proposition. I held the story and production outline of *Zola* on my desk for two years before it was finally approved; my faith in the subject eventually wore down the resistance of the studio. But its success paved the way for the several screen biographies that followed. Diplomatic finesse may not seem to be a part of the director's equipment, but to close one's eyes to its advantages is the sheerest folly. For my part I see no difference in stalking a Hollywood executive for the privilege of making a notable film than in stalking individuals and financial institutions for money as European directors must constantly do.

With a sense of humour, patience and hard work one can make pictures of high artistic standard in Hollywood.

Freedom of creation among the directors of Europe may become the exception rather than the rule. A knowledge of the tricks of their Hollywood confrères can be very useful.

HENRY KOSTER
(1905-   )

Henry Koster had been directing films in Germany and Austria when he emigrated to Hollywood in 1936 to work for Universal. With Joseph Pasternak he discovered Deanna Durbin and directed her in a series of films so popular they were widely credited with saving that studio from certain bankruptcy. Through the 40's he worked for various studios on a variety of respectable if unpretentious projects (*The Bishop's Wife, Harvey*), and he would seem an odd choice as director of the first Cinemascope feature, *The Robe*. While this process was promoted as Fox's answer to the spectacle elements of Cinerama and 3-D, it was secretly hoped that much money could be saved by eliminating the need for time-consuming changes of camera position. With the proscenium-sized screen it was thought that a director could rely on static sequence shots; as Koster says, "I placed my camera in a central spot and forgot about it." Koster's denial of the function of the close-up as necessary dramatic punctuation was not unique, even as late as 1953. Many directors sincerely believed that close-ups were only necessary as a means of allowing audiences to recognize small objects or gestures, and disliked the way they "broke" the dramatic flow of a sequence. This is why Koster can talk about a "close-up" of six people at the same time. Critics have pointed out that the staging finally developed for Cinemascope by directors like Sirk and Ray ultimately did rely on a composition in depth closely related to the 40's films of Wyler and Welles. But the use made of such staging in *The Tarnished Angels* or *Rebel Without a Cause* is considerably more sophisticated than the purely theatrical notions described here by Koster.

DIRECTING IN CINEMASCOPE
HENRY KOSTER

With CinemaScope, a director is at last free of the camera and has an unparalleled chance to demonstrate his ability to move actors logically and dramatically. Now, more than ever before in motion pictures, he has room in which to work. He no longer has to worry about cramping his action because of the hampering restrictions imposed on him by the camera. Now he doesn't have to worry about "dolly shots" and "pan shots" and "boom shots" and all other camera movements; he is free to concentrate on the chief task of drawing superb performances from his players.

CinemaScope places a director somewhere between the stage and the screen technique. On stage, he has great freedom of lateral movement, but he must sacrifice the emotional impact of the closeup. In 2-D movies, he was able to deliver the closeups, but had to forego all attempts at composition of his actors in great crowd scenes. CinemaScope is the happy blend of the two: you have the luxury of the wide screen and the blessing of being almost constantly in closeup—and closeups not of a single person, but of two, three or half a dozen simultaneously.

Let me use a scene from 20th Century-Fox's first CinemaScope Technicolor production, *The Robe*, as an example. Dean Jagger, playing a Palestinian patriarch, has called a meeting of his village, to introduce them to Michael Rennie, playing Peter. Prominent in the group are Richard Burton and Victor Mature. Now, in the old-style movie, I first would have had to shoot a long-shot, to show the villagers coming to the marketplace and to establish the scene. Then I would have gone in close, making individual shots of all four of my principals and perhaps a few locating shots of places around the square. Then

From *New Screen Techniques* (New York: Quigley Publishing Company, 1953). Reprinted by permission of Quigley Publishing Company and Henry Koster.

Henry Koster gets involved in some typical studio promotion for *The Robe* (1953).

I would have made reaction shots from members of the village. Then I would have made some two-shots: Jagger and Rennie, Burton and Mature, Burton and Jagger.

But when it came time to shoot this scene with Cinema-Scope, I placed my camera in a central spot and forgot about it. Because the lens catches such a wide scope of action, you will see Burton and Mature enter from the left, while Jagger and Rennie come from right center and the villagers flow in from all directions. Jagger starts to make his speech—and we see him and the three other men, all in closeup! It is much more effective to watch their reactions to the speech when you can also see the speaker.

Remember, I have not had to move my camera! This is where the director's ability to stage a scene is important. Instead of moving the camera into the actor to get a closeup, I stage their movements so that they walk into the closeup. In that respect it is like the stage—you must arrange the action so that the audience's attention will be focused on the center of attraction.

One thing I found in directing *The Robe* that I did not anticipate beforehand was that the "extras" must act, too. No longer are they shapeless, faceless blurs in the background. With CinemaScope, everyone is in focus at all times. If your extras fail to react, or display the incorrect reaction, it is as glaring an error as if the same mistake had been made by a principal. That is why I found it necessary to interview every one of the 5,000 extras used in the picture. I needed more than "types," I needed actors.

In brief, CinemaScope makes the movie director less dependent upon the cameraman and the film editor. It gives him freedom, but freedom always carries responsibilities with it. The director must now combine the staging ability of a theatrical director, the composition technique of a first-rate painter (because he is working on a large canvas), and the eye for pictorial effectiveness which he has always needed.

To direct the first picture in CinemaScope is the greatest thrill, and the greatest challenge, of my career. Think of it—to be a pioneer at my age!

ARCH OBOLER
(1909-   )

One of surprisingly few directors with a background in radio (Orson Welles is another), Arch Oboler began writing radio scripts in 1936, making a particular success of the famous *Lights Out* series. He directed his first film for PRC in 1946 (*Strange Holiday*) and over the next few years wrote and directed a series of low-budget productions, including the early nuclear disaster thriller, *Five*. In 1952 Oboler wrote, produced and directed *Bwana Devil*, the first film in the three-dimensional Natural Vision process. Made independently on a shoestring, *Bwana Devil* proved a tremendous audience success and was uniquely responsible for the brief but intense wave of 3-D films which followed over the next year. Oboler here predicts that the process will be abused by producers and therefore rejected by audiences, a prediction which was to come true in a matter of months. Exploited as a stunt, 3-D did not survive long enough for serious filmmakers to develop its possibilities, and 3-D films by Hitchcock (*Dial M for Murder*) and Minnelli (*Kiss Me Kate*) were generally shown in flat versions, audience passions having already cooled as a result of the abuses cited by Oboler (as well as sloppiness of projection and print control, which he fails to mention). But while the rest of Hollywood passed 3-D by, Oboler continued to work with the process, exploring on his own the mechanical and psychological factors on which its success depended. In 1967 he completed *The Bubble* in what was billed as a perfected 3-D process known as Space-Vision. Withdrawn after a few limited showings, the film resurfaced in 1976 under the title *Fantastic Invasion of Planet Earth*, but the fate of Oboler's own career remains a mystery.

THREE-DEMENTIA
ARCH OBOLER

Prophecy is an easy art, since generally the prophet, at the date of accounting, is much too dead to be called to task.

However, since the prophecies of which I speak are going to happen in a very near tomorrow, I don't particularly expect to be supporting a tombstone, hence, gentlemen call me to account!

First, I foresee that the first 3-D motion picture to follow *Bwana Devil* into the theaters, will be jumping with what I call "three-dementia." Everything will be leaping madly off the screen. This is a great temptation in making a three dimensional picture, having objects, from bosoms to zombies, sticking out of the screen into space.

But, gentlemen of production, this is a false path. False because if audiences begin to look upon three dimensional pictures simply as a circus, the law of diminishing returns can quickly catch up with the entire advance. For circuses are not a weekly habit; the trick once seen suffices for a year!

I do not mean to say that these excitement devices of bringing action off the screen should be completely deleted from forthcoming three-dimensional motion pictures; I simply mean that there is a great danger in overdoing the spectacular. For the spectacular becomes the ordinary very quickly once it has become familiar.

I am reminded of horror plays on radio; we quickly found that the law of diminishing returns caught up with us when we tried to compound horror on horror. The audiences simply began to turn the dials. Not that they were frightened. Simply bored.

All of you are familiar with similar experiences in the horror motion pictures; at first it was Frankenstein alone, then Dracula, then Frankenstein and Dracula, then Frankenstein, Drac-

From *The Film Daily Yearbook of Motion Pictures*, 1953. Reprinted by permission of Arch Oboler.

ula and the Wolfman. And soon there wasn't room enough on the screen for all the horror men, but there was plenty of room in the empty theater seats.

Three dimension, as ideally used, then, is a frame through which the audience looks into reality. Hyperstereo, that is stereo photography, carried to an extreme, with objects poking through the frame of the screen in a distorted manner, is a special effects touch to be used with discretion.

I underline this because I believe that three dimensions in motion pictures can be more than today's bonanza at the box office; it can be a bright financial stabilizer tomorrow and tomorrow to the business.

But there must be self-policing in the industry re: 3-D; above all a sense of personal responsibility.

For example, I do not believe that it helps the industry or the future of three dimension at the box office to lead an audience to believe that it is seeing a full feature 3-D picture when actually all that is screening are bits and pieces of three-dimension experiments. I do not believe it helps the industry to take amateur type 3-D movies and show them in the professional theater at regular prices. This sort of quick dollar not only harms the particular exhibitor, but it ruins the taste of the ticket buyer for future three-dimensional pictures.

I am told that at a recent showing, for full admission prices, of a collected group of three-dimensional shorts, an irate ticket buyer, after seeing that he had been shortchanged by less than a full feature picture, walked up and down in front of the theater shouting to the passersby to stay out of this gyp theater.

Let not the motion picture industry gyp itself out of a three dimensional financial future.

RICHARD FLEISCHER
(1916-)

The son of animation pioneer Max Fleischer, Richard Fleischer began as a director in RKO's wartime B-unit, and by the 60's his career had climaxed in a series of massive biblical and musical spectacles. It is an open question as to which category is more destructive of a director's own personality and style. Fleischer joined RKO-Pathé in 1942, and served as writer and producer of shorts like "Flicker Flashbacks," then graduated to features in 1946 with *Child of Divorce*. His 1948 documentary feature *Design for Death* won an Oscar for its examination of the cultural conditioning which led the Japanese to war (a fact little noted in the publicity for the director's later *Tora! Tora! Tora!*). Fleischer had only recently emerged from the low-budget ranks when he was asked to direct *20,000 Leagues Under the Sea*, and while the success of this Disney feature assured his reputation it may have sown the seeds of future disaster as well. Now seen as a director of large and elaborate film projects, he soon left behind such taut, personal works as *Violent Saturday* and began specializing in epics like *The Vikings, Barabbas* and *Dr. Doolittle*. The failure of the exclamatory *Che!* and *Tora! Tora! Tora!* finally put an end to this, and Fleischer returned more successfully to films like *The Last Run*, a neglected work which is also probably his best. Fleischer's dilemma has been to find his career strung out between unpretentious but incisive little films like this, and impersonal epics like *Barabbas*, a problem which has haunted all too many post-war American directors.

UNDERWATER FILMMAKING
RICHARD FLEISCHER

"Show the audience what it's like to be underwater," Walt Disney said to me just before I left for Nassau, in the Bahamas, to direct *20,000 Leagues Under the Sea*. "Make it believable. Make it real."

It was quite an assignment. We were going to have more underwater footage than had ever been in a movie before, use more people underwater than anyone else had ever tried, and have them go through action that would have been complicated and involved even on a dry sound stage where conditions are controlled. Fifty-four men, three cameras and twenty tons of equipment were sent to Nassau. There we assembled a fleet of six boats: an LCT, which served as the main base of operations; an LCM, which served as the camera barge; and four speed boats, which we used as "water-taxis." Because of intensive pre-production planning, everything we needed during our eight weeks of underwater location work was at hand when we needed it.

There are four principal reasons why filming underwater is uniquely laborious. First, three natural phenomena are required *in combination:* bright sunlight, clear water, and calm water. Two of the three will not suffice. Great patience with Nature is necessary.

Secondly, actors and crew must wear strange apparatus, breathe compressed air, work under hazardous conditions, suffer—after a while—from exposure and cold.

Third, it is impossible to communicate anything but the simplest ideas. We had to devise a set of twelve hand signals to express such essential film instructions as "Action." "Cut," "Repeat Scene," and such essential underwater needs as "Emer-

From *Films in Review*, August-September 1954. Reprinted with the permission of Films in Review, National Board of Review of Motion Pictures, Inc., 210 E. 68th St., N.Y., N.Y. 10021.

Filming underwater episodes in the Bahamas for Richard Fleischer's *20,000 Leagues Under the Sea.* © Walt Disney Productions.

gency—get me to the surface at once." During the course of production the cameraman, Till Gabbani, and I learned to write notes on a special underwater slate, but this was used only for last-second emergencies.

Fourth, and of controlling importance, is the fact that you can stay underwater for a very limited period. We could allow no more than 55 minutes from the time the first man was "put on air" and buttoned up on the deck of the LCT, until the last man was back on it. Ten of these 55 minutes were required to get everybody down to the ocean bottom, and another ten to bring them up to the surface. Since we depended for illumination on sunlight we had to wait until the sun was high in the heavens, which meant our work day was from 10 a.m. to 4 p.m. Because of the time required for refilling the compressed air tanks after each underwater trip, rest, and lunch, four dives a day was our maximum.

Photographing under water is a five-step process. The first is the search for a suitable location. Cameraman Gabbani, Fred Zendar (our chief diving expert), and I would swim about seeking an area not only appropriate for setting up a set piece, or utilizing a photogenic coral formation, but one with the right kind of ocean bottom (coral or sand).

The second step was taking the cast and crew down and showing them the main features and boundaries of the area we had chosen.

Third, if the scene were not too complicated, I would sketch the action on a blackboard on the deck of the LCT, much in the manner of a football coach diagramming a play. We would mark the location of boats, the camera, the coral reefs, and indicate exactly where certain things were to occur. If the scene were unusually difficult, we would take the water-taxis back to shore and there rehearse the entire sequence, step by step, until everyone was familiar with every movement. This rehearsing on shore was necessary for the underwater burial sequence in *20,000 Leagues Under the Sea*, for which 42 men had to be on the ocean floor—20 in front of the camera and 22 behind it (cameraman, his assistants, prop men, grips, a still photographer, and our underwater "safety" men). The burial sequence is the largest single scene ever photographed under water.

The fourth of the five steps in underwater movie-making takes place simultaneously with the third. While I sketched out the action, or rehearsed it, the crew was underwater placing the cameras, sets and props. The fifth and last step, of course, was filming the scene.

We worked at depths up to 31 feet. Below that the sunlight falls off sharply, and everything is deep blue or black (we used Technicolor film). But more importantly, after the first 33 feet, which are known as "the first atmosphere," you encounter much greater pressure, greater dangers of working, and greater difficulty returning to the surface.

We had two different sets of underwater equipment. Those of us behind the camera used swim fins and the standard aqualung, i.e., compressed-air cylinders strapped to the back with a breathing tube to the mouth, plus a face mask. The actors in front of the camera had a much harder time, thanks to Jules Verne.

He had written that the seamen of the Nautilus were able to walk about on the floor of the ocean in diving suits that had no air hoses to the surface or to the submarine. This is a dramatic and pictorial effect—but it seemed completely impossible when we first discussed filming his book. The only self-contained diving suit—developed by the British—involved a chemical re-breathing device and was considered so dangerous it had been used only in wartime on "suicide missions." Luckily, we did not have to kill any actors to get what we wanted. Our diving and designing experts pooled their respective talents and came up with a practical outfit that resembled the appearance of those described by Verne. It was a combination deep-sea div-ing suit and an aqua-lung. The men wore diving helmets, the full suit, and the heavy boots, and had an aqua-lung rig on their backs. The air was piped to the helmet through an ingenious system of tubes. These self-contained diving suits, the first practical ones ever devised, weighed a total of 225 pounds!

All the time we were in the water teams of expert lifeguards and veteran underwater safety men patrolled the waters above us or swam behind the camera—ready to come to the assistance of anyone who might need it. Zendar organized the diving operations and water safety program so efficiently that there was not a single accident, nor any major interruption in shoot-ing during the entire location.

Hitherto the cameras used for underwater photography have usually been either the Eclair Camerette or the Arriflex, en-cased in pressurized, water-tight "blimps." Both are portable, lightweight, and highly maneuverable. However, we used the standard Mitchell camera with a CinemaScope lens inside a light, pressurized, water-tight case with a built-in power source and precise, external remote controls for adjusting, focussing, and lens stop. Cameraman Gabbani found he could handle the Mitchell underwater with the same movements and precision he was accustomed to on a dry sound stage, including racking the magazine over so he could check composition through the lens. The combined camera and case, weighing 175 pounds "dry," had a neutral buoyancy in the water and one man could swim it into position. It even had its own aqua-lung—an automatic pressure device that kept the pressure inside three pounds heavier than the pressure outside at any level!

Our underwater sound stage usually included a platform, from 5 to 20 feet high, on which we mounted a tripod and the Mitchell. For dolly shots and "swim-through" we used the Aquaflex (an underwater blimped-camerette) equipped with "wings" and a "tail," which made it extremely maneuverable. Gabbani, pushing it in front of him as he swam through the water, achieved some magnificent shots.

The most exciting moment during our two-month location occurred during the shark fight. Local fishermen had trapped several eight-foot sharks for us and while our water safety men stood nearby, armed with spear guns, knives and small axes, we turned a shark loose. The frightened fish bee-dived for the ocean bottom. Gabbani swam right behind him and captured his every movement with the Aquaflex. We covered the shark's dive with the Mitchell and an extra Aquaflex, and thus got several different angles of the one "take."

I was a novice in underwater work and had thought sharks would be our greatest hazard. But they weren't nearly as much trouble as the barracuda and moray eels and the razoredges of the coral formations. Zendar told me that if you swim toward a barracuda he will retreat. I'll never forget the first time I steeled myself to advance on these vicious looking fish. I was wishing I were back in the peace and safety of the Hollywood Freeway. I also remember, in gratitude, the time Zendar grabbed me by the seat of my swimming trunks and pulled me up. I had been so engrossed in seeking a new location that I almost descended into the open mouth of a waiting eel!

The waters of the Bahamas are the finest for underwater cinematography, in our considered opinion. We examined dozens of possibilities—from Catalina to the Caribbean-West Indies area. Nowhere else did we find such a variety of picturesque coral formations, such an abundance of fish life (ranging from the colorful, harmless groupers, to game fish, manta rays, sting rays, sharks and barracuda), and such crystal-clear water, or so many pleasing shades of blue and green. The clarity of the water cannot be over-emphasized. On many occasions we had excellent visibility for distances of 200 feet.

No direct current runs through these waters and there is no problem of silt or mud clouding a scene. There is, however, fine white sand and "coral dust" on the ocean floor, which was easily stirred up when the divers walked on it, and required ten or fifteen minutes to settle. Soon after our arrival we laid sections of heavy hemp matting on the bottom for the divers to walk on and we had no further headaches with murky water.

In any underwater scene you expect to see fish, and so did we. But the noise and commotion of our preparations frequently scared off the "finny" actors. So we employed local fishermen to net large quantities of groupers and angel fish, which we kept alive in wire mesh pens until we needed them, whereupon the prop men put them in one-man mesh baskets out of camera range, ready to release them on cue. By trial and error we discovered that if the fish were released toward a coral head they would swim in that direction rather than toward the open sea. This enabled us to keep large numbers of them within camera range. After a while the groupers became interested, or used to us, and remained in the area after a shot was finished. We were able to recapture and thus re-use some of the fish dozens of times.

TERRY SANDERS
(1931-   )

At the close of the silent period a group of "independent" experimenters existed on the fringes of the Hollywood establishment, privately financing low budget films not merely for the rewards of personal expression, but as audition pieces for entry into the industrial establishment itself. Several of them, particularly Vorkapich, Fejos, and Florey, did in fact manage to insinuate themselves and contributed significantly to the development of Hollywood style. Following the war, however, many avant garde independents turned their backs on the commercial industry, although a significant group, led by Curtis Harrington and John Cassavetes, continued to seek the wider audiences possible only through the established patterns of commercial production and distribution. Denis and Terry Sanders could be considered part of this group of mainstream independents. As UCLA film students they had made in 1953 the short film *A Time Out of War*, winner of both an Oscar and a Venice Festival Prize. This led to an encounter with Hollywood on *The Naked and the Dead* which proved unfortunate, but as independents they managed to produce and direct such films as *Crime and Punishment—USA* and *War Hunt* (in which they introduced a discovery of theirs, Robert Redford). But the difficulties involved in getting these projects moving eventually proved discouraging, and Denis turned to television while Terry specialized in documentary production.

THE FINANCING OF INDEPENDENT FEATURE FILMS

TERRY B. SANDERS

Although independently produced motion pictures are of great importance in the film industry—comprising approximately one third of all United States feature-film production during the past ten years[1]—few people, even within the business, have a clear conception of the unique methods of financing involved in these ventures. Literature on the subject, if not nonexistent, is extremely sparse; those who understand the field best have gained their knowledge through experience which has frequently been very bitter. The ignorance, semi-knowledge, and general confusion concerning motion-picture finance is due in part to the complexity of the subject and in part to the reluctance of businessmen in the film industry to reveal publicly the details of their transactions.

The financing of independent feature films is not a subject which can be discussed in scientific or absolute terms; recourse to general statements, approximations, and qualifying phrases, such as "in most cases," is unavoidable. The designation "independent feature film" is, in itself, somewhat indefinite; but it will be used here to refer to those films of feature length produced by comparatively small organizations which are financed individually (picture by picture), as opposed to films produced by large companies (M-G-M, Warner Bros., Paramount, Twentieth Century-Fox, Columbia, Universal, and RKO) operating upon capital raised on a corporate basis. Each financing arrangement involving an independent feature film is a separate, individual deal, subject to various refinements through bargaining. Moreover, such elements as national economic conditions, public film tastes, foreign marketing condi-

---

[1] Jack Alicoate, ed., *The 1954 Film Daily Year Book* (New York: The Film Daily, 1954), 125.

© 1955 by The Regents of the University of California. Reprinted from *The Quarterly of Film, Radio, and Television*, Vol. 9, no. 4, pp. 380-389, by permission of The Regents and Terry Sanders.

tions, government regulations, court decisions, and tax and banking policies greatly affect the general financing situation and lead to at least year-to-year variations. Nevertheless, although no two financing arrangements are precisely alike, all have certain characteristics in common; and there exists at least a certain established pattern which serves as a basis for negotiation. This general pattern, and the elements and parties involved, will be discussed here.

THE MONETARY ELEMENTS

In general, three categories of money are involved in the financing of independent feature films. They are mainly differentiated by the degree of risk attached to them and must usually be obtained from sources independent of each other. The nomenclature for these types of money is not entirely logical but, since it is fairly widely accepted in the motion-picture industry, it will be used here. The three categories are known as "first money," "second money," and "completion money."

First money.—First money is so termed because, of the three categories of money financing a film, it is the first to be repaid. However, it is usually the last money to be raised by the producing group. First money finances about 60 per cent of the film, and is practically always loaned by a bank at a straight 6 per cent interest rate. For a film not to bring in enough return to repay this loan is unusual. First money entails the minimum possible risk and gets a minimum return.

Second money.—Second money—often referred to as "risk" money—in effect, finances the film. Once it is obtained, the producing group usually has little trouble in raising the first money. Second money—so-called because it is paid off second, after the bank loan—supplies the remaining 40 per cent of the budget needed to finance the film. Because many films fail to make enough money to return their cost, and because the second money does not begin to be repaid until the entire bank loan has been liquidated, a relatively great risk is involved in putting up this capital. To compensate for this, the second-money (or risk-capital) group, which receives nominal interest (2 or 3 percent, if any at all), usually demands 50 per cent of the film's net profit in return for putting up a majority of the second money. The producing group usually raises the remaining amount of second money needed, either in the form of cash or deferments. Deferments may be the director's or the actors' salaries or film laboratory costs, full payment of which is postponed at least until the first money has been paid off. The artists and technicians under such an arrangement take a considerable amount of risk; and, in return, they will demand a percentage of the film's net profit in addition to their salaries. If the producing group has made use of deferments in raising its share of the second money, these percentages will come out of its share of the profits.

The second money (as cash and deferment agreements, if any) must be deposited at the bank which has loaned the first money. This is the bank's guarantee against financing the film for more than 60 per cent if the budget has been overestimated or padded. If the production comes in under budget, the money that is left over goes immediately toward repaying the bank's loan.

Completion money.—Generally, first and second money (including deferments) make up 100 per cent of the budget. However, a film will frequently run over budget and require added money for completion. Since an unfinished motion picture is totally worthless, the bank and the risk-capital group (if it is not itself guaranteeing completion) protect themselves by requiring assurance that the film will be finished. This assurance or guarantee to supply the extra money required to finish a film is known as completion money or a completion bond. Completion money may be in the form of a guarantee signed by a financially responsible person (which means that if necessary he would be able to repay the full amount owing to the bank) or actual cash in escrow. Some banks require a cash deposit along with the completion agreement equal to 15 per cent of the budget.[2]

[2] Herbert T. Silverberg, "Indie Legal Procedure Outlined by Film Attorney," *Hollywood Reporter* (April 27, 1950), 6.

Completion-money arrangements vary greatly. When the guarantor is a personal friend of the producer or when the producer himself is financially responsible, no fee or percentages are involved. Usually, however, the completion-money group will demand a share of the producer's profits (which may range from 5 to 15 per cent) and, sometimes, a fee besides. If completion money is used, there is usually a provision that, for each $10,000 or $20,000 used, an added percentage of the net profit—perhaps 1 or 2 per cent—is given over to the completion group. This compensation is necessary since any completion money spent is not usually repaid until after the first and second money.

THE INTERESTED GROUPS

Many individuals and groups are usually involved in the financing of an independent feature film. Most commonly, they are the producing group, the bank, the risk-capital group, the deferred-money group, the completion-money group, and the distribution company. Each is after a profit; and each attempts to protect its investment, if possible, through guarantees or, if a certain amount of risk must be accepted, through the most favorable terms it can secure. Out of the producing group's successful bargaining and negotiating with the other groups, the final financing arrangement emerges.

The producing group.—The producing group in the independent film field may be a large, long-established organization, such as the one headed by Samuel Goldwyn, or it may consist only of an individual or group of individuals with an idea in the form of a script and little else in the way of experience or financial assets to recommend it. However, the producing group which has a record of financially successful films will, of course, be able to raise capital relatively easily and at terms favorable to itself. On the other hand, the unknown or previously unsuccessful producing group will generally find financial backing difficult to obtain. If the financing is finally obtained, it will be at terms which take away most of the ownership of the film. As has been previously stated, the producing group usually puts up a share of the second money and sometimes guarantees completion of the film.

The bank.—A number of banks lend money for partial financing of independent films. They receive 5 to 6 per cent interest in comparison to 2 or 3 per cent on loans of comparable size to other industries.[3] According to Herbert L. Golden of the Bankers Trust Company, "If you lend money to the independent, the only thing you have as security for your money is the picture which he is going to make. You don't have anything else."[4] But the bank takes little risk. In effect, it secures the loan by rarely financing a film for more than 60 per cent of its budget, by demanding evidence of a satisfactory distribution agreement, by estimating the potential box-office draw of the cast, by securing assurance that the film will be completed, by having first claim on income from the film, and by holding a lien on the story rights and completed film.

After having sustained large losses in recent years through financing motion pictures, a few banks require all loans to be fully secured by bond or collateral. Since few producers can afford a loan on these terms, such stringent requirements are actually these particular banks' indirect way of saying that they are not financing films any longer. Nevertheless, advancing first money for independent films has long been, and continues to be, a profitable and relatively safe business for the few banks which specialize in this field.

The risk-capital group.—The people who put up the risk capital are financial speculators. If the film fails—returning, let us say, only first money—they lose every dollar they invested; on the other hand, if the film is a financial success, they may make back many times their investment. Usually, the investors who put up the risk capital will take about 50 per cent of the profits—always contingent entirely on the individual deal.

The deferred-money group.—The talent or technical service which defers its fee or salary becomes, in effect, a direct investor in the film. Under such an arrangement, a director

[3] *Ibid.*

[4] "Television and Motion-Picture Prospects," *Commercial and Financial Chronicle*, 177 (May 7, 1953), 38.

whose fee is $75,000 for a certain film may take $10,000 in cash and defer $65,000 until after the first or second money has been paid off. Since this is a distinct gamble, he will demand, perhaps, 10 per cent of the net profit. If the film does not return its negative cost (the final, actual cost of the film), he will receive neither the deferred portion of his fee nor, of course, any money from his part ownership of the film.

The people who frequently defer a portion of their fees or salaries include the producer himself, the writer, the director, the actors, the director of photography, the music composer, and the film-processing laboratory. Certain of these people—notably the actors and the cameraman—must, however, receive a basic minimum salary prescribed by their guilds or unions.

The completion-money group.—Various persons may put up the required assurance that a film will be finished. Certain financial speculators specialize in these guarantees; and in return, they try to get as large a share of the profits as they possibly can. Their share, as has been stated, may range anywhere from 5 to 15 per cent, plus a penalty percentage if the film goes over budget. In order to avoid the usually large demands of an outside speculator, the producer will often try to supply the guarantee himself; or, if he cannot, he will find some financially responsible friend or relative to do it. Occasionally, the risk-capital group will also guarantee completion.

The distribution company.—The function of the distributor includes the leasing of the film to exhibitors, the arranging for play dates, the delivering, and the collecting of film rentals or percentages of the exhibitors' takes. For distributing a film in the United States, the usual charge is a straight 30 per cent of the gross (money received from exhibitors, not the money paid in at the box office); abroad, the distribution charge is higher, usually 35 to 40 per cent. The distributor advances the cost of prints and advertising, which on a million-dollar film might come to $250,000. He takes little risk, however, since the print-advertising costs are paid off even before the bank's first-money loan.

The distributor can be directly involved in the financing of a film in two ways. First, unless the loan is fully guaranteed, a bank will not put up first money until it has assurance that the film will get satisfactory distribution. Thus, the distributor, by agreeing beforehand to release the film, puts up, in effect, a portion of the security which the bank or first money lender demands.

Second, the distributing company may put up the necessary risk capital for a film, and also the completion guarantee. At the present time, most of the major film companies are involved in financing independent films which they also release through their distributing organizations.

These, then, are the groups that are generally involved in the financing of an independent film. Although one group will often take on a number of functions, and thus eliminate the necessity for some of the other groups, the pattern remains more or less the same. If one individual puts up both the second money and the completion agreement, he will usually exact separate percentages of the ownership of the film for the separate functions he performs. It remains, now, to see how all of these elements are integrated in the financing of an independent feature film.

FINANCING PROCEDURE

How does the independent producer actually go about arranging the financing of a film? There is certainly no set pattern, especially since, as far as cost, independent films may run anywhere from $50,000 to $1,500,000 and more; but a generalized procedure can be outlined. The producer starts with a script or a story to which he has obtained the motion-picture rights. He makes out a tentative budget. He approaches certain actors to see if they are interested in the film. He approaches certain directors. He begins the difficult task of finding a person to back the film—a person who will put up most of the second money. He also tries to find someone who will guarantee the completion of the film. He shows the script, and whatever tentative cast and director agreements he has, to a distributing organization and tries to get a release commitment. If and when he has all these elements, he takes evidence of them, together with the script and a final budget, to the bank and asks for the first money. The bank will examine everything; and, if all is satisfactory, it will loan the sum. The second money and, if necessary, the completion money is deposited at the bank; and shooting on the film can commence.

Herbert L. Golden puts forth an example:

> The producer, in his role of financial promoter, is generally forced to put on quite a show. He comes to us at the bank and says, "I have Gregory Peck, I have second money, I have completion money, I have William Wyler to direct, and I have a great script. If you will put first money in, I can go ahead."
>
> We act like we believe him at least partially, although we know actually he hasn't got all of those elements. We know that as soon as he leaves us he is going to go to Gregory Peck's agent and say, "I have Bankers Trust Company to put up first money if you come in. I have a great script and a great director"; then, he goes to Wyler and he says, "If you will come in I have Bankers Trust and I have Gregory Peck." Thus, he goes around the circle. Everybody knows what he is doing. Everybody knows he has nothing but an idea. He tries to pull all the strings in, and, gradually, the successful producer finally gets everybody into a room, and he finds he does have all those people.[5] [Mr. Golden omitted the important distribution factor.]

A more concrete example is the experience of a certain producing group in its first independent film venture, which, as it turned out, was extremely successful financially. The members of this group started with a script which they budgeted at the unusually low figure of $80,000. Of this sum, $10,000—representing the fees of the writer, director, and producers—was deferred. The remaining $70,000 was needed in cash. After approaching many people, they finally found an investor who liked the script and agreed to finance the film. The arrangement was that he would guarantee 50 per cent of a $40,000 bank loan. The producers would guarantee the other 50 per cent. Of the $30,000 second money still needed, the investor would put up half and the producing group the other half.

[5] *Op. cit.*, 37.

The producing group, through a financially responsible relative, obtained the completion bond. The profits of the film were divided equally between the producing group and the investor. The film had neither stars nor a prior distribution agreement, and the producers had no established reputation in the field, since it was their first film; but, because the loan was fully secured, the bank was willing to advance the money. The producers had, between themselves, enough money for the guarantee and their half of the second money.

After the success of the first film, these producers were able to raise capital for their second film—budgeted at $300,000—with relative ease.

THE PAYING BACK OF MONIES

Whether or not an investor in an independent feature film will recoup his money often depends upon the precedence which his investment takes when returns begin coming in. This factor—the order in which the various parties involved are paid back—is of the utmost importance and forms the basis for the entire system of motion-picture finance. The general pattern follows.

When money comes in at the box office, the exhibitors, first of all, extract their share. What remains is known as the gross of the film and is collected by the distributor. The distributor begins taking his 30 per cent fee immediately from the time the first dollar comes in. This is a constant charge which continues throughout the release of the film. The remaining 70 per cent of the gross is first applied toward paying back the print and advertising costs, which the distributor has advanced. When the entire cost has been repaid, the 70 per cent is next applied toward paying back the first-money loan plus the usual 6 per cent interest. When the first money lender has been completely paid, the 70 per cent goes toward repaying the second money. Payments of deferred salaries and completion-money debts usually come after the second money, but sometimes they are paid back *pari passu*. This means that payments on these debts are made concurrently with the second money and in amounts commensurate with the proportion of the total debt that they represent. When all debts have been repaid, the 70 per cent of the gross becomes profit, to be divided in accordance with whatever the initial arrangement happened to be.

There are innumerable subtleties and refinements in financing arrangements involving independent feature films; but these must, necessarily, remain untouched by this article. Moreover, the general principles and procedures outlined here are not always significant in every financing deal. What has been presented is a simplification of the general example; it is a basic foundation and a point of departure.

JOSEF
VON STERNBERG
(1894-1969)

With the production of *Anatahan* in 1952 (three years before this essay was written), Josef von Sternberg's stormy directorial career had finally ground to a halt. Von Sternberg and the Hollywood film industry had never been on very good terms, and only when his films succeeded at the box office, as they did in the late 20's and early 30's, was he given the opportunity to function with the latitude he describes here. The control over all aspects of production which von Sternberg demands is similar to the call of other directors for one "film author" per picture. But his Sam Goldwyn story here does more than point out the primacy of the director; it insists on the *totality* of the director's contribution. For von Sternberg, the director's collaborators should not only refrain from speaking, they should be made to understand that they have nothing to say. Even in this basically theoretical discussion he goes out of his way to take credit for anything and everything of value in his films, from the camerawork to the sound recording—glories always accomplished over the protests of dim-witted technicians, at least as von Sternberg recalls it. This lack of generosity was one of the aspects of von Sternberg's ego which won him few friends in Hollywood, and was generally aggravated when he did attempt to take complete command on the set. Credit has always been a subject of controversy in Hollywood, and for von Sternberg the spotlight was only big enough for one man, with no light left over for those outside the charmed circle.

MORE LIGHT
JOSEF VON STERNBERG

Michelangelo was explaining to a visitor a number of additions and alterations which he had made to a statue. "These are trifles," said his friend. "It may be so," said the sculptor, "but recollect that trifles make perfection, and perfection is no trifle."

"Let there be light, and there was light!" God was the first electrician. Before light there was nothing. Light was the climax of creation. Then, according to the Bible, came a minor climax—man was created.

There was also Prometheus who put a torch to the chariot of the sun and brought light to man, reversing the above order of creation according to the Greeks. For stealing the property of the gods he was chained to Mount Caucasus and his liver became the prey of vultures. (And to this day cameramen are bilious.)

Light means fire and heat and life. Without light there is nothing. Darkness is the territory of the grave.

The last words of the great German poet Goethe were: *"Mehr Licht."* He had thought deeply about life and had said things better than most men, but when his eyes grew dim he had only two words to express everything he thought: more light. Without light there is nothing.

The history of light is the history of life, and the human eye was the first camera. It is shaped like a lens, and the image we see is reversed like in a camera—and made upright again by the brain. It took millions of years for man to create a sensitive surface to hold fast the effect of light and a few years more to pile one image on the other and to turn persistency of vision into the motion picture.

Every subject has a moment when light can force its beauty

From *Sight and Sound*, August 1955. Reprinted by permission.

Josef von Sternberg.

into full power, and that brings us to the province of the artist. The artist's duty and function is to capture not so much that which he can perceive—but that which his skill and imagination can endow with full power—no matter what the subject may be. We must learn to behold and to create—not with the camera but with the eye.

The camera is only an accessory to the human eye and serves principally to frame—to include and to exclude. Within the frame the artist collects that which he wishes us to behold— beyond the frame he places what he considers of no value for us to see. It is important to know how to use the camera—but it is more important to know how to use the eye. We cannot see without light and we cannot photograph without it. Therefore the knowledge of what light means is the first step in the direction of what photography means.

Every light has a point where it is brightest and a point toward which it wanders to lose its force completely. Light can go straight, go around, deflect, turn back and pierce through; it can be gathered or be spread, made to sparkle or be blocked. Where it is no more—is blackness, and where it begins is the core of its brightness. The journey of rays from that central core to the outposts of blackness is the adventure and drama of light.

Shadow is mystery and light is clarity. Shadow conceals— light reveals. (To know what to reveal and what to conceal and in what degree to do this is all there is to art.) Each light furnishes its own shadow, and where we see a shadow we know there must be a light. The great Alexander threw his shadow over Diogenes when he asked the man who lived in a barrel to name his wish, and the answer was: "*Stand from between me and the sun!*" This answer does not mean that Diogenes craved the sun, since he attempted to achieve the enviable position of craving nothing—but that he was irritated by a meaningless shadow.

The sun is the brightest light we know. It never ceases to project its rays. When the earth spins us away from it we see the stars only because the sun is still shining. This great source of light never stands still and its movement spells day and night, dawn and dusk. Between the earth and the sun is air. Air is the diffusion—the veil; and when it is too thin the sun becomes destructive and when it is too thick the sun loses its power. Thick air gathered and arranged by winds is called a cloud and when a cloud intercepts the sun the earth is drab. This paragraph is not to reiterate what every child knows, but to call attention that the angle of light and what it has to penetrate is of great importance to the appearance of the subject.

Light has a source, a direction and a point where its strength fails—and every light throws a shadow. If you choose any object and place a light anywhere you are a photographer, but if you can make the light bathe the object with the ever-varying drama of its rays and its shadow—you might be a good photographer. The black box, the glass and the sensitive silver is incidental.

The more light sources you use the more capable you must be. Lights can be friendly to each other or antagonize each other—or, what is worse, duplicate each other's functions—and then the rays are no longer bearers of beauty—they carry confusion. When you learn to photograph, begin with one light; if that one light is mastered, all other lights are mastered too.

The motion picture began by using one light: the light of the sun, and it followed the sun to California where it shone the brightest and the steadiest—and where it is now used the least. This is quaint and humorous though not without its reason. The first studios were built out of glass to permit the sun to enter. Those who built these glass houses thought they were as Joshua and could command the sun to stand still. But the sun, indifferent to man and his problems, moved, and bit by bit the glass was painted black and the sun banished, to be replaced by a sun built by human hands that could move and stand still as ordered. The first lights were of mercury, weak and feeble and flickering, but the lights were made steadier and stronger until an electric arc was invented and actually called "the sun." Equivalent to the power of millions of lighted candles and blinding in its effect, the inventor tried to imitate the power of the sun and the photographer tried to imitate its effect.

Imitation is not art—not even imitation of nature. We all

somehow know that. When an artificial flower is made to decorate a girl's hat the girl will say: *"My, don't it look real!"* but
give this same girl a branch of cherry in flower and she will
say: *"It looks as beautiful as if it were painted."*

The painter has taught us how to see and what to look for.
When I first discussed this chapter with Erich Maria Remarque
he said: *"Whenever I see a painter working in a beautiful landscape I know he is a bad painter."* This means that the painter
is judged by other standards than by the selection of his subject. Cézanne loved to paint common landscapes early in the
morning long before others had their breakfast because the
light was then at an angle, but he loved most to paint apples, a
clock, cloth or a skull: something that didn't move and which
he could inspect and place under favourable light conditions
that could be controlled.

The great painters who have said magnificently all that literature might have neglected, have pointed out with never-
ending emphasis that the subject, however it may reveal the
mentality of the painter, is secondary to the treatment.

They have painted everything they could see and everything
they could imagine and not always the human form and face.
They have painted sailboats, mountains, clouds and flowers but
also the carcass of an ox, and whatever the subject, we have
been taught to observe the values they have given it—that is, if
we care to enter their world. One taught us to see trees, another to see the interior of a room, another dirty snow on old
houses; they taught us to see beauty in the crucifixion, in a
laundry; in an autopsy, in drunken revelry, and in an ugly
body and an apparently ugly face.

The painter's power over the human form and face is of
course terrific. Not compelled to move it as we are, he can fix
the body and the expression to his complete satisfaction and in-
vest the subject permanently with his own nobility. Leonardo
makes his Mona Lisa smile with an inscrutability that may last
as long as the earth. Renoir paints flesh until, as he has said, it is
tempting enough to make him want to bite it. Rubens paints
the figures he desires to embrace, Raphael creates the madon-
nas he wishes to worship, and Michelangelo throws beings into

stone and on canvas like he wants to be, and all painters people their world with their chief interests—though if you see the side of an old wall painted by Utrillo or a clown by Rouault, the chief interest may not be instantly apparent.

The artist lauds or glorifies—invents freely when he finds nothing—protests or destroys that which he does not like—but he never operates without comment.

It is possible for an artist to be a photographer—and for the photographer to be an artist. But in being an artist he is judged as such and must use the standards of art. Being a photographer alone does not even mean that one knows how to photograph.

Those who merely reproduce what they see also have their use—and the frame and angle and the moment they choose to expose, also disclose their viewpoint—they, too, are qualified to photograph—but to the artist the subject is incidental, and what he thinks about it is all important.

The world in which the artist moves is the world of light and only the world of light. Light has strongly affected the imagination of all men, though there are some who are more sensitive to it than others. But light affects not only men but entire races of men, the quality of landscapes, and the animate and inanimate life of a whole country.

Even cities have different lights. The light of Paris and the light of London are dissimilar and the light of California varies from the light of Iceland. All weather affects the light, and rain or snow splits and reflects it. Light operates only when it hits an object but the air is solid too. Though the property of light is clearly noticed when air is condensed to a fog it is also visible to the sensitive eye in the rarest atmosphere, and air too can be made to glow.

Not even the most ignorant photographer is unconscious of light, though he may be at a loss to use it, and though the result may be disastrous. A story goes that before the days of Gutenberg, some simpletons built a city hall in a little German town and forgot to provide for windows, whereupon they formed a bucket brigade and tried to throw light into the dark building with buckets, and when that failed to work, they brought out sacks, cut the rays of the sun with scissors, tied up the bags and tried to empty the light into the building that way. These methods are not far removed from the usual method in photography where light and space is barricaded, wasted and used to no purpose.

We see in terms of light and our work is reproduced in terms of light. It speaks to us in terms of light though it may often be judged in terms of darkness. Let me stop for a second in my discussion of light, and descend with me into the regions of darkness—into the inferno of our particular world. There, when these things are discussed, one kneels, touches one's head several times to the east and mumbles the name of whichever producer, director, author or columnist happens to be the reigning box-office specialist. I'll spare you the names because they have no place in this discussion. Any one of a dozen temporary shibboleths when rubbed fervently into any Hollywood debate are Maxim silencers. Should one dare to mention, for instance, that the photographer and the director in motion pictures should be indivisible one can produce a major tremor in California. Why should the earth quake at this simple and logical ideal? The director writes with the camera whether he wishes to or not, or whether the others permit it or not. He influences and controls the camera as definitely as if he carried it in his pocket and took it with him at night to place it next to his watch beside his bed. What harm is there if a man knows his tools? Ah! shout the film marines, then you don't allow others to function.

Somewhere in "A Thousand and One Nights," a princess is wooed with the condition that the suitor who recognises a certain mystifying object wins her or, failing to distinguish the nature of the puzzling object, his head is added to the pile of the others who had desired the maiden. In our case the "mystifying object" is the finished film. In the Arabian Nights, Scheherezade tells us that the winner took a swift look, recoiled in horror, and cried, " *'Tis the skin of a louse grown large in oil!*" Let us inspect this bloated skin a little closer. When I was an assistant director I worked for Sam Goldwyn, who one day saw the film that had been done for him. In the silence that followed came his still small voice, "*Who directed this film?*" A man by the name of Windon stood up. "*Who wrote the story?*" Another arose. "*Who assisted?*" I stood up. "*Who photographed?*" Another stood. "*Who cut this fine work?*" I lifted my head proudly. "*Who put those actors in the picture?*" My old friend, MacIntyre, jumped to his feet. "*You're all fired!*" Mr. Goldwyn said in penetrant disgust as he left the room. There is a reverse to this false diagnosis. When a film is a success even the man who swept the floor after work is quickly snatched up by a rival studio in an attempt to find the formula. But should my opinion be consulted, I would venture to observe that a scientific analysis would disclose that the only insect which grew the skin in the first place was the director, and no matter how long the skin was soaked to make it monstrous, nothing but the director was the original inhabitant.

There are some directors, among whom I am numbered, who can photograph their own films. Personally I have often preferred to work without a photographer, and where I have worked with one, he has used light and position of camera with precise instruction from me, even when afterwards he accepted "Academy honours." I find it wastes time to instruct in something which I can equal with little effort, and therefore have often combined the technical function of director and cameraman to the intense disgust of the companies I have worked for, who have repeatedly challenged me to stop "fooling" with the camera.

This "fooling" with the camera saves time and energy, as otherwise director and cameraman must outguess each other and waste valuable effort in synchronizing their work. The large companies have iron-clad ideas to the contrary, and so my work has been checked with stop-watches to confirm my loose statement that I can operate twice as fast by "interfering" with the cameraman, rather than to sprawl in a chair and wait for his functions to cease, which cessation can only take place after he has provided light for every possible emergency of the actors, rather than for the movements that only I can cause.

But the factory system (against which I have nothing except that it is wasteful and self-destructive) of motion picture photography is dominated today not by the director, but (a) by

the laboratory whose principal interest is to insure even exposure rather than to expose the real culprits, and (b), what is
more absurd, by men called associate-producers or supervisors
who are paid from one hundred and fifty dollars to seven thousand a week to duplicate and trip up every specialised task in
motion pictures in the name of organising these tasks.

I was once called in by one of these "experts" and to my
astonishment told precisely how to photograph a close-up of a
much-publicised female, and actually shown a frame of film,
containing the face of another star taken from another film;
and I was told to imitate its shaky composition and effect, together with the empty space over her wig to provide ventila-
tion for some purpose incomprehensible to me. I was informed
this was "company photography" and to adhere to it, and
when I suggested that I liked to see photographic space contain interest other than unnecessary air providing solely for the
comfort of a producer, he mumbled something about leaving
everything to him. I left some other things to him with the result that the whole film was shelved for many a day and not
shown until some fifty writers, directors, producers, photographers and editors managed to paste together something which
any one of them could easily have done better alone.

This denaturing method of using the elements of photography is, to state it in my kind and mild fashion—faulty. In contrast the fine use of light creates a world of magic where the
significance of every object, alive or not, is not only revealed
in full essence but endowed with wonderful qualities, intangi-
ble though they may be.

The distance, intensity, sharpness and angle of light is an in-
exhaustible topic, particularly in our work where the motions
of the subject and the movements of the camera constantly
make for new combinations.

Even where we can't move the light we can move the camera, and the technique of the motion picture is based on the
movement of both.

Granted that my own sensitivity to the problem of light may
exceed the need for its normal application, it is nevertheless ad-
visable for the director to have some knowledge of its superla-

tive grace. While working with me, Miss Dietrich became so conscious of the value of light that her emotions dwindled when the lights snapped off one by one and the stage became dark, and when she walked past the power house, where the final switch was pulled to stop the dynamo, she felt as if she had received a blow.

The creation of visual beauty is not an easy accomplishment. We demand of beauty, visual or not, that it heal us from the wounds of life, and infinite care must be used to keep it from being marred by the slightest imperfection. No chain is stronger than its weakest link and if a film could be made, with all flaws eliminated, to show the perfection of the material, it would take instant place beside the masterpieces of the world's art. Part of the Russian experiment years ago, as Eisenstein explained it to me, was to abolish art because it is useless. Of course, that theory was not clearly thought out, since its very virtue is the supposed uselessness. We soon are sick and tired of what is useful alone. The Russian experiment is not over yet, nor is it confined to Russia. There was a good reason for wanting to abolish art. Art creates beauty, and beauty is disturbing to those who wish to contemplate ugliness. René Fülöp-Miller told me that Lenin could not listen to music. Listen to Lenin: *"But I can't often listen to music, it goes against the grain of my nerves. I would like to talk sweet nothings and fondle the heads of these people who can create such beauty in the midst of a dirty hell. But today is not the time to fondle the heads of human beings; today their skulls must be split, pitilessly—though the battle against force is our last ideal—a difficult task."*

Men who create beauty do not split heads pitilessly, and the creation of beauty is not quite so easy as murder. Expressed in various ways, beauty is synonymous with our longing to escape from the commonplace. It is the period of peace, in which we gather our strength for the conflict of life, and it is the reason for such conflict. All we fight for is to make life beautiful. But in fighting for beauty we must distinguish between those who fight to make their own life beautiful and those who fight to make the lives of others beautiful. Force beauty in others and you're in trouble. Each man has his own seventh heaven.

But beauty does not force, it does not clamour—it releases. The artist and the reformer are non-identical. You can teach others to see, but you cannot overcome resistance to beauty with bodily violence or any other kind of violence.

The artist is the officiating priest who administers the sacrament of beauty, and beauty is the business of every form of art. It is maintained that there are some who have no sense of beauty—I never met one who didn't. It may take a curious form, like gazing at a rubber plant with rapture, but in one form or another—though often concealed, it is part of our mortal clay.

The film has two instruments with which to record this beauty. One is the camera and the other is the microphone. Both are merciless.

Every instrument is superior in its inherent potentialities—to the human being using it—though there are occasional masters who can make us feel that the very limit of the ultimate power has been reached. The violin listlessly held before it is placed firmly against the shoulder promises more than it ever performs—and neither the camera nor the microphone has as yet recorded the great power both of which contain when they stand black and silent before touched by human hand.

On our stage these two, the camera and the microphone, are viewed with reverence—more so than the human being. Should something go wrong with the machine, everyone waits patiently until repairs are made, and sits quietly as if in a church. Not so when anything goes wrong with the human being. He is scolded and reviled and is asked to direct or act even when sick and in pain. The human being is usually less respected than a machine, but that may be because we credit the human being with more endurance, or because we erroneously believe that its parts are not really worn out until life ceases.

For a long time our profession endured the tyranny of the camera until it was confronted with the microphone. Its congenital tendency to contradict the camera was recognized by few. The viewpoint of the artist had dominated photography long before the arrival of sound, which returned the film to the primitive stage of engraving an accidental image. The camera even became an enemy, since it made noise—and it was punished and confined in a dog house from where it could only look out behind heavy glass plates. It took two or three years to permit the camera to emerge into its old freedom.

Before the arrival of the microphone, the optical instrument had been played by men, some more talented than others, who used it with austerity. Their world did not consist of what they saw so much as of what they could make us see. The camera had been taught to combat the imitative trend which runs into the dead end of reproduction. Verisimilitude, whatever its value, is a dangerous opponent of art.

Upon entrance into our intimate circle, the microphone was viewed with great interest, like one looks at a Mexican jumping bean. It arrived in the shape of a small black cannon and was held by a human being who tried his best frantically to escape the eye of the camera. Whenever he moved he made noise. Whenever anybody moved the result was noise. Creaking floors received more attention than creaking stories and whenever a bystander sneezed or coughed he was told to either control his nose and throat or to leave. A distant airplane terrorized the stage like in an air raid—and for a long time the camera was forgotten.

The acoustic instrument was used by engineers with skill in transferring precisely what was heard, without the benefit of even the most primitive non-mechanistic viewpoint. The human voice is no doubt a thrilling road to the quality of the human being, but a beautiful voice is not always arranged to dwell in a harmonious body. Moreover it needs the tincture of great inner experience. The camera, however, had collected by virtue of its ambitions human beings to act before it that formed a second Tower of Babel. No two voices matched either in accent or intelligence, let alone in beauty.

Personally I was uneasy at being precipitated into this problem. Biding my time until the microphone could be made subservient to the same control as the camera, I attempted to use dialogue and music only to counterpoint and supplement the work of the camera, rarely permitting both the same function, but, instead, stimulating and provoking associate ideas that brought in scope and distance beyond the ability of either instrument to produce alone. Though often, unfortunately, achieving only artificial instead of artistic values, I nevertheless persisted in attempting to order human speech into an acoustic pattern, regarding all sound whether coming from a lifeless source or not as subject to musical laws.

The profane voice of the average motion picture actor can and does injure the vision of the dramatist if his person has not already done so. The problem of the human voice is entirely different on the screen where the audience is forced to view the vision of the owner of that voice through the eye of the camera—from the problem of the human voice in the theatre where the actor retains the face he puts on when he leaves his dressing room.

Even there the human voice can be damaging. An oft-told anecdote deals with an irate critic leaving the theatre furiously at the end of the first act. When the manager caught up with him and asked him whether he couldn't hear, the infuriated critic shouted at him, fire in his eyes: *"That's the trouble! I heard every word!"*

The problem of the microphone is one that will not long escape the attention of the artist. It was comparatively easy at once to accustom the audience to regard with appreciation the changing of the harsh roar of a train or the sound of battle or a similar strident noise into obvious musical treatment, but the problem of the human voice may take longer to solve.

Intrinsically the sound machine almost from its very inception was capable of mechanical distortion and artistic perception. The present effective though complicated system of mixing sound is already far beyond the ability of any human being controlling it today. I sometimes have fused a dozen different sound tracks into one—reducing and augmenting each one at will. Even the worst sort of film has already adopted what I did at once: to make the voice of the speaker attend the face of the listener, to bring the outer world into a room, to change the exaggerated sound of footsteps into meaning (though even today the architect will paint his wood to seem like marble, forgetting that sound also photographs), to use distant speech and laughter as part of a sound curtain instead of hearing a solo in an empty world, to make echo and the tone of space dramatic ("Academy honours" to my mechanics who protested in writing this proper, essential use of sound), and a dozen other a, b, c, technicalities without which sound is too blatant.

But sound, though important and potentially effective, will always play a supplementary role to sight, as the camera has proven itself to be a diabolical instrument that conveys ideas with lightning speed. Through some curious inherent quality of flattening all lines and making them instantly perceptive and overprominent, it has achieved an anatomical property that analyzes every split second of motion. It exposes imbecility without the slightest hesitation and holds up to contempt both the person who uses it badly and the mistreated subject.

Time and again the news-camera has revealed the stupidity of well-known public figures or has so overpowered the subject that roars of laughter have greeted the person and his utterances which, conveyed to us by microphone alone, or through the radio, succeeded in impressing us. (Winston Churchill was made to look a fool by the news-camera. I sat next to him on the evening Edward VIII abdicated to rock England, and while everyone was waiting for him to express his opinion, he called the head-waiter and said: *"This coffee is very inadequate."*)

The camera, left to its own devices, is an incisive, vivisecting, and often destructive instrument, and the men behind the camera have devoted much time and effort to appease the cruelty of the little piece of glass through which our work is gathered.

The art of cinematography has been falsely compared to the art of painting—which does not depend upon sudden effect and does not vanish before it can be closely analyzed or inspected for any length of time. Moreover it stands still, while the average motion picture contains from three hundred to one thousand variously composed angles, in their turn composed of thousands of fleeting images which must be ordered into a continuity of effect—one viewpoint—while the painter constructs his canvas with its one image to withstand the critical inspection of centuries.

Though the painter, like everyone else, is justified in discussing the value of the motion picture, his work in it can prove completely ineffectual without intense photographic experience. Gifted painters have been at work in our medium and they have proven to be less capable than a less gifted artist who has learned to see in terms of the camera. In Japan, Foujita showed me a film he made for his government, and though he is an able painter his work on the screen turned him into a beginner.

In order to function at all, the artist must make his men, women and other materials move with the grace and efficiency of his vision and speak with a melody which he composes. Whether he is able to do so or not is a matter for others to determine. But it is for no one to determine the principles of art. They have been determined long ago.

The cardinal points of photography are identical with those of painting. They are—material—subject—composition—light— and the most obvious of all—viewpoint. The radical point of departure is—motion.

To begin with the material—still photography as distinguished from motion picture photography has one enormous advantage which some day will cease to be: that is the treatment of the surface of the photograph. Choice of grain in the paper, manipulation of the negative, the enlargement of an interesting detail can salvage otherwise uninteresting work and make it effective. It is only a matter of time when such manipulation will be incorporated into our work.

The subject whatever it be, water, sky, landscape, pavement, machine or face, animate or inanimate, must be viewed with impartial eye and made to reflect its inner values—and the value of the artist. These must be captured and held fast at their best, and it is the duty of the artist not only to engrave the image at the moment of its highest grace but to animate the subject. If the subject is human, this is not easy. It may be possible to inspire a momentary glow but to maintain that glow is unbelievably difficult—both for the subject and for the artist.

The motion picture has capitalised the human being in particular and has not without some justice attempted to state that it is the container of everything that can thrill us. The camera proceeded to explore the human figure from every angle and to concentrate on its face.

The face is in itself an inspiring mask when not maligned, and our whole past and ancestry has left its mark on its surface in ever-varying arrangements no two of which are alike, just as even the whorls of our fingertips differ. There are painters who have painted nothing but the human face and, like Yawlensky, have finally reduced it to a simple pattern which varies only in elementary line and color.

The artist has a great duty to the human face and if he cannot bring to the fore its native dignity, he should at least conceal its shallowness and stupidity—though it is possible that no human being is either stupid or shallow but appears to be so only because it is ill at ease and has not found that corner of its world in which it can be comfortable.

Monstrously enlarged as it is on the screen, the human face must be treated like a landscape and invested with the relief of light and the retreat of shadow. It is to be viewed as if the eyes were lakes, the nose a mountain, the cheeks broad meadows, the mouth a flower patch, the forehead sky, and the hair a cloud.

Color values must be altered as in an actual landscape by the added use of light, filter and manipulation of that which absorbs too much light. Just as I spray trees with aluminium to give life to the blunt green, just as one filters the sky to reduce its whiteness, just as the camera is pointed to catch a reflection on the surface of a lake, just so must the face be viewed to contain the elements that form its chiaroscuro. The skin should reflect and not blot light, and the lights are to be used to caress, not to wipe out, what they strike.

If it is impossible to raise the quality of the subject's face by placing deep shadows into the eyes, it is better to obliterate it in merciful darkness and to have the human face be no more, and no less, than an active pattern in the photographic scale.

When the face is photographed, the result is strongly affected by everything that is visible in the same frame. When I light a face I first light the background and fill my frame with light values that point to the face. The figure too should meet with no other measure, and a walk or its movement through a space should be made into an encounter with light.

But whether face, a letter, a toy balloon, or a street, the problem is always the same—lifeless surfaces should be relentlessly treated to take light, and over-brilliant and flaring surfaces must be reduced to their order: shadows must avoid duplication, and the vitality of the general pattern concentrate toward its chief interest.

Wherever possible in dealing with black and white photography, all colors should be avoided as they provoke bad judgment. My sets and costumes are normally designed in black and white, and where light is difficult to use without exact control I spray black and white paint on anything that is before my camera. The superb virtue of black and white photography is that it automatically makes all color values unreal and changes them to an orderly scale.

Color photography can be of no value, beyond its novelty, until the artist uses unreal and unnaturalistic color on face, costume and background alike and orders each scene into a unit of the entire. The tints now in use in films are not superior to the hand-colored photographs which have been a horror for fifty years.

The value of color is determined by the value of the artist who uses it. There are many great painters alive who excel in the use of color. I am not informed as to the exact time Henri Matisse needed to determine the color he used in a single canvas, but it must be considerably longer than the time used that determines the colors that are poured into our "super" features. W. C. Fields' classic: *"Double superlative! Can you handle it?"* has so far been answered by the film with quite a firm *"No."*

When I took Karl Vollmoeller to a much-vaunted film in color he expressed judgment tersely by saying: *"It would have been bad even without color."*

Until the able color artists enter our menagerie, its chief asset will remain the great use of black and white, its numberless combinations, extensive range and variation, and the dramatic relation of one to the other. A shaft of white light properly used can be more effective than all the color in the world badly used. More than that—with light and an empty canvas and a few ridiculous properties one can produce a landscape that is superior in beauty to most landscapes provided even by nature, unless nature also genially provides, which it rarely does, the proper light to record its bounty. Even then one must use gauze and filter, and the proper lens—controlled exposure, precise shutter, skilful focus and—a point of vantage often impossible to obtain.

But, you see, there is no wholesale judicial committee in dealing with the elements used in art. Each one according to his measure dominates the final result. The slightest detail is influenced by the slightest idea, grandeur or pettiness is revealed—each idea is sifted—through each thought of the artist, and the mentality of the man at work becomes fully apparent in every move.

Of all our problems the simplest is the one of composition. Though it is a fluid one and aligned with the problem of light, it is easily perceived. In its finest sense film composition shifts constantly with each image in motion, and every frame of our work should relate to the sum total.

But above all—the greatest art in motion picture photography is to be able to give life to the dead space that exists between lens and subject. Smoke, rain, snow, fog, dust and steam can emotionalize dead space—so can the movement of the camera. The camera can advance and retreat with or against the action it photographs—it can expose in every second an orderly and rich pictorial progression. (This does not mean movement for the sake of motion, which one can often see in the labour of those who come to our work from the theatre and are excited by the discovery that the audience can be made dizzy. The movement of the camera should be made to subscribe to the rhythmic conception of the entire work.) The camera can release by virtue of its motion a dynamic force which will give the perfect motion picture its ultimate rating and will remove it finally from the stigma of being what it so often attempts to be at present: a subsidiary of other arts which can be used more powerfully.

Were I to instruct others how to use the camera, the first step would be either to project a film upside down or to have the film viewed so long until the actors and the story made the students yawn, if they failed to do so immediately. To eliminate the factors which do not contribute to the study of the camera is very difficult as the untrained eye is apt to confuse the reason for the faults and the virtues of the camera. (Note to the universities of the future: The camera collects all faults and virtues but does not produce them all.)

The speed with which the eye can absorb visual information must also be learned. The motion picture camera has specific effects that must be mastered. Slow motion can seem swift in interest and quick motion can appear to be never-endingly dull. The motion picture camera has no limits that circumscribe its artistic functions—its limits are—if any, the limits of the human eye.

Its greatest asset—superb and unique—is motion, not only outwardly visible but inwardly concealed and felt; and in order to master the laws of motion one must first master pause and rhythm. In other words: the laws of art—and the lawlessness of it, too.

MICHAEL CURTIZ
(1888-1962)

Curtiz was a major figure in the flourishing central European film industry of the silent days, directing many films in Hungary, Germany, Denmark, Austria, Italy and France between 1913 and 1926. Gifted with the ability to squeeze lavish results out of restricted budgets, and notorious as a fast worker, he was signed by the Warner Brothers to come to Hollywood and direct films for their financially shaky little studio. But soon after his arrival the Warners hit the jackpot with their Vitaphone talking picture process, and Curtiz found himself top director for the industry's fastest-growing studio. In his prime it was nothing for Curtiz to direct five or more films a year, and he quickly developed a reputation as a hard-driving taskmaster with little regard for his actors or crew. His best 30's films, like *Captain Blood* or *The Walking Dead*, made bold use of sweeping shadows and camera movements, and of the somewhat expressionist scenic designs of Anton Grot. After such memorable 40's productions as *Yankee Doodle Dandy*, *Casablanca* and *Mildred Pierce*, Curtiz's films seemed to lose much of their energy, but the 50's did bring his greatest commercial success, *White Christmas*. Ironically, it would be hard to imagine a more atypical Curtiz picture. N.B.: Curtiz's memory of his early days is particularly faulty. He may have been signed by Harry Warner in Paris in 1926, but not while directing *Sodom und Gomorrah*, which he made several years earlier in Austria. And a gap of four years and eleven pictures separates *The Third Degree* from *Under a Texas Moon*.

TALENT SHORTAGE IS CAUSING TWO-YEAR PRODUCTION DELAY

MICHAEL CURTIZ

With the many problems the industry faces, it seems unbelievable that the greatest of these is the supply of talent, of personalities the public will pay to see. With thousands of hopeful people, some old as well as young, beating upon the gates of Hollywood, working to be discovered, to show what they can do, this seems a paradox. But out of a million hopefuls, we might find one who has that elusive quality that makes a star—personality—and sufficient acting ability to back it up. Given some talent to work with, we can teach anyone to act with time and hard work; but personality cannot be learned. It is something you were born with. You have it or have not.

To show just how rare a quality it is—how much goes into creating a star—the greatest box office names of today are those who started in pictures twenty years ago. Most of these underwent a period of apprenticeship in smaller parts and featured rôles, then having once attained stardom have continued to reign as box office favourites, successfully outdrawing droves of newcomers, over a period of a decade or two. Very few of the stars established in the past five or six years can compare with the old-timers.

The public (and the cinema owners who in a sense represent this public to us here in Hollywood) constantly clamours for new faces, but we have learned that they are very particular and selective in admitting newcomers to their circle of favoured box office greats.

Down through the years, major studios have spent sizeable sums in searching for and presenting new talent. We have worked to develop our own and taken from other reputable sources. We have had some success at these endeavours, but never enough. The problem of a constant sufficiency of new

From *Films and Filming*, June 1956.

Michael Curtiz on location for *The Lady Takes a Sailor* (1949).

talent possessing the potential of stardom has never been solved.

To make our talent situation worse, our list of established stars is dwindling. We are responsible for this ourselves in a sense. We have let some top stars get away to other media. Some are prospering so on television, or the stage, that they are no longer available to us except occasionally. Then many established stars have formed their own independent companies; some are interested only in participation or package deals. This has made it extremely difficult for a studio at times to cast a picture properly. In fact, the casting problem has become bigger and bigger. Many productions have been postponed a year or two because the producer cannot find the right star. It all adds up to the fact that the studios must develop their own new talent or face the alternative of becoming releasing agents only.

On the subject of new talent, we are both open-minded and scared. We want it, but we are afraid of it. We too often lack the courage to entrust big, costly pictures to unknowns.

I think this is a mistake, particularly if these unknowns are qualified, and if the pictures that serve to introduce them are well made, with intelligently written stories and competent production. There must be a three-way combination of sparkling talent, excellent story and able direction, or the whole effort is wasted.

We must take these risks—risks not as frightening as they might seem, if the right amount of careful preparation is gone into in advance—if our industry is to continue to grow and prosper.

It is demonstrable, I think, that an outstandingly good picture made by these standards will do well on quality alone. Take *Marty*, for a recent example. Here is a picture peopled by relative unknowns, but who have that certain magnetism of personality which is essential; with an appealing, human story of great charm; and direction which illuminates and blends the highest values of the other creative talents.

Maybe one reason I feel so strongly about new faces—those who have the qualities of stars of tomorrow—is that I have had the good fortune to encounter so many of them as they were starting out, and been able to give them a helping hand.

I think more than that, I have a sympathetic feeling for young people trying to become established, because I remember my own early days as a young actor and director. I can never forget the struggling, the hoping and praying for a break.

My own came when as a young man of 26 [*sic*] I was directing *Sodom and Gomorrah* for a French film company in Paris. We had many visitors, including one man unknown to me, who was there for three days running. On the third day our schedule called for a very big crowd scene so I told my assistant to close the set to visitors.

Five minutes later he returned to me, his face white. He told me the man was Harry Warner, of Hollywood. Naturally, we invited him to stay.

That night I signed a contract to direct pictures for Warner Brothers. It was intended that I should do the Biblical spectacle, *Noah's Ark*, but as it turned out that was to come three years later. Meanwhile, I, as a foreigner, was assigned to do *The Third Degree*, an American gangster story. My next one was another piece of Americana, *Under a Texas Moon*.

In the course of directing these and many other pictures since coming to America, it has been my good fortune to give some wonderful young players their first big breaks. All had that magnetism of personality which is a must, plus talent and the capacity for hard work.

In the past year at Paramount, I have had a hand in adding several other newcomers to the list through two pictures—*The Vagabond King*, in which we introduce Oreste; and *The Scarlet Hour*, an exciting modern drama in which the cast is headed by Carol Ohmart, a brilliant young actress from radio and television who should go far in motion pictures. The latter film also introduces Tom Tryon, a talented leading man who makes a fine impression.

Jody Lawrence's story, I feel, is particularly interesting. She had tried hard to establish herself as an actress without success. Finally, quite discouraged, she got a job as a waitress in a local candy store. I found her there and, after a screen test, assigned her the ingenue lead in *The Scarlet Hour*. She gives a fine, sensitive performance.

I will be the first to admit that introducing newcomers is not easy, any more for the director than it is for the sales department. An established actor with talent and experience usually needs little individual direction; but it is a different story with a newcomer. The director must have a great deal of patience. He must guide the player carefully. He must see that he keeps his emotions under control, that he keeps the character simple and believable.

I realise how important to the industry are the big established stars whose names will practically guarantee large receipts. I wish we had more of them to make it easier for directors and producers to cast pictures and thereby solve the biggest problem the motion picture business faces at this time. It is to augment this small group of top names that we must develop and gamble on new talent. We must have stars for the future.

It is a great gamble and it takes courage for a studio to put an unknown talent in a picture which costs millions of dollars to make; but it is all the more rewarding when the gamble pays.

NICHOLAS RAY
(1911-   )

Although Ray has long been tagged as a loner in the Hollywood system, even an outcast, this article on the genesis of
Rebel Without a Cause shows him to have had a particularly well-reasoned grasp of the interrelated functions of
producer, director and writer. While many of his fellow
directors rant incessantly about the corrupting touch of all
producers, Ray clearly charts the positive contributions of
the best of them, and gives special credit to David Weisbart, with whom he worked on *Rebel*. Once a student of
Frank Lloyd Wright, then an associate of Elia Kazan and
John Houseman in the New York theatre, Ray directed his
first film, *They Live by Night*, in 1947, but it was not generally released for two years. A romantic treatment of the
same story later filmed by Altman (*Thieves Like Us*), it
introduced the themes of adolescent alienation which
would later recur in so many of Ray's films, including
Knock on Any Door and *Rebel*. In these and other films
the Ray hero is typically isolated, sometimes physically
(*The Savage Innocents*) but more often spiritually and
emotionally, a single element of a large and hostile universe
(*In a Lonely Place*). According to Ray, his films all share
the common working title, "I'm a Stranger Here Myself."
Ray's last commercial films were the Samuel Bronston epics
King of Kings and *Fifty-Five Days at Peking*, since which
he has been announced for any number of unrealized projects. In the early 70's he taught at New York's Harpur
College, and with his students made the film *We Can't Go
Home Again*, an unusual stylistic experiment which has
been given only rare public screenings.

STORY INTO SCRIPT
NICHOLAS RAY

The innocent public has learned much about writers and producers from the drawing room anthropologist, who arrives in Hollywood for a short visit and a series of brisk interviews and writes a book about the place with plenty of references to primitive society and the tribal unconscious. To say anything more is, perhaps, inviting confusion. Yet, though the parallels with initiation ceremonies in Polynesia may be exhausted, personal experience has still something to tell.

I have been lucky enough, in Hollywood, to work for two outstandingly good producers. "Producer" in this sense means not the executive in charge of everything that goes on at the studio, but a member of his staff delegated to supervise scripting, casting, budgeting and the general approach to an individual film. Leo Rosten, whose book *Hollywood—The Movie Colony* contains the best straightforward analysis of producers I know, remarks that movies are what the executives "encourage or *allow* their battery of creative talents to make of them." True enough; but this privilege ideally belongs to the director, and his task is to take it over as soon as he can in the creation of a film.

A sympathetic and imaginative producer can be enormously helpful, not only in the creative ideas he brings to a picture, but in fighting the director's battles with the "desk set" for him. He needs, of course, courage as well as imagination; and this is what makes him rare. The inept or insecure producer, unfortunately, is not so rare, and his existence formed the subject of a pamphlet by the Screen Directors' Guild a few years ago. Simply through what he cannot or will not do, he may cause much damage to a picture—by creating a climate of confusion and mistrust in which the director's relationship to his

From *Sight and Sound*, August 1956. Reprinted by permission of *Sight and Sound* and Nicholas Ray.

After setting up a complex Cinemascope tracking shot, Nicholas Ray (hands on hips) gives a last word of advice to James Dean and Natalie Wood during the shooting of *Rebel Without a Cause*.

writers and technical crew, as well as to the front office, is affected.

At Warners I found another good producer. Rather to my surprise, the studio offered me a choice of any of their contract producers, and I decided on David Weisbart. He was the youngest; he had two teenage children, which made me think he would bring a personal interest to the subject; and he was also an excellent worker with the celluloid strip (a rare attribute among producers). Previously he had been a film editor, and had cut *A Streetcar Named Desire* for Kazan, who told me he had liked working with him, thought he and I would get along, and that Dave would be a *contributing* producer. He was.

When Dave read the outline of *The Blind Run* and listened to me talk some more about it, his first reaction was as if he had swallowed a hot potato. (Later, of course, he knew he had.) This was not surprising. To begin with, he was faced with an original story—less a story at this stage than an idea—and not the comfortable basis of an existing novel or magazine story or Broadway play. Also, the subject itself was potentially explosive.

I think he remained in a state of shock for some time. But when the story was at last taking shape and we were nearly ready to start shooting, he became passionately involved in the film. Not the least valuable thing he did for me was to accept, with patience and understanding, the two false starts over finding a writer, and allow the search for the right one to continue.

2

Finding a writer is for many reasons more difficult than finding a producer. The producer, anyway, usually finds you. There is a traditional writer-director hostility in Hollywood, and it is a unique kind of hostility. Basically, each resents his dependence on the other. The writer needs the director for his story to be realised; the director needs the writer to give him a story in a form he can realise.

From this situation springs a good deal of misunderstanding and bitterness. The writer claims that his creative contribution is under-estimated—the director and stars nearly always receive more publicity and acclaim than he, and yet hasn't he created the characters and the story, written the dialogue and evolved the structure?

If the writer's case were as simple as this, he would be the most ill-treated professional in the film industry. Unfortunately for him, it is not. First, there are perhaps a half-dozen first-rate writers in Hollywood. Most outstanding creative writers will prefer literature or the drama, to which their contribution creates no ambiguity. The famous novelists who come to Hollywood and write a script seldom arrive with an open mind about the new medium they are exploring, and seldom learn very much about it. Nearly all of them return with an ironic, rueful image of the monstrous director or producer. The writer, they claim, is not *understood*.

In the same way, a few writers who have attained fame and influence in Hollywood will turn to direction in order, they claim, to preserve the integrity of their scripts. This is an admirable theory but, on the whole, a deplorable practice. To bring it off requires the exceptional talent of a John Huston or a Preston Sturges at their best. There are many writer-directors whose films are unsatisfactory precisely because they overestimate the writer and under-estimate the director. The writer-director is much too indulgent to the writer, reluctant to cut a word of that brilliant dialogue, a sentence of that verbose scene.

The most talented Hollywood writers are those who recognise the special nature of writing for the movies and acknowledge the creative claims of the director. ("One of the functions of the director," says Gilbert Seldes in *The Movies Come From America*, "is to save us from the writer enamoured of his own wit; another is to save us from the players enamoured of their own personality; and a third is to save us from the producers. . . .") This involves, sometimes, a difficult kind of abnegation for the writer, who is working in a medium in which the image and not the word has the final impact. "It was all in the script," a disillusioned writer will tell you. But it was never all in the script. If it were, why make the movie?

There is a revealing story told in this connection by the German director Fritz Lang. When he made his first Hollywood film, *Fury*, in 1935, he knew about thirty words of English. (This did not prevent him from working on the script.) The brilliant picture that emerged was considered too controversial and disturbing by a distinguished front-office executive. Irately he summoned Lang to his office and accused him of having changed the script. Lang replied that his lack of English made this impossible; comparing the script with the finished film, he showed that not a line of dialogue nor a situation had been changed. All the same, the executive complained, the film was entirely different from the script.

Starting from an original idea, the tendency of most writers is to make it "literary," to present situation primarily in terms of dialogue. The director has to fight against this, and the result is often to make the writer accuse him of being illiterate. There may be a scene in which a writer is especially proud of his dialogue; it may be good dialogue; but what is really needed for the scene is not good dialogue but a visual conception. And the dialogue has to go. What replaces it may seem, to the writer, banal—and here another misunderstanding can arise. Someone remarked that a fundamental tenet of Stanislavsky's system is to help an actor say "What time is it?" and mean one of maybe twenty different things—"I want to leave" or "I want to stay," "I love you" or "I hate you," "I'm worried" or "I don't care," and so on. In this sense the most apparently banal line of dialogue can achieve dramatic meaning. Out of the inner moment, the state of being and the urgent need, comes the whole accent of what is said or done. Only the director is in a position to help the actor create this effect.

If writers were able to work more closely with directors from the beginning of a film's conception, the results and the mutual understanding would improve. Most directors, when they start making films, are handed complete (though often impracticable) scripts a few days before shooting is due to start. Later, they still have to fight to work with a writer of their own choice. (Often the difficulty is that a studio likes to use one of its own contract writers, for obvious economic reasons.) This is a battle Hollywood directors have been fighting for twenty years, and it is not yet won.

The complaints are not all on one side. Studio executives work under the anxious pressure of having to account to their stockholders, and they can do this only by keeping up a regular supply of profitable product. An executive's first instinct is to oppose anything that will interrupt the supply or increase the budget. It is inconvenient and often wasteful to postpone a shooting date, to juggle with actors' commitments. Why can't the director get on with making the picture he has been signed to make?

Nobody sets out deliberately to make a bad picture, though a lot of people set out just to make a picture. The economics and the mechanisation of the system demand it. The difficulty starts when a film-maker's personal convictions interfere with the mechanisms of a business operated for profit. To object to the movies because they are "commercial" is idiotic; to accept that honesty and originality are necessarily "uncommercial" is impossible.

Yet good films somehow get made—and not, as some embittered humorists like us to believe, simply in spite of the front office. Producers, directors and writers have many misunderstandings among themselves. For the front office this is merely an additional burden to bear. It has every reason never to take a risk. Yet it does, and surprisingly often. The decision that enabled a *Grapes of Wrath*, a *Citizen Kane* or *A Place in the Sun* to be made uncompromisingly, the way their creators wanted, could not have been an easy one. And in one case at least it could not have been easy to appease the stockholders.

Production methods, then, are one factor. Another is human insecurity. In making films, creative people and businessmen and administrators have to work together. There is a hatchet of tradition to be buried. There is an intensely competitive atmosphere. Credit and fame are not only matters of personal pride but professional necessity. In the process of discarding ancient instinctive hostilities, some unexpected alliances may be formed. In the producer-director-writer triangle it is not necessarily the "artists" who form the base. To gain a point, the producer may decide to drive a wedge, and it is not difficult for him to do so; separately and secretly, writer and director may seek the producer's support in an unresolved issue.

An insecure producer tends, on principle, to keep writer and director apart—in some cases, even to the extent of refusing to allow the writer to visit the set, thereby making it virtually impossible for him to learn more about the medium.

An insecure writer always decides his first obligation is to the producer, rather than to the story or himself—except his economic self, that is, for a writer commonly assumes it is only the producer who gets him the job.

An insecure director has a wider field in which to operate. Basically he can be insecure because he doesn't know what he wants—from the writer or from the actors, from the technical crew or the cutter (and, in a few unfortunate cases, from any of them). As a result his potential victims are legion. The case has been finely put by Arthur Hopkins in his book, *Reference Point*. It is about the theatre, but the parallels are deadly and apt.

He prays for delivery:—

"From the director who inflicts his barbed jokes on defence-less people.

"From the director who suffers the tortures of the delivery room.

"From the hysterical director, a fugitive from the home for wayward girls.

"From the director who keeps actors waiting while he is prostrate with exhaustion.

"From the director who keeps actors sitting around while he tries to make up that rumpled bed—his mind.

"From the director who stages a big scene which he has planned for his own stellar appearance."

This makes it only too clear that we can be the most danger-ous of all.

3

The Blind Run was an original idea for a film, without dramatic structure but with a point of view. The problem in developing it was to create situations and dialogue that reflected this point of view. On occasion I have earned my living as a writer. For most of my films I have supplied ideas for situations or changed existing ones, and written some dialogue scenes. But I don't regard myself as a writer. (Ideally I would prefer not to write at all, being no doubt even more indulgent than a professional to the few lines I've written that have pleased me.)

Warners wanted me to use one of their contract writers, and suggested Leon Uris, whose *Battle Cry* had just made a successful film. This didn't prove he was the kind of writer I was looking for, but he was enthusiastic about the subject, seemed to share the point of view, and there was an intriguing episode in his personal history. Before becoming an established writer, he had been a distribution supervisor for a San Francisco newspaper. To the forty boys working under him, who came to him with their problems, he had acted as a father confessor.

Uris began by spending ten days as an apprentice social worker at Juvenile Hall, the detention centre where all kinds of children and adolescents who have got into all kinds of trouble—from getting lost to setting fire to a house, or even murder—are held for examination and interview by social workers and psychiatrists before their cases come up in court.

We had first approached Juvenile Hall and the Juvenile Bureau of the city police department some time earlier, uncertain of the reception that might be forthcoming. Richard Brooks had told me that, through no fault of his own, he had failed to get any official cooperation on *Blackboard Jungle*. He had been advised to tell the authorities that he had no script, for fear that certain scenes would meet with objection or disapproval. This was bad advice, as the deception was discovered, the authorities were angry, and Brooks was refused even an interview and told by the police to expect no cooperation at all.

I could truthfully say, on my first visit there, that I had no script. But I knew what I wanted, and explained it frankly to Judge McKesson at Juvenile Hall, and to Dr. Coudley, chief psychiatrist there. They liked the approach and offered us everything we needed: talks with social workers and psychiatrists, admission to interviews with young delinquents and to courtrooms, going out on riot calls in a police car.

Out of all this had come confirmation of my original point of departure. In listening to these adolescents talk about their lives and their acts, two impressions always recurred. What they did had a terrifying, morose aimlessness, like the 16-year-old boy who ran his car into a group of young children "just for fun." What they felt, when asked about their families, was a bitter isolation and resentment. All told similar stories—divorced parents, parents who could not guide or understand, who were indifferent or simply "criticised," parents who needed a scapegoat in the family.

4

Leon Uris approached his first treatment with diligence and research. As a way of feeling himself into the subject, he began by writing a short history of the imaginary small town in which the action was to be set: sketching the growth of one of those quiet "normal" communities now astonished by the number of juvenile delinquents in their midst.

The treatment itself, however, gave me the ungrateful task of explaining it was not what I wanted. One of the most difficult things for a writer is to try and follow somebody else's point of view, to create a story for an imagination not his own. On an adaptation, he can discover concrete instances of the director's attitude towards the material. On somebody else's original, he is working in the dark. It was like an eye test at the optician's—could he read the characters in my mind as he might a chart on the wall? We did not, it seemed, perceive the same characters on the chart. The search had to continue.

Of the writers available at the time, Irving Shulman seemed the likeliest. Apart from his work as a novelist and in films, he had been a high school teacher. He was also deeply interested in sports cars, which suggested a promising point of contact with Jimmy Dean.

By this time I had seen *East of Eden*, had met Jimmy and knew he was the ideal actor for Jim Stark. It was still far from certain, although he was interested in the project, that he would play the part. One side of the difficulty was personal. Since beginning to know him a little, I had realised that, for a successful collaboration, he needed a special kind of climate.

He needed reassurance, tolerance, understanding. An important way of creating this climate was to involve him at every stage in the development of the picture. Accordingly, he met Shulman one afternoon at my home.

The result was disappointing. After a brief spurt, the talk of cars dwindled away to nothing. Suspiciously, rather menacingly, as happened when rapport was not forthcoming at a first encounter, Jimmy withdrew.

Shulman at once set about constructing a screenplay in some detail. Unlike Uris, he considered active research unnecessary and did not visit Juvenile Hall or talk to any of the people with whom I had made contact there. His talent for inventing or remembering incidents led us quickly forward, however, in some directions.

We started by discussing the school gang, and Shulman remembered a newspaper item about a "chickie run" at night on Pacific Palisades. A group of adolescents had assembled in stolen cars on the clifftop plateau. Drivers were to race each other towards the edge. The first to jump clear before the rim of the cliff, the drop to the sea, was a "chickie." On this night one of the boys failed to jump in time. The "chickie run" on the plateau replaced the original blind run through the tunnel.

We discussed Plato, the lonely boy trying to escape from his drab indifferent family, and tried to find a more definite character for him. Although in Shulman's screenplay he became more overtly psychotic than in the final version, we arrived at a new background, a new basic situation, for him. His loneliness now came, like Jim's and Judy's, from a well-to-do home; hesitant, craving affection, filled with violent inner struggles, he lived in a large house with his neglectful, pleasure-seeking mother, and had contact with his father only from a cheque that arrived with a typewritten note pinned on it—*for support of son*. For some reason the front office at Warners had strong objections to this. I could only reply that for me it had an equally strong reality, as I have two sons in that situation, and it was an idea drawn only too directly from personal experience.

These were developments, but they did not reach the heart

of the story. *Romeo and Juliet* has always struck me as the best play ever written about "juvenile delinquents." I wanted a *Romeo and Juliet* feeling about Jim and Judy—and their families. Out of this came a conviction about the shape of the story. "Try to follow classic form of tragedy," I noted one day. "Make sure the unities are comprehended." The main action should be compressed into one day, beginning for Jim Stark in trouble and confusion, but ending, for the first time, in something different. Another note was: "A boy wants to be a man, quick." The problem was to show, during this day, how he started to become one.

Weisbart and I also had an idea for a school scene. The students go to an astronomy class at the Planetarium. Confronted with a giant replica of the sky, pinpointed planets and constellations glittering on it, they listen to a dry cosmic lecture. The voice drones on, of universality and space and the immense cycles of time, and concludes with a vision of the end of the world. Flashes of light explode across the sky. And while the other students mock or whisper, Plato suddenly shivers from an awareness of his own solitude.

Later, an idea for another scene at the Planetarium occurred to me. At the climax of the story, when Plato believes that Jim, his only friend, has deserted him, I thought he should return to the deserted Planetarium at night, seeking shelter under its great dome and artificial sky. It was the kind of unexpected dramatic reference I felt the story should contain; there was for me a suggestion of classical tragedy about it. Discussing the scene with Jim and with Leonard Rosenman—who, after seeing *East of Eden*, I had decided should be the composer for the film—I was encouraged that they agreed, and thought it would be one of the best scenes in the story. Shulman, however, tenaciously disagreed. He thought Plato should seek refuge in his own home.

This was a crucial point for me because it symbolised the more violent statement, the more sweepingly developed conflict that I was searching for and that Shulman seemed unable to accept. It was a gesture of anger and desperation that matched the kind of thing I had heard at Juvenile Hall.

The issue made me decide that our points of view were essentially different. In spite of the valuable things Shulman had brought to the screenplay, we were once again at a dead end.

5

According to Robert Lindner, author of the original *Rebel Without a Cause*, we were at a dead end anyway. I met him at a cocktail party sponsored by the Hacker Foundation at the Beverly Hills Hotel. He was in Hollywood to give two lectures: "The Mutiny of Adolescence" and "Must We Conform?" There was, naturally, some tension to overcome at our first meeting. He knew I had rejected his book, though he soon made it clear he was not piqued by this—only genuinely bewildered.

His own book, he told me, contained the most searching basis possible for any film on deliquency. "You must do it this way. You must make a developmental film." In his lectures he was going to discuss the conflict between protest and conformity that faced young people today. The problem of the individual's desire to preserve himself in the face of overwhelming demands for social conformism was, he felt convinced, at the heart of the subject.

As this nervous, handsome man in his early forties (his remarkable career as a criminal psychologist was to be abruptly ended by death a year later) talked excitedly of protest and rebellion, I could not restrain the impression that he was grappling with a delayed rebellion of his own. The idea of filming his study of the young delinquent who related fantasies of violence under hypnosis seemed almost to obsess him. He almost begged me to do it; he offered his services as consultant.

I explained that one strong reason for my not wanting to film his book was that I had already made *Knock On Any Door*, about an adolescent who drifts into crime as the result of poverty and wretched upbringing, and I didn't want to repeat myself. His security, however, was unshakeable. So, in its way, was mine—though behind it lay some pressing doubts.

It was now towards the end of November. Nearly two

months had passed and I was still without the script, or the writer, that I wanted. Not surprisingly, Warners were anxious to set a date for shooting to begin. As so often happens when preparations for a film do not run smoothly, the rumours had started that it would never be made. A technician at the studio, someone reported to me, had laid a bet of $250 to this effect. Dave Weisbart was having his front office troubles, and after we had started shooting told me there had been talk of abandoning the project. On a higher level, Steve Trilling as executive producer was also having to justify his faith in an idea that, although money was being spent on it, was still no more than an idea.

I made another note: "Dave and I should be considering the new young writers as possibilities. Someone who will stay right there and work with us through the rest of the show. . . ."

ELIA KAZAN
(1909-   )

Elia Kazan's introduction to Budd Schulberg's published screenplay of *A Face in the Crowd* deals less with that film than with the newfound respectability of screenwriting itself. Although Kazan remembers the 40's as a dark age when good material had to be "licked" before it could be brought to the screen, those were the years when Billy Wilder, John Huston, Robert Rossen and others first brought a measure of recognition to the screenwriter by equating the value of his contribution to that of the director, and then became writer-directors themselves. By the 50's such ideas had become much more widespread, and the bad old days, when studios assigned writers by the team to work on various projects, were definitely fading fast. Schulberg's scripts for *A Face in the Crowd* and *On the Waterfront*, and Paddy Chayefsky's for *Marty, Bachelor Party* and *The Goddess* represented a high-water mark in the literate 50's screenplay. Incorporating lessons learned on the New York stage—and even at times from New York television—these screenplays emphasized character over action, and strove above all for a surface of psychological realism. Kazan was well suited to transfer such material to the screen, his work with the Group Theatre and later The Actor's Studio (of which he was a founder) having been instrumental in shaping these new concepts of writing, acting and staging. If "the method" became household jargon in the 50's it was largely through the influence of Kazan in his films with Marlon Brando, James Dean and Montgomery Clift.

INTRODUCTION TO
A FACE IN THE CROWD
ELIA KAZAN

I arrived in Hollywood in 1944 to make my first motion picture, *A Tree Grows in Brooklyn*. I went from the train to the
hotel and then checked in with my producer, Louis Lighton.
He was a fine man, an oldtimer, a fine producer, too. His eye-
sight was failing and I found him bent close over his desk peer-
ing through a very large magnifying glass. He was working
on the script. He had before him Betty Smith's novel, as well
as several earlier versions of the screenplay. These were being
cannibalized—as they say at plane repair shops—in a search for
usable parts. Laboriously and with practiced craftsmanship, the
producer was putting the incidents together into sequences,
arranging these for climax and shaping the whole into what he
always called three "acts." Bud Lighton knew what he was
doing; he'd done it since the days of the silents.

The screenplay was credited to Tess Slesinger and Frank
Davis, but in all the nine months I was in Hollywood on this
project, I never met these two people. Years later in New York,
I heard of Miss Slesinger's death. I still hadn't met her. Another few years passed and one night at a party a strange man
came up and introduced himself. It was Frank Davis.

I was fresh from the theatre and this separation of the writers
from the director—and from their own work—came as a shock
to me. I was to learn that it was regular practice.

I remember my first day at lunch in the Twentieth Century-
Fox commissary. Behind the closed doors of the executive
dining room, I was told that Mr. Zanuck ate in state, flanked
by his producers. I didn't care about them. To me, the figures
of glamour were the famous directors—gods! There they were,
ranged along the best wall, looking out over the enormous

From "*A Face in the Crowd,*" *a Play for the Screen* (New York: Random House, 1957). Reprinted by permission of Budd Schulberg and
Elia Kazan.

Elia Kazan

dining room, each at his reserved table with his favorite waitress, also reserved. The center tables were taken by the stars.
They were surrounded by their favorites and sycophants:
makeup men, hairdressers, stand-ins, agents, girl- or boy-
friends. At other prominent tables sat the big men of the
back lot, the cameramen. Each had his heads of departments,
his gaffers and key grips and so on: an Homeric catalogue.

Only after several weeks did I notice and explore a sorry
group at a remote table. Their isolation was so evident that it
seemed planned. There was no mixing with this group, no
tablehopping to their table. They seemed out of place. Their

dress was tamer. Few had the fashionable suntan that a Beverly Hills success carries right to his grave. They laughed in an hysterical way, giddy or bitter. The writers . . .

Some of them were admitted hacks and some were unadmitted hacks. Some were top screen writers. There would be an occasional Pulitzer Prize playwright or a famous novelist who had come out to do one screen assignment. Every last one of them seemed embarrassed to be there, and the embarrassment expressed itself in a bitter wit. They specialized in long sagas about the idiocy of the motion-picture business. There was a never-ending competition of appalling anecdote. They razzed everything and anybody—including themselves. A wealth of talent spent itself in mockery.

My education continued on the set of *Tree*. Since I was a total stranger to film, Lighton assigned me one of Hollywood's best cameramen, Leon Shamroy. I was to stage the scenes "as if they were happening in life" and Leon would decide how to photograph them. He would get onto film various angles that could subsequently be cut together to make an effective cinematic narration. Leon was a new experience to me. As I say, I'd come from Broadway where the writer was god and his lines were sacred by contract. Now I'm sure that Leon read the script, or most of it, before he started on the picture, but I know he didn't look at the day's scenes before coming to work each morning. This wasn't negligence; it was policy. There was a superstition that to look at the literary foliage would blur one's sense of the essential action. When I came on the set in the morning, he was usually there, a victim of sleep (too much or too little) and ready for the ministrations of the set porter. In those halcyon days, each set had its porter. In a daily ritual, Leon was presented with coffee—a Danish—*The Hollywood Daily Variety*—*The Hollywood Reporter*. While he read, I would earnestly rehearse the actors. In time, Leon would lower his *Reporter* and ask, "Well, what's the garbage for today?" The garbage was the dialogue. If he had a criticism, it was always the same one, "What do you need all those words for?" On his benign days, he didn't say garbage. He said, "The nonsense."

The writers were in a humiliating position. The motion-picture makers insisted on referring to themselves as an industry. An industry aspires to efficiency. They were supplying fifty-odd pictures per major studio per year to the market. They tried to supervise the manufacture of scripts by methods that worked splendidly in the automobile and heavy-appliance industries. The system, with variations, went something like this:

An "original property" (a novel, a play, a "story idea") was bought outright. By this act, a studio acquired material and at the same time got rid of a potential troublemaker, the "original" author. (One of the tales that the writers told was about a studio head who bought a highly regarded bestseller. He strutted into his dining room and boasted, "I just bought a great story—but I think I can lick it!") The next step was an executive conference about the property and, usually, the casting of the stars. The "original property" was then turned over to a "construction man." His job was, precisely, to "lick the story." In other words, he was to bring the material into digestible shape and length, twist it to fit the stars and to eliminate unacceptable elements. These last included: elements banned by the Code; elements which might offend any section of the world audience; unentertaining elements such as unhappy endings or messages ("Leave them to Western Union!"). There was a word that governed what was cut out: the word "off-beat." This covered anything, really, that hadn't been done before, that hadn't been, as the marketing experts say, pre-tested. The "construction man," to put it simply, was supposed to lay down the outline of a hit. (For one reason, at this time, Middle-Europeans were highly regarded for this job. Their knowledge of our language and country was slight but they were hell on structure and continuity.) Since the "construction man" was a specialist, the time came when his usefulness ended. Then, through his agent, he was invited to step out. A "dia-logue man" was brought in. (The verb "to dialogue" was added to the Hollywood writers' glossary.) After the man who dialogued it, there frequently followed a "polish man." The script was getting close. (They hoped.) There was a good chance that an "additional dialogue man" would spend a few weeks on the job. His instructions might be very simple, as: "Put thirty laughs in it."

What was wrong with hiring a specialist in each field? It should have been efficient.

Trouble was, the final shooting script was so often preposterous. Characters went out of character. Plot threads got snarled. Climaxes made no sense because the preparation for them had got lost somewhere on the assembly line. If it was a "B" picture, they usually shot it anyway. But if it was a "big" picture, the producer, like Lighton, would find himself late at night compiling a *last* final shooting script out of bits and pieces of all the previous versions. More often, it was the director who did this. Or sometimes, a brand-new writer was called in. The Screen Writers Guild put in a lot of time ruling on which writers were entitled to what screen credit for a picture that none of them could altogether recognize.

II

It was all confusing, as I said, to a director fresh from the theatre. The theatre was Eugene O'Neill and Sidney Howard and Robert Sherwood and S. N. Behrman and Thornton Wilder and Clifford Odets and twenty others. The least newest greenest playwright shared the aura and the rights that the giants had earned. The rest of us—actors, directors and so on—knew that our function was to bring to life the plays they wrote.

But, I was told, pictures are different. . . . The difference comes from the power of the camera. Film is a pictorial medium. The strip of celluloid ought to tell the story with the sound track silent. There are crucial artistic choices that can't possibly be anticipated in a script. They have to be made hour by hour on the set and in the cutting room. A director stages plays; he *makes* pictures.

This was all true and I must confess that I took to it rather readily. Since I happened to be one, I was disinclined to quarrel with a line of reasoning which thrust power and pre-eminence upon the directors.

I was a good while longer learning certain other facts about picturemaking. They are equally important. I learned them as I tripped up on inadequate scripts—including some that I vigorously helped to shape. I can state them with painful brevity:

There can't be a fine picture without a fine script.

There can't be a fine script without a first-class writer.

A first-class writer won't do first-class work unless he feels that the picture is *his*.

I doubt if the writer's place in pictures will—or should—ever be exactly the same as in the theatre, but I've been thinking lately about just what happened in the theatre. It's relevant and salutary.

Take 1900-1920. The theatre flourished all over the country. It had no competition. The box-office boomed. The top original fare it had to offer was *The Girl of the Golden West*. Its bow to culture was fusty productions of Shakespeare. Either way, the plays were treated as showcases for stars. The business was in the hands of the managers and the actor-managers. The writers were nowhere. They were hacks who turned out new vehicles each season, to order. A playwright had about as little pride in his work, as little recognition for it, as little freedom, as a screen writer in Hollywood in the palmy days. And his output was, to put it charitably, not any better. . . . Came the moving pictures. At first, they were written off as a fad. Then they began to compete for audiences and they grew until they threatened to take over. The theatre had to be better or go under. It got better. It got so spectacularly better so fast that in 1920-30, you wouldn't have recognized it. Perhaps it was an accident that Eugene O'Neill appeared at that moment, but it was no accident that in that moment of strange competition, the theatre made room for him. Because it was disrupted and hard-pressed, it made room for his experiments, his unheard-of subjects, his passion, his power. There was room for him to grow to his full stature. And there was freedom for the talents that came after his. For the first time, American writers turned to the theatre with anticipation and seriousness, knowing it could use the best they could give.

III

Well, now it's 1957 and television is the "industry." It's a giant —and a growing giant. It's fated to be much bigger than pictures ever were. Even now, it's overwhelming. We've all seen that. During the elections, during the World Series, during political crises, homes from coast to coast are tied to a few networks on the same cable, on the same timetable. Whether it's good or bad or both, one thing is certain: it's here.

Television is the subject of this second picture that Budd Schulberg and I have made together. It's also the force that's shaken up the whole picture business. It's our turn now. We in pictures have got to be better or go under.

When TV appeared, the motion-picture people put up a struggle. They didn't give up easily. First, they pretended that it wasn't there. Then they tried to combat it with every conceivable technical novelty. They tried big screens in all sorts of ratios of width to height. They tried the third dimension, with and without goggles. They tried multiple sound sources and bigger budgets. As I write, the novelty is long long long pictures. They tried just about everything except the real novelty: three-dimensional material, new and better stories.

There are signs that they are being forced to that. It was hard to miss the meaning of the most recent Academy Awards. For 1953, *From Here to Eternity*; 1954, *On the Waterfront*; 1955, *Marty*. Of these, only the first came from a major studio. All three used ordinary old-fashioned screens. All three were shot in black and white. And different as they were, each of them was plainly, undeniably, "offbeat." People simply didn't care what size the screen was. They went to see those pictures because they had life in them.

The writers rejoiced in a recognition that went beyond their Awards, and notice, in each case the writer carried through from start to finish, working actively with the director. James Jones had written a hot novel out of his war experience. Daniel Taradash made the material his own, turned it into a fine screenplay and worked closely with Fred Zinneman, the director. Budd Schulberg did an original screenplay out of long research and conviction and feeling, consulting with me often as he wrote, and standing by during much of the shooting. Paddy Chayefsky expanded his own television sketch into a picture and was consulted by Delbert Mann as it was being shot.

To get back to the picturemakers, they're in trouble. The box-office barometer dipped down, recovered, dropped again. Picture houses are closing, going dark. There is a rumor that one of the big studio lots is to be sold for a real-estate development. In such moments of confusion and panic, executive imaginations make unaccustomed flights. It has begun to occur to them that the writer—that eccentric, ornery, odd, unreliable, unreconstructed, independent fellow—is the only one who can give them real novelty.

The first sign that the old order was changing came in an odd but characteristic way: there was a certain loosening of the industry's self-imposed censorship Code. There were departures from the frantic and crippling rule that *You must please everybody; you can't offend anybody*. An older law was operating at the box-office: if you try to please everybody, you don't please anybody.

At the same time, the unwritten taboos began to be relaxed. The superstition about "offbeat" material took a new turn. There seemed to be some mysterious plus in the "offbeat." Warily, story departments were instructed to look for subjects with this peculiar quality.

So now the writers—the fellows who used to sit in that clump in the farthest corner of the studio commissary—are being brought forward. A number of them have been moved "up" to non-writing jobs. They have been made producers and/or directors. Since it would seem obvious that writers are needed as writers, this may sound as inscrutably silly as other Hollywood behavior I've described—but it is at least a fumbling recognition that writers "have something" and that whatever it is, it's needed now. More reasonably, books and other stories that used to be thought unsuitable for pictures are being bought and tried. In a surprising number of cases, the "original author" is being asked to make his own screen version. Above all, writers are being invited, cajoled and very well paid to write original and serious pictures. This last is the big step and the big hope.

Another sign of change is the growing number of small independent units being financed by the big studios and operating with a freedom that was unimaginable ten years ago. The mood is, "Let them try . . ."

I'm one of the ones who's trying. I've formed my own company, Newtown Productions. I like being my own boss. I make my own pictures the way I want to make them. Also, I make my own mistakes. One of the things I've done, against all business advice, is to upset the traditional balance and make the writer more important than the stars. I don't think it's a mistake.

You see, I think we have a wonderful chance right now. The breakdown of the old standardized picturemaking has made room for creative people. It is a boon to anyone who has something personal and strong to say. For art is nothing if it is not personal. It can't be homogenized. By its nature, it must disturb, stir up, enlighten and "offend."

I'd like to make one last point about the writers because it's important. To go back to the Academy Awards winners, Dan Taradash and Budd Schulberg and Paddy Chayefsky, notice that they don't sneer at pictures. They don't think that screenwriting is beneath them or that it's somehow an inferior form. The first time I met Budd, he had published three important and successful novels but he said to me, "God, I'd like to write a really good picture some day." I heard Paddy use almost the same words back in 1951 when he was a young TV writer. They have both done it. I think Budd has done it again.

Turn a few pages and you'll be reading his screenplay for *A Face in the Crowd*. The very fact that it is published bespeaks a new dignity. The way the picture was made tells a lot, too. I said earlier, we made it together. That tells the story.

After *Waterfront*, Budd and I decided to make another film, to be based on his short story, *Your Arkansas Traveler*. The impulse came partly from the story itself but even more from a series of conversations we had about—well, about everything. About TV—its power—hypnotic, potentially most dangerous and still, at times, brilliantly effective for good. We talked of how much more powerful Huey Long would have been if he had had TV at his disposal. We talked about the famous Nixon broadcast, when the question of his financial backers turned somehow into a defense of his children's dog. We talked of the harm that Senator McCarthy did his own cause when he whispered direly to his young assistant in front of the cameras. We talked about the way public figures are now coached for their broadcasts and how the medium can make a performer or a politician overnight—or break a man that fast, too.

As we discussed the story, we began to watch programs much more than either of us had before. Every once in a while, something brilliant comes out of the box, like the reportage called *The First World War*, the Basilio-Saxton fight, Ed Murrow's interview with Colonel Nasser and his provocative visit to Clinton, Tenn., Yogi Berra leaping into Don Larsen's arms, Mary Martin and Ethel Merman. But TV, having won first place in the entertainment field, has the burdens of the victor. It has become the staple. It can't "offend." It's standard brand. And no matter how deeply you're drawn into what they're showing you, one of those fellows has got to come out and tell you with horrifying cheerfulness about soup or soap or cigarettes.

We took cognizance of the new synthetic folksiness that saturated certain programs and the excursions into political waters by these "I-don't-know-anything-but-I-know-what-I-think" guys. We wondered about the power of television to sell synthetic personalities as it sells the soup and the soap.

We went to Madison Avenue like explorers going into a strange country. We talked with performers and account executives and writers. We had interviews with bigshots and lunch with medium-sized shots and drinks with little shots. We are indebted to all of them—not least for permission to sit in on a conference about the photographing of a catsup bottle.

We listened and we read and we made notes and we compared notes and always we discussed what we had seen. Out of these conversations and the mutual desire to say something about this giant of our times came the shape of our picture.

Budd was the original source and, perhaps, the conscience. I was at his call and often at his side in the months he was writing it. He was at my side when my active work began. He was there during the casting and all the other preparation. We went to Piggott, Arkansas, together and decided that was the place to shoot the country scenes. He came there on location and, also, to Memphis. He has been on the set every day in New York and made essential contributions. I never worked more closely with an author in the theatre.

And as for the lunch hour, we ate together.

BILLY WILDER
(1906-   )

Billy Wilder began his career as a journalist, first in Vienna and later in Berlin during the final years of the Weimar Republic. He was scriptwriter on *Menschen am Sonntag* (1929), on which he worked with Zinnemann, Ulmer and the Siodmak brothers, and soon began a busy career as a writer of early German talkies—*Emil und die Detektive* being perhaps his best known work. He fled the country with the rise of Hitler and eventually wound up in Hollywood, but his lack of English made things extremely difficult for him, and at one point (according to one historian) he was sleeping in an unused ladies' room in the Chateau Marmont. Wilder finally gained a foothold in Hollywood when teamed as a writer with Charles Brackett, and the pair scripted some of the most famous Lubitsch (and pseudo-Lubitsch) films of the late 30's. In 1942 he moved over into direction in order to protect the integrity of his scripts, in the process becoming one of the decade's first writer-directors. The partnership with Brackett continued even after this, however, with Wilder directing and Brackett producing their screenplays of *The Lost Weekend* and *Sunset Boulevard*. Drawing no doubt on the residue of his experiences as a Weimar journalist, Wilder created some of the darkest and most cynical examples of the Hollywood *film noir*, from *Double Indemnity* to *Ace in the Hole*. But since then his career has been an unpredictable series of ups and downs, with both Wilder and his critics at a loss for explanations.

ONE HEAD IS BETTER THAN TWO
BILLY WILDER

Some people become directors because of their wives, others in spite of them. I became a director because of my scripts. I wanted to protect them. When I arrived in Hollywood in 1933 I could not speak a word of English; but with my experience as a journalist and screenwriter in Europe I was determined to make my stories speak for themselves.

I dragged my carcass up and down Hollywood Boulevard for over a year before I sold two original stories. Then I was lucky enough to be teamed with Charles Brackett, and together we turned out such screen-plays as *Bluebeard's Eighth Wife, Hold Back the Dawn* and *Ninotchka*.

Many times I am asked by some aspiring newcomer to this business: "How do I become a director?" I never have the answer. From cutting, maybe. By being an assistant director, certainly not. When I started to write my way into films it was like building a house: and I struck oil underneath it.

Writing is not an easy way into films. Few of us can face that tear-stained Olivetti every morning.

There is a traditional hostility between directors and writers. Without a director the writer will never see his story brought to life; and without a writer who can present a story in cinematic terms, a director has no basic material with which to work. It is easy to understand why many writers feel that their contribution to a film is under-estimated, why some may be resentful of the kudos given the director and his artists.

I have never written novels. I visualize situations and characters in terms of images and movement, not of dialogue alone. Distinguished novelists have frequently made the trek to the West Coast and returned some months later to their Greenwich Village attics, disillusioned if not disgruntled. No one has

From *Films and Filming*, February 1957. Reprinted by permission of Billy Wilder.

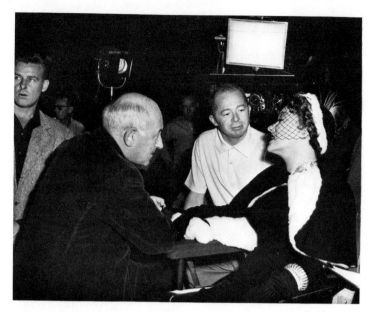

Billy Wilder directing Cecil B. De Mille and Gloria Swanson in a scene from *Sunset Boulevard* (1950).

doubted their writing ability. The fault is that too often the writer, not trained to the film medium, makes his script a thing to be read instead of a blueprint for the camera.

A good story, fascinating characters, well-turned dialogue . . . all can be thrown away if the writer does not primarily think in terms of pictures.

It is not easy for a writer to follow a director's conception of a story. Few good writers want to shape a story into which some other person will breathe life. The remarkable thing, human nature being what it is, is that so many fine films have resulted from this struggle (or collaboration, call it what you will) between writer and director.

As I have already said, I became a director to protect my script. I am not alone in taking this defensive action. Most of the creative film-making in Hollywood (and other world studios) today, is the result of the writer-director autonomy.

I do not champion any causes in my film-making. Films are

an entertainment; and I believe in keeping them that way; but entertainment does not have to lack intelligence. Sometimes I feel gay. Other times I want to make drama; or, so even my best friends tell me, I am cynical and turn out a script like *Sunset Boulevard*. Cynic, maybe, but to me, that film *is* Hollywood —the writer, the agent, the fading star were all portraits from life.

Having decided on a subject, I visualise it in terms of specific artists. However talented the star may be, none is without limitations. The final result on the screen is almost certain to be better if you bend your script to the personality rather than trying to force a performance from an artist against type and beyond his or her limitations.

One result of such a writing approach is that last minute changes become inevitable. I rewrote *Sabrina Fair* in a matter of days when Cary Grant decided not to play the part. I had to change *Sunset Boulevard* when I knew William Holden would be playing the part I originally conceived for Monty Clift.

Many people in Hollywood have the impression that I improvise on the set, working from only a rough scenario. Actually, what is not on paper by morning will never be on film in the evening. Can you imagine me down on the stages trying to think of dialogue on the spur of the moment while the stars and a highly paid crew stand and wait? Just as a skilful acrobat must conceal his anxiety and heavy breathing while performing a difficult feat, a director of light comedy must conceal from the audience that task of making things look easy.

When I began my latest comedy—*Love in the Afternoon*, with Gary Cooper and Audrey Hepburn—the script was not finished. My scripts never are finished; but that is quite different to shooting off the cuff. Up to the last minute, up to the morning of the tear-soaked Olivetti, my collaborator and I are improving the script to our own satisfaction.

As far as possible I plan every detail of the work that must be done on the stages. For example, the routine of bottle-hiding in *The Lost Weekend*. Putting a bottle in a lampshade was not just an idea thought out on set; Brackett and I planned it as an important part of the action during the script stage. Similarly, the *Stalag 17* script specified in detail how the messages should be hidden in the chess pieces.

Of course no writer is perfect; and no director is perfect. The advantage of being your own writer as well as director is that on-the-spot changes become much easier. Sometimes a line of dialogue does not come out right, an action you planned on paper looks untidy in frame, or some other unforeseen emergency necessitates a change. The writer-director can make the alterations with the minimum of delay.

The enigma of film-making is that it is at once a dictatorship and a democracy—the dictatorship of the creator who makes the absolute his conception of how the script should be transferred to the screen; and the democracy of scores of highly skilled technicians who must work as a team, pooling their knowledge and experience, to make that transition from script.

I do not think a director needs to be a highly skilled technician, in the sense that he should be able to work cameras, light a set or make imitation smoke. He can rely on the technical experts in his unit to give him advice. A director does need a hidden sense, a sense that instinctively tells him what cuts with what. A good film is more likely to be a film that has been shot in a manner that makes the final cutting a comparatively simple process, than a film shot so loosely that the cutter has to go on a strict diet of water and aspirin for a month.

I like to tell my stories with the minimum of camera interruption—camera movement, close-ups, quick cuts, must be used like punctuations in a novel. They must emphasise and not distract, surprise but not weary by overemphasis. My scenes tend to be broken down into longer takes than would be used by many directors. My scripts contain no detailed reference to camera angles and movements, which become obvious as the scene is rehearsed on set.

Film-making is an exacting task. Our critics sometimes seem to think a director deliberately sets out to make a bad film. If I stop to think of the things that can go wrong I am sometimes surprised that my films are as good as they are. My best—and by that I mean the film with fewer mistakes in scripting and shooting—was *Double Indemnity;* but then I refuse to look back at old pictures. Reviving an old picture is like taking up an old love of twenty years ago—woman or film: it can never be the same again.

MERVYN LEROY
(1900-   )

Television was all but ignored by Hollywood for as long as realistically possible, but as theatre audiences continued to disappear a variety of accommodations were investigated. The arguments Mervyn LeRoy gives here for supporting Pay-TV are remarkably similar to those advanced twenty years later in favor of Home Box Office and other current cable attractions, but his hymn of praise should be taken with a large grain of salt. LeRoy's attempt to shrug off television's effect on Hollywood by claiming that "movies are still being made, and with more enthusiasm than ever," would have been hard to demonstrate. True, films were still being *made* in Hollywood, but with weekly attendance dropping from 90 million to 39.6 million between 1948 and 1958 the enthusiasm must have been growing a bit thin. If Hollywood could shift its idle production facilities over to television work, however, that lost audience could be recaptured and much industry unemployment alleviated, all through the use of the very medium responsible for the trouble in the first place. LeRoy, a successful producer as well as director, was well aware of the production and distribution problems involved, and his long career with Warner Brothers and MGM was dotted with canny accommodations to the shifting tastes of an unpredictable audience. Twenty years later, the debate on cable television still rages, and the positions of the exhibitors, the broadcasting networks and the FCC remain remarkably similar. Only the role of the studios has changed significantly, a function of the mergers that have turned most into subsidiaries of widely diversified conglomerates.

MOTION PICTURES AND PAY TV
MERVYN LEROY

Hollywood, which thrives on crises and romance, nervously finds itself on the threshold of a royal marriage. Having played an elusive philanderer for almost a decade, the motion picture industry, for whom television has been a beguiling and convenient mistress, is about to make an honest woman of its faithful paramour through a proposal of marriage with pay TV; if it should come to pass, despite opposition which has reached clear to the floor of Congress, this royal wedding could have far-reaching repercussions. It may well trigger another bloodless revolution in the field of mass entertainment comparable to that set off thirty years ago by the bold-visioned Warner brothers when they startled a bemused nation with the first talking picture, *The Jazz Singer*.

There are two powerful groups not radiating joy over the impending liaison. The exhibitors who own the nation's 20,000 movie houses and those who control the destinies of the giant television networks have a common cause in opposing the marriage of motion pictures and pay TV. Although normally competitors, their billion-dollar investment has brought them together in a mutuality of interest as their newest rival bids for public affection. With stakes so high, the entire subject is fogged in mists of intense partisanship. Charges and countercharges, debates in public forums, and millions of words poured out in the press have made it increasingly difficult for the American people to distinguish fact from propaganda.

In this area the television networks undoubtedly have had a willing ally in Madison Avenue's top-drawer advertising agencies, for whom the preservation of the status quo in television is an economic must, in view of the handsome commissions they

Mervyn LeRoy with Jack Lemmon on the set of LeRoy's *Mister Roberts* (1955).

pocket on the millions of dollars their clients spend for TV sponsorship. It would not be surprising if Madison Avenue's professional hand were behind a highly vocal organization with the name "Committee Against Pay To See TV." This committee has been sounding the theme that not only is freedom of the air waves an established American tradition, but that pay TV—by its very name—is a threat to every red-blooded American's right to life, liberty, and the pursuit of happiness. In the same dire vein, Marcus Cohn, counsel for the committee, has stated: "If the American public is ever told it will have to pay for its TV programs the Boston Tea Party will fade into an insignificant skirmish."

So well has the propaganda war been waged that Chairman Emanuel Celler of the House Judiciary Committee warned the Federal Communications Commission—which regulates television broadcasting—to keep its hands off pay TV and let Congress decide. He also introduced a bill imposing a five-year prison term or a fine of $10,000 or both on anyone attempting to impose a fee on home TV viewers. When the FCC authorized a wide test of pay TV, Representative Celler stated he would press for early action in the next session of Congress.

As is usually the case when the kettle is called black, pay TV is not the ogre its opposition has made it out to be. If this statement implies an ulterior motive on my part, it is motivated by a point of view that thus far has not been heard. In the tumult and shouting of recent months, very little, much less an opinion, has been heard from the one group which really has the most to say: the directors, producers, stars, writers, cameramen, art designers, costumers, and many other creators whose collaborative efforts in Hollywood make possible most of America's entertainment.

I have been identified with the production and direction of motion pictures since 1928. I have spent the better part of a lifetime making responsible and costly movies for a mass audience. I have loved the audience challenge. A successful movie at the box office is seen and enjoyed by millions. I have had more than a fair share of success at the box office, and intend to keep making pictures, because there will always be a demand for good pictures. I do not necessarily regard pay TV as a cure-all. But I am for its marriage with motion pictures. It is a healthy alliance because it opens up exciting new horizons in audience penetration.

Let me make plain that I understand the threat that pay TV poses for many movie exhibitors. I wholeheartedly sympathize with them. Their apprehension is understandable because of their enormous investment in land, theaters, and equipment. But progress, change, evolution—whatever you care to call it— invariably takes its economic toll. The crude nickelodeon of the 1910 era was replaced by comfortable, attractive movie houses. In turn came huge cathedrals of screen entertainment like Radio City Music Hall. A few years ago came a further refinement in movie-going, the drive-in. It has mushroomed in popularity for a familiar reason, convenience.

The emergence of a new competitor like pay TV will not

destroy America's zest for movie-going. Quite to the contrary, it will stimulate a desire to see movies. As a people Americans are gregarious. The bright lights of Broadway, Chicago's State Street, San Francisco's Market Street will always be a magnet for audiences to crowd first-run theaters.

Pay TV is not a rule-or-ruin situation. It was said that movies would ruin the legitimate stage. They haven't. Pessimists said radio would hurt motion pictures. It didn't. When television arrived, the prediction was freely expressed that Hollywood was about to be engulfed in a catastrophe. Movies are still being made and with more enthusiasm than ever.

There are plenty of resourceful exhibitors who will come to grips with the competition of pay TV and capitalize on it. One exhibitor has already shown the way. Early in September, a chain operating one hundred seventy-five theaters in the Southwest began a practical pay-as-you-see operation in Bartlesville, Oklahoma. For a subscription fee of $9.50 per month, residents of Bartlesville are being offered a daily fare of first-run movies. The Bartlesville project is the beginning move for other exhibitors to apply for pay TV franchises throughout the country, using such systems as Telemeter, which I regard as the best developed.

Pay TV will eventually be the bridge that will transport new and old audiences to attend fully-equipped movie theaters, because of the dramatic difference in screens. The wide screens which today enable theaters to project such processes as CinemaScope, Warnervision, Vista-Vision, and Todd-AO offer a depth and dimension that home screens cannot match. As the mass distribution of paperback editions has augmented reader volume for the book business, pay TV will create a fresh audience for motion picture theaters.

Unlike the exhibitor's situation, the opposition of the television networks to pay TV is frankly indefensible. The intensity of their apprehension is a clear reflection of the excesses they have committed against the American public in the name of good entertainment and standards of quality. There are things television does superbly well. In the broadcasting of fast-breaking news events, political conventions, sports, debates, travelogues, educational projects, it has been exciting and topical. In such undertakings as *Omnibus* or *Wide Wide World*, television also has functioned with great effectiveness.

But the reverse side of the coin is anything but shiny. Such entertainment hodgepodge as giveaway panels, unspectacular spectaculars, warmed-over dramatic hours, and a plethora of situation comedy shows has alienated and wearied many television viewers. The responsibility for this is split three ways between the networks, Madison Avenue's advertising agencies who call the turn, and the big-time commercial sponsors who foot the bills.

In the last analysis Madison Avenue mirrors the prejudices, ideas, and tastes of hardheaded sponsors who know next to nothing about show business but are willing to pay for it as an acceptable interlude between commercials. Since there is no box office in television, Madison Avenue has devised systems for measuring popularity on TV such as the Nielsen, Trendex, and other ratings. Each week these ratings purport to reassure the uncertain sponsor by reporting the number of Americans glued to his show. The net effect has been to drive a score of talented performers from the network channels.

If anything justifies the marriage of pay TV with the motion picture industry it is television's indiscriminate, wholesale appropriation of old movies. With no particular regard for standards, the television networks and their station affiliates have bought up for reshowing on home television screens hundreds of films made prior to 1948. Many of the films range back to the early thirties. In the outpouring of movies to the TV public, fine films and trash have been lumped together. I know something about old movies on television. Some twenty of my pictures, including such well-remembered favorites as *The Wizard of Oz*, *Fugitive from a Chain Gang*, *Thirty Seconds over Tokyo*, *Little Caesar*, *Waterloo Bridge*, and *Random Harvest*, to name a few, have appeared on television screens. I have been pleasantly surprised to receive many letters from TV viewers who have enjoyed seeing my pictures despite the barrage of interrupting commercials.

These letters are important as a barometer of the audience

that is building for the appearance of quality, first-run motion pictures via a convenient and nominally-priced subscription TV system. And I am firmly convinced that these good films will drive out the bad.

No matter where the chips fall for the exhibitors or the television networks, pay TV's marriage with motion pictures cannot be halted, because of the inexorable changing social scene in America since the end of World War II.

America is changing its entertainment patterns as radically as it is changing its way of living. America is on the move from the cities to suburbia. Decentralization has led to such social phenomena as all-inclusive shopping centers and do-it-yourself projects. The home again is a focal point of interest. Americans are marrying younger—because of better economic conditions—and raising families. Classes of society are upgrading themselves. What was once an upper-lower class has become part of a big middle class. Because it has a zest for living, this middle class has become a tremendously important consumer market.

From the creative standpoint, a marriage of pay TV and motion pictures promises to open up exciting new horizons in mass audience exposure. Unlike some freewheeling thinking in Hollywood that anything will make money on pay TV, this mass audience will create exacting standards that should prove rewarding to those who artistically meet the acid test.

Pay TV will represent a wonderful coming of age for the talented writer, director, and producer. Great screen properties, like great plays or novels, are never plentiful. The acute demand that exists today in Hollywood for good story material will be accelerated by pay TV. It will also encourage bolder writing, which in turn holds promise for a widening maturity of themes on the screen.

The amalgamation will be healthy on many creative fronts, particularly in opening doors to new talent in the fields of producing and directing. Let me warn, however, that pay TV represents no short cut to success. A meticulous and intense apprenticeship is still a prerequisite for authority and skill as a producer or director. Pay TV, with its critical audience, will be no less exacting than the audiences in the movie theaters.

Finally, pay TV will not only provide a golden showcase for the talented star and the exciting personality, but will, of necessity, spur a fresh and unending search for new talent. Star dust is never easy to come by. The discovery of new stars will take on a new zest and purpose.

When the cultural history of twentieth-century America is written, its outstanding characteristic may well be the acceleration that has taken place in the field of mass communications. Consider the developments in a single lifetime: the telephone, high speed presses, the teletype, motion pictures, radio, the phonograph, television. Pay TV is clearly part of this exciting evolution.

Some skeptics in the motion picture industry persist in saying that it is impossible to tailor full-length movies made for the theater's wide screen to the home television screen. What about a *Ten Commandments*, a *Giant*, they ask? My answer is that the yardstick of quality is not the size of the screen but what you put on it. Nothing suffers on the screen if it's good. A bad picture is bad whether it plays Radio City Music Hall or your living room. A good picture will prove its quality on a small screen in your home or on a wide screen in your favorite theater. It's as simple as that.

ROBERT SIODMAK
(1900-1973)

Although born in Memphis, Tennessee, Robert Siodmak was educated in Germany and gained his first theatre and film experience there in the late 20's. One of the group responsible for *Menschen am Sonntag*, he soon became the director of such important international productions as *La Crise Est Finie*, with Danielle Darrieux, and Stefan Zweig's *Burning Secret*. The war brought him to America, where he directed for Universal such Germanic thrillers as *Christmas Holiday* and *The Phantom Lady*. If the early *film noir* style in America may be traced to the influence of Hollywood's large colony of wartime refugees, then Siodmak's contribution is certainly one of the most important. His post-war output, particularly *The Killers* and *Criss Cross*, continued in the same darkly convoluted fashion, but in the early 50's he left Hollywood and returned to Europe, presumably because of the studio interference he refers to here. His recent films, like *Custer of the West*, were unworthy successors to the stylish thrillers of his Hollywood period. Although Siodmak complains here about the vogue of location shooting for gangster films, and the implied "realism" which it contributes, his *Criss Cross* was a particularly influential early entry in this cycle. Yet even there, Siodmak managed a highly dramatic stylization of his locations, exploiting the poetry of real exteriors as Dassin and Siegel exploited their documentary qualities. Like Lang, Ulmer and the rest of Hollywood's German colony, Siodmak realized that newsreel-style realism was "cinema's gift to television," and a distracting intrusion for those capable of creating their own world on a darkened sound stage.

HOODLUMS: THE MYTH
ROBERT SIODMAK

I like making gangster pictures. Not that I had much choice when I went to Hollywood 18 years ago because at that time the crime picture was very much in vogue. I was under contract to Universal-International, and as is usual in the film city, if you are successful at making a certain type of picture then you are given more of them to make. You have to be one of the boys!

Why do I like making gangster pictures? That is easy to answer. Because these pictures contain big emotions: love, hate, jealousy and more often than not, cold-blooded murder. In fact they contain the basic elements of life and as any good picture should, they reflect life in all its various shades.

Life's basic emotions fascinate me and the good gangster script lends itself to deep exploration of character and motivation. Although the best crime film cannot avoid elements of violence, I try to avoid showing violence. Often it is far more effective to suggest this aspect of the screenplay by implication.

The gangster film is always the target for critics. It is often blamed as a cause for the increase in juvenile crime. To me, this criticism is quite ridiculous (as are those people who really believe that rock-'n-roll is a bad thing for the younger generation). Many young people the world over are gangster film enthusiasts and yet they do not turn to murder for a livelihood.

It might interest critics and other interested parties to know that psychiatrists and psychologists regard children as basically bad human beings! Looking back to your own childhood you may remember tearing the legs off spiders or cutting the wings off house-flies and killing little animals. It would seem that at that age you were a mass-murderer. Are you now?

From *Films and Filming*, June 1959.

Robert Siodmak with Dorothy McGuire on the set of one of his most successful *film noir* thrillers, *The Spiral Staircase* (1946).

In my opinion newspapers are just as guilty (if not more so) as gangster films. Crimes are played up very sensationally and detail all the lurid facts. And newspapers can be read and read over again.

What is the ideal hero for a gangster film? Naturally a man who is on the side of the law. Unfortunately gangster films would be very dull if this were always the case. One usually settles for a hero who has failed in life and has therefore committed a crime. How to make the audience bother about such a man? Very simple. If you give him a good enough motive for the crime the audience will want him to win through.

For instance in one of my favourite films, *The Suspect*, I directed Charles Laughton as a murderer. He had killed his wife. But she was such a bad woman everybody in the audience, I am sure, had great sympathy for him.

Should we go back to the gangster film style of the 'thirties —*Scarface* and his friends? No certainly not! Seeing those films today one would be horrified at the lack of character of the principal parts. They were either black or white and as such would be laughable to today's sophisticated audiences.

The cinema, if not in technique, has progressed in character motivation. Today people want to know much more about their cinema heroes and villains. They are no longer satisfied at the sight of Capone mowing down his rivals. They want to know what motivated these senseless killers. The question "Why?" is always at the back of the cinemagoer's mind and it is up to the writer and director to supply a logical answer.

I have always favoured the fictional gangster to the factual. I feel that the documentary approach to the gangster film is strictly B picture treatment. The days when a crime film opened with bold, black headlines and screaming police cars coming down Main Street are finished. They are cinema's gift to television!

The "headline" picture as these were called presented types and not characters. I am interested in character above all else. The first gangster film that I made in Hollywood was called *The Killers*. Here the criminals were not just a mob, each man was an individual, a separate entity. Of course, scripts of the calibre of *The Killers* do not come along every day. This one happened to be written by my friend John Huston from the Ernest Hemingway story. Incidentally, the Hemingway original has only 18 pages which were used only for the opening. The rest was invented. The amazing thing about *The Killers* is that it is the only film of a Hemingway story that Hemingway actually likes! (We gave him a print of the film and I know that he has run it over 200 times.)

It is becoming increasingly difficult to find good screenplays for gangster films (and for that matter other types of subjects as well). Your audience has seen everything before, so nowadays the scriptwriter has to be much more inventive. You can no longer make the conventional "whodunit" without audiences guessing who did it half-way through. They have seen so many variations on this particular theme that their natural inclination is to plump for the man who is least likely to have done the murder. Not surprisingly they are usually correct!

Of course there is always the gimmick picture. I recently made a half-hour "pilot" film for a proposed television series employing this technique. I had three men committing a crime. I laid on suspense to such a degree that nobody could quite understand what was going on. In the end it turned out that the three men were detectives re-enacting a crime in the hope of solving it. I have so far found no backers for the series. The people I tried to sell it to said that it was too intelligent for TV (Thank God!).

In cinema I find the best way of approaching the crime film is to let your audience in on the secret. Not to ask them who did it, but rather to let them follow the story line from one character's point of view. For instance, you can have a man murdered in a Turkish Bath by a knife made of ice. A few years ago the director would have asked "how was it done." Today the much more important question is "why was it done?"

As far as the technical side of film-making goes, I always insist on editing my own pictures . . . although on some of my Hollywood pictures the studio interfered with the final scenes of a film and would re-shoot the ending in which case I no longer cared how the film turned out. The importance of crisp editing is often overlooked in these days of vast technical resources and million-dollar budgets. To me the final shape of a picture can only be got in the editing room under the direct supervision of the director.

I am often asked why don't I shoot in the streets? For two reasons. First, because I prefer the studio. One has much more control over action and artists. Secondly, because the streets are for young people. I am old enough no longer to care when the sun rises or sets, it only means I have to get up a couple of hours earlier!

Of all the films I have made which one do I like the best? A question that is impossible to answer. If I said one of my earlier works (which at the time I made it satisfied me particularly) a cinemagoer seeing it now would think me mad because it would no doubt appear terribly dated.

The best story I have told is, I think, *The Suspect*. It has happy memories for me, not least among them my friendship with Charles Laughton, an actor I admire tremendously.

What is the best training for a young man aspiring to direct? Film editing without a doubt. Here he can learn the basic technique of film. It is like tailoring your own suit.

What don't I like about modern cinema? That is easy to answer. The basic clumsiness of technique. After 40 years it hasn't changed a bit. There are still 60 people standing around one actor with 40 lights trained on the star. It all seems too stagy and not what one expects from *motion* pictures.

Do I like all my pictures? No, there is only five minutes in each of them that I really like. Lastly, what do I promise the audience that comes to see my films? Well, I never promise them a good picture . . . only a better one than they expected.

ANDREW MARTON
(1904-   )

Second-unit direction is one of the most important of Hollywood craft skills, and one of the most misunderstood by those outside the industry. The staging of the *Ben-Hur* chariot race described here by Andrew Marton was a four-million-dollar expenditure for which Marton barely received screen credit. Even today most reference books omit any mention of his contributions and credit the entire sequence to Yakima Canutt, the better-known stunt director. While there is a tone of self-aggrandizement here, Marton is certainly justified in drawing attention to his work, and his claims are backed up in the authorized biography of William Wyler, which quotes at length from this article. Marton was born in Budapest and came to Hollywood in 1923 with Ernst Lubitsch. A few years later he returned to Europe as an editor and director of such films as *The Demon of the Himalayas* (an expedition picture filmed in Tibet) and throughout the 30's he directed in Germany, Hungary and England. In 1940 he began a long career directing minor Hollywood films, of which *Men of the Fighting Lady*, *Green Fire* and *Crack in the World* remain the most interesting. The career of a director like Marton is hard to analyze. His own films are generally minor projects which would hardly rate him a mention in any history of important directors—indeed, only the most complete reference books even refer to him. By the strictest criteria Marton is hardly a notable *auteur*, but as a director of sequences for films like *The Red Badge of Courage*, *Fifty-Five Days at Peking* and *The Longest Day* he is certainly a *metteur-en-scène* to reckon with.

BEN-HUR'S CHARIOT RACE
ANDREW MARTON

The late Sam Zimbalist was a close and respected friend and when he asked me to stage and direct the chariot race sequence for *Ben-Hur* I had mixed feelings. It was a challenge but it also meant anonymity, in accordance with the motion picture industry's archaic rules for screen credits.

I had been disappointed before. I directed the mountain battle scenes in David O. Selznick's *A Farewell to Arms* and was "lavishly" rewarded with a screen credit which read in effect: "Many thanks to Andrew Marton for his valuable contribution." What contribution? Audiences never knew.

However, the challenge of *Ben-Hur's* chariot race was there. Zimbalist was there. And William Wyler, whom I respect greatly, was there. I had directed a sequence for Wyler before —the so-called "Dunkirk" sequence in *Mrs. Miniver*.

So I said: "Let's go."

Zimbalist gave me carte blanche, except for one warning. It was not to be just a race, but a race to the death that carried the implacable hatred of Ben-Hur (Charlton Heston) and Messala (Stephen Boyd) to its logical conclusion. The problem was not who wins the race, but who stays alive. In other words, Zimbalist wanted the most exciting and dangerous race ever— BUT. His one warning: if anything happened to Heston or Boyd there would be no picture.

MGM started building the arena for the race in January '58 at the Cinecitta Studios in Rome. Since the arena in the story is in Jerusalem, its architecture was not Roman, but more barbaric and primitive. Only this one arena was needed, since the film does not show how Ben-Hur, during his stay in Rome, got to be an expert charioteer. We do see him near Jerusalem crit-

From *Films in Review,* January 1960. Reprinted with the permission of Films in Review, National Board of Review of Motion Pictures, Inc., 210 E. 68th St., N.Y., N.Y. 10021.

icizing the training of some Arabian horses intended for the race. But the first time we see him in a chariot is when he enters the arena for the race.

While this huge set was being built we hunted for suitable horses—and matching teams, which were essential. The race was to be run by nine chariots drawn by four horses each, but since certain teams had to be duplicated, and there had to be "understudy" teams for the "star" teams, we required 82 horses of the proper physique, and harmonious colors. Horses can go lame, and anything can happen in a race.

The horses were finally obtained in Yugoslavia and in late January we began active preparations for the filming of the race. Actual shooting was to be in May and June.

In order not to interfere with the building of the arena, an identical track was built adjoining it so we could start training the horses and chariot riders, and lay out camera shots.

The *surfacing* of the race track proved to be a troublesome problem. Research in Roman libraries turned up nothing on the composition of the surfacing of the race tracks of two millennia ago. The surface of our track had to be hard enough to hold the careening chariots and horses, had to have a drainage system in case of rain, and had to have a sanded top, because cement would lame the horses.

So we started with a ground rock debris, which had to be steam-rolled. That was covered with 10 inches of ground lava—against my and Yakima Canutt's judgment—and *that* was covered with 8 inches of crushed yellow rock.

This lasted only one day when actual shooting began. It was used only in the first long shots, in which there were 6000 extras. The horses were slowed so much we almost wasted the entire day's work—a day on which 6000 extras were paid to watch the race. We removed the crushed yellow rock and left only a 1½″ layer of lava. This worked fine—and even enabled the chariots to skid around the corners.

While the set was being built and the surfacing was being worked out, the Yugoslavian horses underwent a spectacular change. They began to fill out, their ears perked up, their nostrils began to flare, and stubborn individual farm-horses began to be cooperating teams of four. The credit for this belongs to trainer Glenn Randall, who even had to teach the horses to react to commands and reining different from the ones they had been used to all their lives. I still don't know how Randall turned them into race-horses. Consider only the stabling of all those horses—the grooming, feeding, shoeing, and keeping them healthy.

The drivers were mostly the elite of stunt and rodeo riders from the US, but there were also some Italians. The charioteers began training as early as February, as did Heston and Boyd. The former had the easier time, for he was experienced in Westerns and has strong hands and tremendous shoulder muscles. Boyd's hands became blistered and bloody. We tried to loop the reins around his wrists, but that didn't help, for his wrists also chafed. We tried quite a few chemicals and ointments to toughen up his hands. At times he had to stop practising for a day or so to allow his hands to rest.

I had three 65 mm cameras at my disposal, at all times, during the shooting of the race. Except for one stand-by back in Culver City, there were only two other 65mm cameras in Rome—in fact in the world. The other two in Rome, of course, were used by William Wyler.

The limitations these new cameras impose quickly became apparent. The best lens to use with 35mm film for a close-up of a charioteer that retains the horses in the picture, is a 4-inch lens (also called a 100mm lens). The equivalent of a 100mm lens in the 65mm medium is a 200mm lens. But the 200 could not be focussed closer than 50 feet, and I had to get closer than 50 feet in order to get a good dramatic close-up. So I used a 140mm lens instead and moved closer to the horses, the hooves, and the danger. For certain scenes we achieved the effect of the horses stepping on the camera car!

Heston and Boyd did all the chariot driving they seem to be doing except for two stunts. We tried but one scene with a dummy being dragged by a chariot. It didn't work. Boyd looked at the ripped and torn dummy, and asked: "Me?" I nodded. He shrugged and did it. We protected him with some steel coverings here and there on his body, but he still was bruised and abrased. However, we got a real and untricked close-up of Boyd being dragged under his own chariot.

Despite the best of precautions, accidents did occur.

The best position to photograph a curve is at the far end as the chariots swing out of the curve. Once two chariots smashed into two of our cameras when they came out of the turn too fast. Fortunately, no horses were lost, or even lamed, and the crew and cameras were only bruised, thanks to a heavy wooden barricade we had had the foresight to erect. But the production schedule really suffered. The cameras had to be repaired and tested before we could use them again, which took several days.

One simple shot turned into a nightmare. It was a fast moving shot, but since it was on a straight run and did not swing around the corners I did not expect any complications. It went this way: the camera car was followed by Heston and Boyd, at full speed, and their chariots were followed by the seven other chariots. We were in the middle of the fastest run when suddenly the motor of the camera car backfired, stuttered and died, and there we were in front of the onrushing Heston-Boyd horses, chariots, etc. I could not help recalling Zimbalist's warning when I had insisted that for realism we had to have Heston and Boyd in these shots: "If you curl one hair on their heads!"

The fine Yugoslavian horses saved the day. They swerved and missed us—all nine chariots. If any of those horses had had split opinions, two going one way and two the other—but they didn't.

One of the stunts in which we used a double for Heston was as follows: We had established for the audience the fact that when a crash occurs during the chariot race workers rush out and clear the track. But when Boyd causes two chariots to go down in a spectacular double crash the workers were unable to clear the wrecked chariots off the track before Heston and Boyd complete another lap and head down the straightaway toward the wreckage. Realizing his advantage, Boyd forces Heston directly into the path of the crashed chariots. There seems to be no escape—Heston either has to pull up and lose the race, or try to take his horses and chariot over the seemingly insurmountable obstacle.

The stunt was easy to put on paper, but not at all easy to put on film.

Yet it was done. Yakima Canutt, who was wonderful in his rigging of the falls in *Ben-Hur*, allowed his son, Joe, to double for Heston in this stunt. Joe is 22 and an excellent stuntman, but perhaps a little too eager. Anyway, he started out toward the wreck at great speed and Yak and I, in one voice, screamed: "Too fast, too fast!"

Joe, of course, could not hear us, *and was committed*. The four horses sailed over the wreck beautifully, but when the chariot came down it hit hard and bounced. Chariot and charioteer sailed into the air. When the chariot landed again Joe was flipped into a head-stand and thrown out between the horses. He instinctively grabbed the cross-bar between the horses, but nevertheless he was dragged some feet.

We rushed him to our emergency hospital just outside the track and a few minutes later I heard a tremendous roar from the crowd. I looked around and saw young Canutt, with only a cut on his chin (four stitches), returning to work.

His is the most spectacular stunt I have ever seen. It will do for him what the *Stagecoach* stunt—jumping between the horses—did for his father.

Naturally, the script was re-written to allow Heston to repeat the falling out of the chariot in a close shot and then to swing himself back up and go on to win the race.

In our search for new angles we tried to get the camera under a chariot, but flying dirt thrown up by the horses' hooves kept covering the lenses. We mounted the camera behind Heston and tried to shoot over his shoulder. I found the flying dirt so heavy I had to hold a small piece of plywood over the lens until the chariots reached their fastest speed. Then I uncovered the lens and for ten seconds, until the lens was blotted out again, I was able to get a shot.

There are seven laps in the race and my detailed script for the race had six pages for each lap. Each stunt, each over-taking by Heston or Boyd, each crash, was carefully planned. Each had to take place within 23 seconds after the run started, since it took that number of seconds to run the length of the track. If a particular scene had to happen on a curve, the time allotted was even shorter.

After the first few days we found that, because of the arena's size, the most effective shots were the ones for which the camera moved *with* the race and *in* the race. I decided, therefore, that once the flag was down and the race began, we should participate in the race with our lens. This, of course, necessitated a rethinking of the race, as well as a rescheduling.

We did not have an actual shooting schedule. Zimbalist's orders were to make the race as good as was humanly possible. I made it as good as I humanly could in ten weeks shooting time, and also made it humanely—without the loss of a single horse or man.

Our concept of how the race should be shot somewhat resembled a musical score in that there were constant crescendos and de-crescendos.

The going around the end-curves required the camera operators—both of them Italians—to compensate for the centrifugal force encountered in the curves. The best shots on the curves were achieved not by the camera car but a specially built rubber-tired and independently sprung camera-chariot!

The heat of Rome was a serious handicap, for the horses could take only seven or eight runs a day. Each run had to be planned in detail if we were to finish the race at all with an average of only seven takes a day! Because of this, almost all scenes were done in one take. The only shot I did over was the one in which Heston's chariot runs over a centurion. At the critical moment one of the chariots got in between the lens and the falling warrior, blotting out the action.

The most difficult shot?

Toward the end of the race—when the wheels of Heston's and Boyd's chariots are interlocked, and Boyd starts to whip Heston.

In order to show the immediate danger in which they were, I decided to pan from the interlocking and splintering wheels to the two antagonists in vicious combat. To get this effect we had to chain the camera car to the two chariots. I didn't have time to realize that if one horse stumbled, the whole contraption—horses, chariots, stars, camera-car—would crash and pile up in disaster.

A pessimist, or merely a worrier, could never have directed this chariot race. And nobody could have done it without the help of MGM's prop-shop and special effects department.

I have been asked how the staging and directing of the *Ben-Hur* chariot race differ from those of the exodus from Dunkirk in *Mrs. Miniver* and the mountain battle scenes in *A Farewell to Arms*. It is in the *number* of separate shots. To my knowledge, never before in one motion picture were there so many *short* cuts in a sequence of 11 minutes duration. Some of the cuts are only a foot or a foot-and-a-half of film!

I was deeply gratified when William Wyler told me he thought the chariot race was one of the greatest of cinematic achievements.

But I didn't feel so good when I saw the screen credits. I share a credit-card with, I believe, five other people and am listed as one of three "second-unit directors"—the minimum credit requirement stipulated by my contract with MGM.

I cannot help thinking that if Sam Zimbalist had lived I would have received the simple credit I wanted: "Chariot race directed by Andrew Marton."

Nevertheless, if today someone asked me to tackle a similar cinematic challenge, I'd again say: "Let's go."

ROBERT ALDRICH
(1918-   )

Robert Aldrich had an extensive apprenticeship in film-making, serving as a production clerk, script assistant, associate producer and assistant director through most of the 1940's. In this last capacity he worked with Renoir, Rossen, Milestone, Losey and Chaplin, as prestigious a schooling as anyone could ask for. His first film as a director was *The Big Leaguer* (1953), and for the remainder of the decade he polished his skills on a wide variety of projects, most notably a series of brutal action pictures like *Attack!* and *Kiss Me Deadly*. In the late 50's he moved to Europe, where he directed the two films he discusses here and very frankly refers to as mistakes. But Aldrich is among the most adaptable of filmmakers, and on his return to Hollywood his career soon revived when he directed *Whatever Happened to Baby Jane?* Aldrich's 60's films were marked by the same excesses of violence that characterized much of his early work, but his European stay did teach him a few lessons at least. He admits here (1960) that his films have been "too talky," but in *The Dirty Dozen* or *The Grissom Gang* this no longer seems a problem for him. And while his films still tend to a greater than average length, a factor which makes them vulnerable to the shears of the distributor, this has more to do with Aldrich's expansive narrative sense than with simple dialogue problems.

LEARNING FROM MY MISTAKES
ROBERT ALDRICH

In some ways it is extremely flattering to be continually queried concerning my personal reactions to having shot my last two films in Europe. But this "flattering feeling" is tempered by the knowledge that in most instances the individual asking the question is well aware that these two specific films were not well received, either commercially or critically. So the question, despite how politely it may be phrased, is in essence a gentle needle. This is particularly true when such a question is put by European journalists, because they are more familiar than American reporters with the fact that heretofore my films have met with a bit more success and recognition abroad than they have at home. Consequently, such a query from a European also carries about it a degree of confused perplexity.

The facts of the matter are really quite simple. Both films *The Phoenix* and *Angry Hills* were pretty bad, and to a large degree I must accept the responsibility for their being less than they should have been. By "large degree" I mean up to at least 50 per cent of the responsibility. Perhaps it would be simpler to take both pictures separately, and then generalize after this individual inspection.

In the case of *The Phoenix*, one of the principal problems was the script, which I co-authored from the exciting war novel of that name by Lawrence Bachmann. The scenario was too long, too superficially philosophical, and far too talky. (The last trait is a common fault of mine that I seem unable to overcome.)

These inherent shortcomings would have hurt this film regardless of its point of production origin. Consequently, they can have no effect on any evaluation of what "making the pic-

From *Films and Filming*, June 1960. Reprinted by permission of Robert Aldrich.

Robert Aldrich in action on the set of *Whatever Happened to Baby Jane?* (1962).

ture in Europe" had to do with its lack of success and acceptance. Another contributing factor to its being indistinguished,
however, is that, after doing two fine films with Jack Palance,
we both ran out of the ability and/or capacity to continue our
professional rapport. Perhaps for persons of our complicated
psyche, it was just too much to expect that we could "get
along" for three pictures. But in *The Phoenix*, Palance's was
the pivotal part, and when I lost control of him, and he lost
confidence in me, the resulting damage to the final film was
catastrophic. Again this is a deficit that must be charged against
the director . . . the involvement with a difficult personality
notwithstanding. In terms of physical production, the picture
was most satisfactory. Charles Smadja, of United Artists, made
a fabulous, bordering on brilliant, deal with Ufa for the use of
their Berlin studios, staff and equipment; and from a monetary
point of view, the picture was beautifully produced at an
amazingly low cost.

At the outset, there were some minor collisions in the blend-
ing of an American cameraman, a staff predominated by
British, and a German crew; but these difficulties were reason-

ably remedied in the first two weeks of shooting. There were continuing minor irritations that had to do only with the conflicts of customary procedure between my personal method of shooting and the style to which the German crews have (since the war) become accustomed. Even though we had an extraordinarily able art director (Ken Adam), we were constantly reminded that one of the many admirable German traits of sturdy workmanship is regrettably prevalent in their unique conception of set construction. Despite design, few (if any) of the interior set walls were "wild," for example, which inevitably caused aggravating and unnecessary delays. Also, I am a constant user of a small camera crane on interiors. Regrettably, the one that Ufa had was of an early vintage, and far from small, and this particular instrument had not seen service for quite some time. This, too, was somewhat of a speed handicap.

And there was, as always, the problem of a partial language barrier. But despite these minor, if constant, irritants . . . the productivity, energy, dedication and interests of the crew and staff (regardless of nationality) were tangible contributions to the making of the film. Of course, many of their methods were different from mine, and some of these were considerably more efficient than our own; and I would, if given an opportunity, eagerly accept another German picture with no misgivings whatsoever. My personal preference would be to make it in the winter, as there seems to be a far larger and more diverse talent and labour pool to draw from during that period, since most German producers appear to prefer to shoot in the summer . . . all of which doesn't really pinpoint or crystallize what went wrong with my film, because none of the above could importantly detract from the unfortunate end result. But what did damage the picture tremendously is not dissimilar to what hurt *Angry Hills*, and should be left for a general summation.

In terms of *Angry Hills* (extensive exteriors in Greece . . . interiors at M.G.M., Elstree), there are three specific reasons that this picture was not all that it could have been. Two of them are peculiar to *Hills* . . . the third is the same deterrent that prevented *The Phoenix* from being what it might. The principal problem that concerned *Angry Hills* is that, because of contractual commitments, we were forced to commence principal photography with a script that was only one-third finished. Consequently, the rehearsal periods were sporadic, and even these never had any overall direction, since none of us knew where the film was really headed. Thus the film lost that most important cohesive quality. The necessity for commencing in this fashion probably was unavoidable, but the reasons for getting into that sad situation in the first place were most definitely *not* unavoidable.

The picture was taken from a novel by Leon Uris, and told of the Greek resistance movement as it functioned during the first months of the German occupation. In this regard, there was only one real problem: neither the author nor the producer had ever been to Greece. So consequently the novel (and Mr. Uris's first draft screenplay) was far from being realistic or believable. When this was politely pointed out, the Producer countered by sending Mr. Uris on a quick, six-day, all-expenses tour of that magnificent but tortured country, in a fervent, if foolish, hope that such a jaunt might furnish sufficient impetus to stimulate and inspire the author to some dedicated and prodigious effort. It was already the middle of May and the film was scheduled to start on the first of July . . . and we still had no script! This then, should be laughingly labelled Problem No. 1.

Problem No. 2 was my inability to find any personal or creative or even emotional routes to discover whatever it is that must be discovered to make Robert Mitchum really function as an actor. I have seen Mr. Mitchum be too excellent too often to doubt for one minute that he is an extremely accomplished and gifted artist . . . he is. And since the performance that I was able to extract from Mitchum was neither sensitive nor accomplished, nor in any regard gifted, it is impossible to escape the conclusion that my failure to "connect" with Mitchum is a liability that I alone, and not the actor, must also assume.

As an American picture-maker, I had heard many disparaging and uncomplimentary comments about English crews, their attitudes and working patterns. This was compounded by the head of a large British studio (also an Englishman) who, before I started to shoot, gave me a long pontifical pronouncement about how much of a disciplinarian I would have to be if I expected to get a day's work in exchange for a day's pay from his indolent countrymen. In refutation of this, all I can say is that I found all this hearsay nonsense to be in complete contradiction to the facts. I had a marvellous crew and staff, a collection of wonderful people who, without exception, gladly and enthusiastically contributed to the making of the film; and this contribution was continually proffered under some of the most difficult and unpleasant circumstances that I have ever had the misfortune to experience. They were a cooperative, helpful lot, who undersotod perfectly our production problems and did their utmost to overcome them. There were a few moments in the early stages of our location shooting when a full spirit of joint cooperation did not exist between the British and Greek crews; and even now it is difficult to say whether this was an outgrowth of the then current political crises (the Cypriot situation was at its worst), or due to some temporary production office foul-up. But whatever the reason, the early tensions were short-lived; and after the first few days, we all got along extremely well, both professionally and personally. The degree of rapport with the British (and Greek) crew is a memory that I shall long cherish, and have every intention of quickly renewing.

The principal contributing factor to the making of a marginal film—a picture that is not really good, but could have been a lot better—in Europe by an American director, lies in the fact that he is completely devoid of any sort of final control over his work, even more so than he is in his own country. Despite the fact that, in general, the Europeans treat directors (even Americans) with considerably more respect and deference than they receive elsewhere in the world, the final evaluation will show that few, if any, American directors are granted final contractual control over their European-based films. So, when their work is finished a person, or collection of people, whom the director has battled throughout the production, at long last have their belated innings. Regrettably, the results are all too obvious. I am not copping any particular or personal plea in regard to these two specific pictures of mine. They weren't good films. Perhaps they couldn't ever have been really good pictures, but both could have been twice as acceptable and representative than they finally emerged.

The Phoenix when I finished my cut, ran 131 minutes. It was released at 89 minutes. Naturally, much of the cohesion and sense was lost.

Angry Hills, in my version, ran a little under two hours. The release time was very little over an hour and a half. Again the conclusion is inescapable. The obvious question is: doesn't this also happen in America? And the answer is: quite often, but to a large degree (at least in my personal framework of reference) it can be controlled in as much as usually a film can be cut, scored, dubbed, previewed and recut before being submitted to that divine, final arbiter—the almighty distributor—for his studied, knowledgeable and thoughtful perusal.

By then the director will have the anticipatory advantage of seeing and responding to many audiences' varied reactions and is thereby fortified with certain built-in defenses that, if he is at all adroit, usually are impregnable. In such cases, the film usually goes out with only minor and unimportant alterations. But regrettably, such is not the case (because of the time-distance-money factors involved) with Americans who undertake directorial chores for European producers. And surprisingly, this is true regardless of the level of "importance" of the American director involved. And another melancholy comment is that quite often the distribution company itself lends its "supposed" good offices to this wanton butchery.

Recently, for example, I saw a rather good John Ford—Jack Hawkins, British-made, Scotland Yard type picture that had been ruthlessly cut to 55 minutes, in order to make it a convenient, comfortable second-half of an already undistinguished double bill. The tragic impact of seeing it forced home the inescapable conclusion that, "if this can happen to Ford, it can happen to anyone."

Is there a solution or a possible answer to this dilemma? I think so.

I feel strongly that if all American directors who plan (or hope) to do European-based films stood together and collectively demanded that their contractual protection be such that they, and they alone, would be responsible for the cutting, editing, scoring, dubbing and previewing of their film up until the time it was delivered to the distributor, many of these tragic misapplications of time, talent and energy could be avoided.

If such a system came into practice, it would force the distributor into an *honest position* of being an arbiter (between the producer and the director) after the fact; and the distributor's perspective would be conditioned on a fully completed and audience-evaluated production. It seems to me that this is the only reasonable route away from today's disastrous and destructive procedures.

STANLEY KUBRICK
(1928-   )

Perhaps Stanley Kubrick's great success in the direction of elaborate screen narratives lies in his understanding of the relationship of thought and action as expressed in novel and film. In this respect his comments on the proper filming of literary material should be carefully contrasted with those of Richard Brooks (q.v.), who offers a more conventional (if equally thoughtful) perspective on the problem. Kubrick was in England filming *Lolita* at the time he wrote this, and his approach to Nabokov's work did, in fact, derive from his conviction that the novel of interior action was best suited to screen treatment. "How did they ever make a movie of *Lolita*?" was not only the film's advertising slogan, but a useful question which Kubrick felt needed an answer, part of which he provides here. Significantly, Kubrick's background was not in theatre or literature, but in photo-journalism. His first short films were photo-journalistic exercises which projected the insights of a still photographer into documentary film terms, while his early features displayed a similar sense of journalistic observation. Kubrick's association with Kirk Douglas on *Paths of Glory* and *Spartacus* established him as a bankable director, and since that time he has enjoyed the luxury of operating completely on his own terms—a rare, if not unique position. But it is possible that the financial debacle of *Barry Lyndon* (produced with Warner's millions, but without any effective studio supervision) may somewhat restrict his future activities, at least on the giant budgets he has grown accustomed to.

WORDS AND MOVIES
STANLEY KUBRICK

The perfect novel from which to make a movie is, I think, not the novel of action but, on the contrary, the novel which is mainly concerned with the inner life of its characters. It will give the adaptor an absolute compass bearing, as it were, on what a character is thinking or feeling at any given moment of the story. And from this he can invent action which will be an objective correlative of the book's psychological content, will accurately dramatise this in an implicit, off-the-nose way without resorting to having the actors deliver literal statements of meaning.

I think that for a movie or a play to say anything really truthful about life, it has to do so very obliquely, so as to avoid all pat conclusions and neatly tied-up ideas. The point of view it is conveying has to be completely entwined with a sense of life as it is, and has to be got across through a subtle injection into the audience's consciousness. Ideas which are valid and truthful are so multi-faceted that they don't yield themselves to frontal assault. The ideas have to be discovered by the audience, and their thrill in making the discovery makes those ideas all the more powerful. You use the audience's thrill of surprise and discovery to reinforce your ideas, rather than reinforce them artificially through plot points or phoney drama or phoney stage dynamics put in to power them across.

It's sometimes said that a great novel makes a less promising basis for a film than a novel which is merely good. I don't think that adapting great novels presents any special problems which are not involved in adapting good novels or mediocre novels; except that you will be more heavily criticised if the film is bad, and you may be even if it's good. I think almost any novel can be successfully adapted, provided it is not one

From *Sight and Sound*, Winter 1960-61. Reprinted by permission of *Sight and Sound* and Stanley Kubrick.

Stanley Kubrick and Peter Sellers in the war room set of Kubrick's
Dr. Strangelove (1964).

whose aesthetic integrity is lost along with its length. For example, the kind of novel in which a great deal and variety of
action is absolutely essential to the story, so that it loses much
of its point when you subtract heavily from the number of
events or their development.

People have asked me how it is possible to make a film out of
Lolita when so much of the quality of the book depends on
Nabokov's prose style. But to take the prose style as any more
than just a part of a great book is simply misunderstanding just
what a great book is. Of course, the quality of the writing is
one of the elements that make a novel great. But this quality is
a result of the quality of the writer's obsession with his subject,
with a theme and a concept and a view of life and an understanding of character. Style is what an artist uses to fascinate
the beholder in order to convey to him his feelings and emotions and thoughts. These are what have to be dramatised, not
the style. The dramatising has to find a style of its own, as it
will do if it really grasps the content. And in doing this it will

bring out another side of that structure which has gone into the novel. It may or may not be as good as the novel; sometimes it may in certain ways be even better.

Oddly enough, acting comes into the picture somewhere here. At its best, realistic drama consists of a progression of moods and feelings that play upon the audience's feelings and transform the author's meaning into an emotional experience. This means that the author must not think of paper and ink and words as being his writing tools, but rather that he works in flesh and feeling. And in this sense I feel that too few writers seem to understand what an actor can communicate emotionally and what he cannot. Often, at one point, the writer expects a silent look to get across what it would take a rebus puzzle to explain, and in the next moment the actor is given a long speech to convey something that is quite apparent in the situation and for which a brief look would be sufficient. Writers tend to approach the creation of drama too much in terms of words, failing to realise that the greatest force they have is the mood and feeling they can produce in the audience through the actor. They tend to see the actor grudgingly, as someone likely to ruin what they have written, rather than seeing that the actor is in every sense their medium.

You might wonder, as a result of this, whether directing was anything more or less than a continuation of the writing. I think that is precisely what directing should be. It would follow, then, that a writer-director is really the perfect dramatic instrument; and the few examples we have where these two peculiar techniques have been properly mastered by one man have, I believe, produced the most consistently fine work.

When the director is not his own author, I think it is his duty to be one hundred per cent faithful to the author's meaning and to sacrifice none of it for the sake of climax or effect. This seems a fairly obvious notion, yet how many plays and films have you seen where the experience was exciting and arresting but when it was over you felt there was less there than met the eye? And this is usually due to artificial stimulation of the senses by technique which disregards the inner design of the play. It is here that we see the cult of the director at its worst.

On the other hand, I don't want to imply rigidity. Nothing in making movies gives a greater sense of elation than participation in a process of allowing the work to grow, through vital collaboration between script, director and actors, as it goes along. Any art form properly practised involves a to and fro between conception and execution, the original intention being constantly modified as one tries to give it objective realisation. In painting a picture this goes on between the artist and his canvas; in making a movie it goes on between people.

JOSHUA LOGAN
(1908-   )

Joshua Logan's career as a film director has been devoted almost entirely to screen adaptations of Broadway plays and musicals, many of which he had originally directed himself. The most successful of these, *Picnic* and *Bus Stop*, were two very well received adaptations that benefited from exceptional performances and scripting. His later films, particularly such titanic musicals as *South Pacific*, *Camelot* and *Paint Your Wagon*, did not fare nearly as well with critics, although *South Pacific* at least proved one of the biggest box-office hits of the 50's. Throughout the decade American filmmakers moved out to actual locations with increasing frequency, leaving the old Hollywood stages more unused than ever. One reason for this was the supposed availability of cheap labor and lack of costly studio overhead on location productions, but even more important was the sense of physical realism offered by location shooting. The improvements in color photography during the 50's, and the concurrent introduction of wide-screen and wide-film processes like Cinemascope and Vistavision, made suspension of disbelief in the face of studio settings extremely difficult to achieve. Once exposed to real New York, Paris or Marseilles backgrounds, audiences were spoiled for the Hollywood reconstructions of Richard Day and the other great studio art directors. As usual, surface realism seemed all that could ever matter, but some films were definitely hurt by the use of natural surroundings, and even genres like fantasy and the musical became weighted down with a misguided documentary "realism."

MY INVASION OF MARSEILLES
JOSHUA LOGAN

Fools rush in where angels fear to tread, and American movies are here to prove it.

Recently I led an American invasion of Marseilles, the largest city of Provence. It was my pleasant duty to make the motion picture *Fanny*, which is a combination of the three stories Marcel Pagnol wrote in the late 'twenties and early 'thirties called *The Marseilles Trilogy*, consisting of the plays and movies, *Marius*, *Fanny*, and *César*. The trilogy is a modern French classic with a peculiar flavor of its own. Scenes from it are reprinted in French schoolbooks. Phonograph records of the original sound track spoken by the great French actor Raimu, with Pierre Fresnay and Charpin, are collectors' items. The "game of cards" is remembered by most Frenchmen as the funniest scene in modern French literature. Plaster statuettes of the game of cards are sold as souvenirs all over France.

It is said that Marcel Pagnol has been collecting an enormous yearly income from the replaying of the three French films. Surely it was because of this work that he was made a member of the Académie Française and allowed to wear its embroidered uniform and sport its bejeweled sword.

But to the French it is not Pagnol's property; it belongs to them. All France seemed to bristle when I arrived with my associates to start choosing locations in Marseilles. The French newspapers dealt with the subject in heavy sarcasm. "This giant Texan"—I am rather large and I was born in Texas—"dreams to make an American picture out of *Fanny!* It can't be done! It's ridiculous, impossible, and typically American to think that it can! And even if it is good, we won't like it!"

The only one who dared to disagree with the newspapers was M. Pagnol himself, who had been my friend for several

From *Harper's Magazine*, July 1961. Copyright 1961 by Harper's Magazine. Reprinted by permission of Joshua Logan.

Joshua Logan on location in Marseilles during the shooting of *Fanny* (1961).

years. I had directed the American musical comedy based on the trilogy in 1954.

"You will make a great picture, Josuah," he said to me, pronouncing my name very much as the French spell it—with the "h" at the end. "Of course, my esteemed countrymen say that I have traded my soul for money and that this project proves I will do anything for that miserable commodity, but I really believe that the picture will be great. It doesn't have to be played by Raimu. Raimu was a monster." (Monster, in modern French, is a very handy expression meaning either prodigy or devil.)

The fact that I had persuaded France's two most famous exports, Maurice Chevalier and Charles Boyer, to play the leading roles of Panisse and César, seemed to impress nobody in France. Pagnol says that any Frenchman who makes a success outside of France is without honor to the French. "We are the greatest snobs in the world," he says with a combination of sneering distaste and twinkling pride. "Don't let them frighten you. Go right ahead and make a great picture. I will enjoy being famous in the outside world."

I rented an office in Paris in the Studios de Boulogne and started casting. I still had to find a young French girl to play Fanny. Leslie Caron had refused because she also didn't believe any foreigner could make an American version of these French masterpieces.

This was not my first wrestling match with the problems of *Fanny*. When S. N. Behrman and I tried to translate the three plays into acceptable English for the musical comedy which we did together, with Harold Rome's music and lyrics, at first Pagnol's Marseilles phrases seemed to defy translation. Even though the trilogy is a sweetly sad and rueful story, it is told in broad comic terms. The Marseillais are cavalier boasters: they talk and gesture with bravura. Alphonse Daudet in *Tartarin de Tarascon* blames it on the sun. He says the sun is so hot when it glares down on the Midi that it acts as a magnifying glass and tends to enlarge everything—gestures, voices, even the content of what people say. It's not lies the people of Provence tell—merely elephantine truths.

Behrman and I had to conjure up English that would taste as salty as Pagnol's French and yet dodge every hint of English or American slang. Harold Rome had the same problem; he could only write lyrics that used a kind of classic, timeless English.

In our version we kept the character of Panisse alive until the curtain was coming down at the end of the play; in Pagnol's trilogy Panisse died at the very beginning of the last third of the story, leaving little suspense. Pagnol, upon reading our version of the play, wrote me a letter saying, "At last you have found an ending for me."

In preparing for the motion picture, Julius Epstein was engaged to rewrite our version and make it into a scenario. After many meetings with him and executives of Warner Brothers, we decided to do a non-musical version of *Fanny*, using Harold Rome's warm score to underline the moods of the picture but avoiding all songs. It was mostly a question of length. Songs take time, and we wanted to tell more of Pagnol's story. Also, the French do not like the American musical form in pictures; neither do the Germans, Italians, or Swiss. Without the European market everyone felt it would be too great a risk.

Julius Epstein watched the three pictures again, using their sound tracks and our libretto as his main sources. He then proceeded to add scenes that had had to be eliminated from the musical version.

I passed out copies of the script to all my French associates, who were bilingual. There was uniformity in the reaction to it. Each looked up after having read the last lines of the script and, with enormously surprised eyes, said, "Why, it's *good!*"

My two biggest problems at that time were to get a girl to play Fanny, and secure a square-rigged sailing ship which represented the *femme fatale* of the piece. This ship was to lure the young boy, Marius, away from Fanny's arms. The time for shooting was getting closer. Michel Romanoff, my assistant, took off in an airplane to scout all the ports in the Mediterranean for a square-rigged ship. I flew to England to try and persuade Leslie Caron to change her mind. She finally capitulated when she realized that Charles Boyer, whom she had long admired and who was as French as she was, had agreed to play the part of César which Raimu had created. It was not because of me but the thought of playing with Chevalier, Boyer, and Horst Buchholz that finally captured her.

Time was getting short. Dresses and hair pieces were being made in England for Leslie. The huge sets were beginning to be constructed. A crew of workmen took off by train and car to start building the scaffolding on the Old Port in Marseilles. The sets were to represent the weather-beaten buildings which had been torn down during the war on the right side of the port; and they were to camouflage the new concrete structures there. The left side of the port, capped by Notre Dame de la Garde, was still almost intact.

My little office at Boulogne was like a small lifeboat. In every corner of the room were French actors practicing English so that I could decide if they could play in the picture and still be understood.

A telephone call came from Palma de Mallorca from Michel Romanoff. He had found the perfect ship! She was the *Verona*, an English barkentine built many years ago by Mr. Singer, owner of the Singer Sewing Machine Company. Recently she had been re-rigged with square foresails to be eligible for the tall-ships contest of last year's Olympic Games. Her captain flew up to see me in Paris. Yes, she could sail into and out of the harbor in Marseilles, just making it, and dangerous it would be.

Salvatore Baccaloni, the Metropolitan buffo, arrived from America, ready to play the ferryboat captain. Lionel Jeffries flew over from England to discuss playing M. Brun, the tall and lanky customs inspector. Since M. Brun was supposed to be from Lyons and a foreigner in Marseilles, we felt we could take the liberty of casting an Englishman in that part.

Huge, wonderful Georgette Anys walked into my room. She was obviously Fanny's mother, Honorine the fishwife. But she could scarcely speak English. We decided to take the chance; she went into intensive diction lessons.

Suddenly, the cameraman we had been counting on to photograph our picture became unavailable. Zinn Arthur, my public relations assistant, suggested that we try for Jack Cardiff, the master cameraman of the early days of Technicolor. Cardiff had just directed *Sons and Lovers*, to be shown at the Cannes Festival. He was now a full-fledged director, and a distinguished one. Perhaps he would consider the job of cameraman a step down. By some miracle he did not then have another directorial offer, and decided to come with us. That was a good day.

A frantic telephone call came from Marseilles. It was our art director, Rino Mondellini. Permission to build our sets had been rescinded. The people of Marseilles were up in arms that their beautiful sidewalk had been disfigured by several hundred holes dug into it by pneumatic drills. "Yes, we gave you permission, but we now take it back." Without the poles we could not put up the supports; without the supports the sets would blow down during the mistral. "With all those holes," said Rino, "it's the biggest golf course in the world!" We laughed but we didn't feel like laughing.

We all flew to Nice to see if we could use the old harbor there and make it look like Marseilles. But I was stubborn; I had come this far to photograph Marseilles and I was not going back without accomplishing the mission.

Again to Marseilles. What could we do? If we pointed our camera in the direction to the left of the port, it was all right. Once we swung to the right, Marseilles looked like a modern city of bland, square concrete. We decided to photograph all the scenes two ways. As the camera looked left, we would be in Marseilles. When we swung to the right, we would move to a little town called Cassis where there were old buildings along the right side of the harbor—and then by cutting the two angles together we could recreate the old city. This was complicated, difficult, but possible. Peace was restored.

An army of technicians, actors and their families arrived in Marseilles. Half of us lived in Cassis, seventeen miles away. Horst Buchholz arrived from America where he had been filming *The Magnificent Seven.*

Meantime, everybody in Marseilles began to harangue us about our casting. Taxi-drivers said, "How can Maurice Chevalier play Panisse? He's a Parisian! Charles Boyer in the great Raimu's part? Impossible! He hasn't got the accent! And what about this German boy?"

A fishwife at the vast covered fish market on the left bank of the old harbor asked me, "Who is going to play Fanny?"

When I said Leslie Caron, she turned and looked at all of her associates as they exchanged those French grimaces and shrugs which can mean almost anything. "Don't you like her?" I ventured.

After a long pause, she spoke in a very careful voice. "She's a good *dancer*." That is all I could get.

But the waiter who served Mr. Buchholz his orange juice the morning before we took off, looked him over in such a critical way that my heart almost stopped beating. Finally, he nodded his head in approval. Yes, Horst Buchholz looked like Marius. The waiter was willing to let us proceed.

The first shot I planned to get was of Marius up in the shrouds of the square-rigged ship, sailing past the Chateau d'If, looking back toward Marseilles. For this we had brought a helicopter and crew from England. And then I learned an awful fact. The wind that fills the sails of a square-rigged ship is the opposite wind to the one that is needed to photograph from a helicopter. The helicopter had to force itself against the wind in order to remain steady. Also, if the wind was right for the sails, the sun seemed in the wrong direction; if the sun was right, the helicopter could not fly. Horst Buchholz remained up in the rigging for hours as the helicopter made pass after pass, trying to photograph the scene.

When we came back that afternoon, exhausted, discouraged, we did not know that we had filmed the most exciting shot in the picture. We met a jubilant crew who had been waiting for us. "Marseilles has capitulated! The picture is going to be a great success!" Michel Romanoff and the production staff were exultant. "We are going to get all the co-operation we need now."

"What happened?" I said.

Michel replied, "The helicopter! The citizenry was very impressed that you would go to such trouble and expense as to actually bring a helicopter to photograph their city. Now they believe it actually has a chance!"

Soon our problem was not their disapproval but their exhausting enthusiasm. Would we use their restaurant for the actors to change their clothes? Could five hundred people come in and look at the set? Teen-agers swarmed around Leslie Caron and Horst Buchholz for autographs and conversation. Would we come to dinner with the mayor? Would we have lunch with the port director? The assistant mayor? The assistant port director? The head of police?

Each evening we had to attend an "*apéritif*" given by various members of the crew, which meant drinking a Cinzano or pastis at a nearby bar before taking off for our hotels.

The sun shone brightly all day long—the hot sun of the Midi. Alphonse Daudet was right. Adjectives soon became superlatives. It was the best cast, the greatest crew, and the finest story ever told. We loved Marseilles and Marseilles loved us. The cast loved each other. We patted each other on the back after every scene. Kisses, hugs, handshakes, *apéritifs*, bouillabaisse, *ailloli, vin rosé*. Euphoria!

A movie company is apt to become slightly high under the worst conditions. They are displaced persons working in an unfamiliar place against enormous odds of weather and time. But put them under the hot sun of the Midi and the cup of truth runneth over.

As I write this, it is six months since we stopped shooting the picture. Throughout these months I have been running the film in the cutting-room, trying to get it into the correct shape to be distributed for an American audience. I am no longer in the hot Midi sun. The shadow of New York brings realism back to me.

I am optimistic that Americans and Britishers will like *Fanny*, but I worry about the French. Would we like to see a French company come to the banks of the Mississippi and make a movie of *Huckleberry Finn?* No matter how good it was, no matter how faithful to Mark Twain, could we accept a freckled-faced boy in a tattered straw hat smoking a corncob pipe who spoke *French?* Or think of Jim! Aunt Polly! The widow Douglas!

Oh, no! Like Fanny, the idea's ridiculous—and only a fool would try it.

JOHN STURGES
(1911-   )

In any large film industry many directors become identified with particular narrative genres, and in Hollywood
this has included musicals (e.g., Vincente Minnelli), thrillers (Hitchcock), comedies (Tashlin) and westerns (Ford,
Mann, Boetticher and many others). Among the most pro-
lific of western directors of the 50's and 60's was John
Sturges, director of some of the most influential "official"
westerns of the day. These prestige films followed in the
wake of Zinnemann's *High Noon* and Stevens' *Shane*, and
included *Gunfight at the O.K. Corral, Last Train from
Gun Hill* and *The Magnificent Seven*, all very efficient but
hardly to be counted among the finest of post-war westerns.
Sturges entered the film industry in 1932 as an assistant in
RKO's blueprint department, then worked as an aide to
producer David O. Selznick. During the war he worked on
some forty-five documentary and training films for the military, including *Thunderbolt*, on which he assisted William
Wyler. After the war he directed his first feature, *The
Man Who Dared*, and soon came to specialize in elaborate
action films. While some, like *The Great Escape*, display
considerable enthusiasm and organizational skill, the rest
share with *The Hallelujah Trail* and *Marooned* a deadly
quality which overwhelms the work of actors and director
alike. Although Sturges admits to learning from Stevens
and Wyler, and to using "a lot of Kurosawa's stuff," he
has never mastered the simple lesson which John Ford offers
him in the last line of this revealing piece.

HOW THE WEST WAS LOST!
JOHN STURGES

Three things are essential to every western. The first is isolation—this is an absolute must. In *High Noon*, the first question is "Why don't you call the Marshal?" and the reply "I can't reach him." In *Bad Day at Black Rock* they ask "Why don't you call for help, mister?" He can't, the lines are cut. So the first thing you have to do is isolate people from any help, they can't go to the government, they can't go to the next town. Next thing is that issues are resolved by violence. By gunplay. The third thing is that one man, or one group of men, have to take law and justice, right and wrong, into their own hands, whether they want to or not, whether they may die doing it or not.

Now those things have nothing to do with the west, but they're three of the most powerful situations that you can find to make a story. And they all happen in the west. You add one more ingredient—colour: the look of the mountains, the clothes. Anybody who doesn't like to see a man ride a horse is a rarity. And whatever you want to say you believe. Actually the west wasn't really as we show it at all.

Everybody in the west was young, a man of 30 was an oddity, and most of them were foreigners—Swedes, French, and so on. We age the town, too. I'll never forget a reviewer who wrote that the town looked so new it was pathetic. But all western towns were brand new, some only six months old. Dodge City was put up in three months. But we can't do that, it's become an artifice of the imagination. The first thing you do in a western street is to go around filing the boards, bleaching and ageing them. But you can see pictures of a western town where they haven't even painted it.

People's minds like discipline, so, like the ballet, westerns are

From *Films and Filming*, December 1962. Reprinted by permission of John Sturges.

Lee Remick and John Sturges take a break during location shooting for *The Hallelujah Trail* (1965).

always done the same way. If you go to hear Beethoven, you don't complain that it was played exactly like the last time. It's not supposed to be different. And a western is a controlled, disciplined, formal kind of entertainment. There's good and bad; clearly defined issues; there's a chase; there's a gunfight. You like to see the same formula and the same technique done well. Most people who try to do "different" westerns have fallen right in the fire. The answer is to do the same western better and in a different way.

Though *The Magnificent Seven* was a western remake of the Japanese film, *Seven Samurai*, the styles of the films were totally different. I certainly used a lot of Kurosawa's stuff because they were marvellous things, and I was greatly affected by his ideas and his construction, but the way we told the story and moved the camera was completely different. The moment when the character of Britt is sitting waiting for the bandits to come back to their tethered horses, and he becomes fascinated with some flowers and studies their petals—that we stole.

We followed Kurosawa's opening pattern completely with

321

one exception. The bandits were faceless and anonymous, you never really knew who they were, they never said anything. And we created the character of the bandit leader; we departed there. Otherwise we began just as he did. We showed a little town, the bandits came and said "We'll be back when the crops are ready." The people got together and said "What are we going to do?" and nobody knew so they went and asked the old man. And he says "Hire Samurai" ("hire gunfighters"). They say "They're proud people and want a lot of money," so he says "Fine, get hungry gunfighters."

The feud over whether or not the Indian should be buried on Boot Hill was our own invention, but we wanted the same combination of courage and humanity to be displayed as in the corresponding sequence in the original film.

The part played by Horst Buchholz was a combination of two characters. Mifune is a great comedy talent, and I didn't know anybody who could play his part. Secondly, the Japanese film was set about 400 years ago and there was a quality about swords and samurai and the terrible need to be identified as something important; but it would have kind of oafish overtones if you were going to tell it with gunfighters. A gun is a small thing, not like a sword, so it didn't ring true to me. So we took two characters, the fellow who wanted to be the samurai and the young kid who wanted to be a samurai, and we put them into one.

There are not many stories that can be adapted to a western setting. *Pygmalion* would make a hell of a western. I've seriously considered making this as a film. A newspaper man is with some fellow at a bar in a little town, and they're talking about gunfighters. This fellow says "Look, the public want to have heroes, legends—they create these things. I don't believe there's a gunfighter who's killed one-twentieth of the men he's supposed to have done." Then he says, "See that kid over there. Never mind if he can hit anything with a gun or not, if he wants to be a hero and if he's got any guts at all I could make him the most famous gunfighter in the west." The other one says, "Oh come off it." So he goes over to the kid and tells him what to do. The kid's never fired a bullet, never killed a man.

Six months later he's the terror of the west. When he comes into the bar everybody stands back. Then he discovers the meaning of fear. He recognises the power of having people straighten up like this, and he starts bluffing down real gunfighters, who back off. He turns on his mentor, and says, "Don't tell me what to do." Then he comes home and runs into a real gunfighter. He challenges the guy, who says, "I can take one look at you and see you're bluffing." The kid is trapped. He draws, and is killed.

If you can make a western out of *Pygmalion*, I guess the sky's the limit.

My latest film, *The Great Escape*, I'm producing myself. I'm essentially a director though—the only other film I produced was *The Magnificent Seven*. Everyone says "Why make a war story, or prisoner-of-war story?" But this is a story of courage, gallantry. And several aspects of it are unique. Anybody who makes a film, particularly one that's expensive and involves a lot of time and effort, has to make one that nobody's seen before. It's the story of men who take action in terms of life and death, rightly or wrongly, into their own hands and do something about it. It's a pretty good example of the price of freedom. The men in the camp are from every country, every race, every rank, with one common denominator—the determination to get out and be free.

An aspect of the story is that this was not a brutal camp. The men were well fed, reasonably well housed. The Geneva convention was scrupulously observed by the camp until the escape, so it made a pretty good case for the men to sit out the war. But they arrive at the camp with a determination to be free, to strike a blow at the enemy from behind. Also there is the moral that this is good conquering evil. It lends itself to being told in very striking visual terms. All you have to do is look at the camp, then at one of the pows, and that's the story. Just as surely as in *Bad Day at Black Rock* when the streamliner comes into this desert town and the fellow in a black suit, with one arm and a bag, gets off. If you dump these fellows into the camp, slam the door on them, and have the guards looking at them and them looking through the wire at the guards, there's got to be a story. Immovable body, irresistible force. Something's got to blow!

Most of the story is told with the camera, with what you see. The technique is to try to get the audience to be with the escapee. There are a lot of ways to tell a story in visual terms. There's the one you could call the "eye of God" technique—the only person who could see what you show on the screen if it weren't a film would be God. A fellow is wandering around a room, and I could have a shot inside a desk showing that it has a time bomb, which will go off if he opens the drawer. Only the audience sees this, and a director can show it to them. In this film we're going at it in a different way. Everything's played off from the point of view of the people who are participating. If I'm successful the audience will share the same suspense and excitement as the people involved.

An awful lot of things I've been given credit for have come from other people. George Stevens has probably influenced me more than anyone, except maybe William Wyler. Stevens used to say repeatedly "Get a format in your mind on how to shoot a sequence. (As you get more experience you won't have to do that.) Then when you go on location, forget it. Get out and look at the place, let things happen to you and you'll find you learn the facility of staging scenes where it's effective. If you draw diagrams in a book and go around looking arbitrarily for certain mechanical arrangements then you'll never get anywhere at all." And with actors, Stevens said, "Always let the actors do what they want to do first, you're in control and if you don't like it you can change it. But good actors are very bright people, they make a contribution of their own taste and talent within the concept of the scene and how it should be staged. It might be very good, and if it isn't there's no harm done."

Hal Wallis is a favourite man of mine to work for because he has such a marvellous organisation. You certainly profit by working with staff over and over. It makes it a lot easier, but it's a trap you can fall into, too. I've worked with some of the best cameramen in the business. You try to take the fellow that goes along with your style, and he in turn stimulates you. But it's foolish to try to mould cameramen or actors, or dictate style to them. If you tend to compose scenes for the camera then you can get into trouble, the cameraman doesn't go your way. I don't do that, I compose them so that they can look at a scene from any angle. I don't care so long as there's a general pattern of film that will cut together. Some very bad things can happen to you if you become pre-occupied with the composition of film as composition. The idea is, what's the shot for? I also try very hard not to get arty, it's absurd.

I was a cutter for years, and before you start cutting film it takes you about four years to be able to run film through the moviola without standing on it, or to cut it without tearing it. This is *long* before you can cut anything. And directing's like that too. All film is shot with an awareness of how to cut it, unless you're a real square. That's part of the craftsmanship.

You never know when the camera's moving. I've had people say to me "You never move the camera." That's baloney, it moves all the time. I like to try and get the excitement of the kaleidoscopic effect of film. I try very hard to avoid intermediate distance. If it's going to be a long shot I really get back so that I can't go further. If it's going to be a close-up, I get right up. And if you're going to move, *move*. I hate little fussy things.

There's nothing more visually interesting than a face. John Ford came out one day when I was completely socked. We were out in the desert somewhere with miserable weather and I couldn't see anything. I said "Look, what are we able to shoot out here, Mr Ford?" and he said "The most interesting and exciting thing in the world, a human face."

HENRY KING
(1892-   )

By the end of his career Henry King's reputation had suffered a severe decline thanks to the uniformly poor reception of his last few films, particularly such ill-advised efforts
as *The Sun Also Rises, Beloved Infidel* and *Tender Is the
Night*. When he wrote this article on the need for reviving
the old-style star system he seemed a back number, and in
fact he retired from direction that same year. Even the
more adventurous critics had small use for King, and in
1968 Andrew Sarris had no idea where to rank the director,
whose work he found "turgid" and a pale shadow of John
Ford. How satisfying, then, that Henry King has been able
to enjoy in the 70's a revival of some substance, as festivals
and retrospectives replay his masterworks of the 20's, 30's
and 40's to increasingly more appreciative audiences. King
entered films in the rough and ready days of the industry,
and had several years of experience behind him before directing his first great film, *Tol'able David*, in 1921. The
command of the medium evident in this early work is still
exceptional, but more important in light of King's later
career was the love of the countryside and its people which
would become a hallmark of his most personal films. While
King's style was unquestionably deliberate, who could
quarrel with the pacing of *Margie, Twelve O'Clock High*
or *The Gunfighter*, films which would be destroyed by
more fashionable rhythms? King was a consummate studio
craftsman, and throughout the talkie period Fox was his
studio, an identification which might not always have been
to the good. Tied so closely to one company, his fortunes
ebbed and flowed at the whim of forces outside his command, and if King faltered in the 50's, one might look to
CinemaScope for the reasons.

NO END OF STARS
HENRY KING

Prophets forecasting the end of the "star system" will join the Hindu astrologers who recently predicted the end of the world.

Hollywood has gone through several self-made crises over the predominance of stars, during my own tenure as a director. It will happen again.

The king is dead, long live the king—that's the star system in a nutshell.

I have been privileged to officiate in the launching of many great stars from Richard Barthelmess, Ernest Torrance and Ronald Colman to Gary Cooper, Tyrone Power, and Jennifer Jones. I expect again and again to see a new rising talent bring a picture to life and to greatness.

We may have come to expect too much of our stars. They share our fault, claiming too much for themselves. The greatest and most durable stars through the years have not tried to produce and direct their pictures.

We had learned through trial and error that a star cannot successfully produce and direct himself. The misinterpretation and denial of this truism lies at the root of problems which individual stars have raised in their efforts to control and direct their own vehicles, during the current scramble for top names. A star's belief in his omniscience about all decisions is a dangerous fallacy, like the old divine right of kings. Democracy works better.

A parallel axiom is the actor's lack of sound judgment on the basic story. Proverbially, actors are noted for making the worst story selections. A fat role does not necessarily make a good story. The wisest actor relies on director and producer judgment about the basic value of a story.

From *Journal of the Screen Producers' Guild*, December 1962. Reprinted by permission.

Henry King discusses a scene for *Beloved Infidel* (1959) with Gregory Peck and Deborah Kerr.

Talented actors with star quality are built up to great heights by director and writer. A fine role in a good story creatively directed can make a star overnight out of a relative unknown if he or she has the inner spark. There is some mystic rapport through the camera's eye that kindles excitement in the viewer and leads to a new name topping the marquee.

I have the greatest respect for the actor who takes his profession seriously, and contributes his own essence to the part he is playing. I should be the last to underestimate what a brilliant actor can infuse into any rewarding role. I have seen that lightning strike too often to be a skeptic.

The star can make a great contribution in talent and intelligence. We don't pay these fantastic prices just because an actor carries weight. We never buy stars by the pound.

We have been guilty of buying stars by the price-tag, which may not always correspond to the box-office. *Caveat emptor* applies in casting. But the laws of supply and demand work, in the long run—those who defy them go broke. Eventually the star must be worth his price, and is.

Hollywood should not panic because a few stars make over-publicized mistakes. I can remember past scandals and tragedies that reduce recent events to their proper proportions. Hollywood and the star system survived then and will now. Let's get some historical perspective, instead of hysterical invective. Stardom brings its own peculiar problems. Even a tinsel crown causes an uneasy head. Fame is a burden and a problem, as well as a reward.

Hollywood isn't slipping, except into periodic moods of pessimism. The public will still pay to see top pictures and top stars. They pay to the tune of more millions than most old-time pictures could hope for. The proper combination of story and star unlocks Fort Knox. The public wants entertainment and will pay for the best.

Even motion pictures' deadly rival, television, presents daily evidence of the vitality of moviedom. Look at the high popularity of Hollywood's past star products, even in direct competition with the latest and best the new medium can offer. The goal of every new TV idol or series star is to make the grade in motion pictures. Some of our new stars may come from TV, as Charlton Heston and others have done.

Only Hollywood's wide screen, color, and epic scope can give the popular idols of telefilms a proper opportunity for real greatness. The motion picture industry must not underestimate its primary position, in panic or self-criticism. This is still the big time, and will be unless there is some major technological change like wall-screen pay-TV. If such a major change does take place in the future, I venture to predict that the motion picture industry will be there in the forefront, greater than ever.

Temporary setbacks and economic swings must not blind us to the long-range dominance of our industry—and in turn to our dependence on the stars. Without great talents and great names, we are shadowboxing or settling for half portions.

Let us therefore not balk at giving the star his due. He—and especially she—is the backbone and mainstay of the industry, our flag flying proudly in the breeze, our marquee top, call it what you will.

Instead of trying to play down our stars or circumscribe them with taboos and limitations, we should return to our old policy of glorifying them.

Whatever happened to the "big build-up"? Remember when studios spent literally millions to promote their stable of stars? I should not say "spent." The word is "invested." The returns were lasting and fabulous. If our present economic structure of free-lance stars and independent producers precludes such build-ups, then in self-preservation we must invent a new economic structure which will be mutually profitable.

Let our bankers and backers work on this problem, since they are so determined to insist on the "insurance" of big names. It is to the star's benefit to cooperate—it's their future that will be aggrandized. Whether the answer is multiple deals, cooperative efforts without violating anti-trust, or whatever, let us devise a new pattern for star-building.

Above all, let us aim at glorifying stars, not demoting them.

Women stars should again revive the glamorous style traditions of Gloria Swanson, Barbara Stanwyck, and Joan Crawford, to name but a few. Whole audiences of women flocked to the theatre when the word got out that a star's costumes were really spectacular in her new feature. Jennifer Jones, Ava Gardner, Elizabeth Taylor, Joan Crawford herself, and others in the same milieu, have a golden opportunity to set the pace for modern style and make Hollywood again the fashion capitol, on screen or off. Hitching motion pictures to the vast fashion business will be an irresistible force to benefit both industries.

I shudder a little at the jeans-clad publicity photos of so many modern luminaries, even if it is the popular vogue of the younger generation. Those very youngsters will thrill to more glamorous attire in the proper setting, never fear.

This is just one facet of re-glorifying our stars with conscious, planned, elaborate efforts. They will repay the investment.

My opinion on the star system, therefore, is simple. Hollywood has no choice but to follow its star.

ANTHONY MANN
(1906-1967)

Anthony Mann was originally an actor and director on Broadway, first gaining attention for his direction of *Thunder on the Left* and *So Proudly We Hail*. David O. Selznick signed him as a talent scout, and in 1942 he directed his first film, *Dr. Broadway*, for Paramount, then specialized in low-budget thrillers for companies like Republic, RKO and Eagle-Lion. Here he began to work with the cinematographer John Alton, whose dramatic visual style was to have a great impact on Mann's later work. *T-Men, Reign of Terror* and *Devil's Doorway* were the most important Mann-Alton collaborations, highly styled examples of *film noir* lighting applied to a wide range of genres. Mann's most interesting work came in the 50's, primarily in such James Stewart westerns as *Winchester '73* and *Bend of the River*. Between them, Mann and Stewart created some of the most intriguing examples of 50's Americana, breathtaking landscapes peopled by an exotic array of rugged, if neurotic, loners. Needless to say, American critics took little notice. As Andrew Sarris has pointed out, anything emerging from Universal-International in the 50's was snobbishly avoided by the critical establishment, the films of Mann and Douglas Sirk included. Mann writes here about the third phase of his career, the spectacles which occupied him through the early 60's. Such projects seemed irresistibly tempting to even the best directors of the period, but few were able to emerge unscathed. In the move to blockbusters Mann's fate was not dissimilar to that of the ancient Romans.

EMPIRE DEMOLITION
ANTHONY MANN

The reason for making *The Fall of the Roman Empire* is that it is as modern today as it was in the history that Gibbon wrote: if you read Gibbon, like reading Churchill, it is like seeing the future as well as the past. The future is the thing that interested me in the subject. The past is like a mirror; it reflects what actually happened, and in the reflexion of the fall of Rome are the same elements in what is happening today, the very things that are making our empires fall.

I did not want to make another *Quo Vadis?* (which I worked on, by the way; I did all the burning of Rome in that picture in 1950—I was the night shift), another *Spartacus*[1] or any of the others because these stories were the stories of the Christ. Those films gave the impression that the Christian movement was the only thing the Roman Empire was about, but it was a minor incident in the greatness of the Roman Empire.

This is not a film based on Gibbon. No film could digest his *Decline and Fall*. I have not even read the complete Gibbon (it would take my lifetime to read); but the inspiration was the Oxford concise edition of some fifteen hundred pages. Not only having read Gibbon, but having also read Edith Hamilton's *The Roman Way*, William Durant's *Caesar and Christ*, Plutarch's *Lives*, Caesar's *Wars* and many more, I came across one very exciting thing about the period, which made our storyline possible. All the historians spoke of the creativity of Rome. It was one of the great adventures of all history—Rome gave us greater law, greater understanding, greater concepts of peoples. All the historians picked the time of Marcus Aurelius as the beginning of the end.

[1] Mann was also the original director of *Spartacus*, before Kubrick came onto the picture.—R. K.

From *Films and Filming*, March 1964.

Anthony Mann with the Ultra-Panavision 70 camera used to photograph *The Fall of the Roman Empire* (1964).

Edith Hamilton did it through writers. She said that all creativity of writers and of law ceased to be after the end of Marcus Aurelius' age. Gibbon used Christianity as his great enemy of Rome. In Durant, Caesar and Christ were the two great figures, Caesar the beginning and Christ the end: but he did something that Gibbon didn't do, he said that this was the resurrection of the Roman empire, because out of it came the Papacy and Rome today is as alive as it was in those days.

Whether you accept such theories or not is another matter. What we wanted to do was to find a point where we could start the picture. A spectacle film is only as good as the internal story, the development of characters that people can understand and accept. Aurelius' life was a fantastic one. He had two children. He had a son, Commodus, who destroyed everything that Marcus Aurelius did and this was the beginning of the end; from then on there were thirty Emperors and Rome became a dictatorship put up by the military. His daughter,

Lucilla, fought very hard to uphold everything that Aurelius believed and tried almost to create an Eastern Empire with him. It is a story of a family; it is the story we tell against this terrific background of Rome, which internally starts to destroy itself. Our theme, which is essentially that of Durant's book, is that no civilisation can be destroyed from without, but it destroys itself from within.

As Hadrian trained Aurelius to become an Emperor, so Aurelius trained other men to be Emperors; but he did not feel that his son was right for such authority. In the old days Nero and Caligula had merely inherited the throne and at its height, the Roman Senate decided this was no longer healthy for the empire; so that the Golden Age of Rome was the hundred years when there was no war, the only time in the history of the world when this was so. We picked this climatic moment to open our film. There were many places where we could have started it, but as we wanted to tell the Roman story and not the Christian story we went to the time of Rome's greatness.

The film was originally my idea. I was walking down Piccadilly and I passed Hachards bookshop and saw the Oxford concise edition of *The Decline and Fall* in the window. I had just finished *El Cid* and I said to myself, "Now that would make an interesting picture." Samuel Bronston wanted me to direct another epic picture for him, so I took him the subject and said I had no idea what the story was going to be but would he let me work on it.

Basilio Franchina, a fine Italian writer, did an enormous amount of research for me; and it was he and Ben Barzman who did the original work on a script. After several discussions we all agreed that this was the period we wanted to concentrate on. We found fantastic and interesting things that are so modern today. For instance, when Aurelius was up in the northern frontier trying to stop the barbarians invading, all he wanted to do was to capture their leaders and try to convince them to live as Romans. He made an experiment by taking twenty thousand barbarians and putting them on Roman soil and treating them as Romans, trying to teach them to be Romans so that there need be no more barriers or frontiers if they could only be made to understand. But the experiment was a failure. It was one of the many failures that made it impossible for Rome to survive. Contraception—because the barbarians were breeding like the Chinese today, while the Romans were not. The laws that the Senate worked under were as modern as today's laws. Yet the Senate at one time could be bought, the armies could be bought: and that marked the beginning of the end.

The reason I wanted to make *El Cid* was the theme "a man rode out to victory dead on a horse"; I loved the concept of that ending. Everybody would love to do this in life.

I found on *El Cid* that Spain is great for locations because there are so many different kinds of country. It is ideal for making a spectacle film. But one must be careful not to let the concept of the spectacular run away with you. In *Fall of the Roman Empire* I have concentrated in the first part on establishing the characters in simple, human terms—meeting characters doing the things that they did in those days, the sacrifice of a bird or simple things that we ourselves would do in our everyday lives. Then the spectacle is done entirely differently to what you would expect, because the whole of the Empire comes to Marcus Aurelius in the mountains with all their different coloured chariots, their different religions and so on; and he makes a speech to them, and the speech is what the empire *was*—so that in very simple terms we show the empire and its vastness through the eyes of one man. The story is told through the eyes of individuals rather than having chunks of spectacle and little characters in between. The first half of the picture is an intimate story of life and death, and the characters bring you into the spectacle rather than it being imposed on you without dramatic reason.

In the film we have Sir Alec Guinness, James Mason, Stephen Boyd, Sophia Loren, Mel Ferrer, Anthony Quayle and a newcomer to most cinemagoers, Christopher Plummer, who plays the destructive son, Commodus, opposite Guinness' Aurelius. Plummer, I believe, is one of the great new actors, capable—and this is so important in a spectacle—of making the character as big emotionally as the physical impacts of sets, costumes, crowds of people and breathtaking locations.

But characters can only come from good writing; and I believe if you are going to use a writer you must use all his talent, and all his talent is not all his talent if you impose something upon him. So once we had decided the focal point for our film, I left Barzman and Franchina free to construct a script about the people and the period. It was a 350 page treatment. They knew the kind of feeling I wanted because they had worked on *El Cid*. They could write anything; I didn't mind how wild it went. Bronston's script supervisor, Philip Yordan, would come in once in a while to inspire the boys to make this the best picture that has ever been—we were all trying to make a great film.

After this first draft we worked very closely together on formalising the characters, to make them living beings. We actually wrote six scripts. Even the sixth script, which I finally used as my "hanger," developed itself while we were shooting. This writing took us more than one year. We did not have artists in mind when we were writing; but we wanted characters with memorable scenes to attract artists of the calibre of Guinness to want to play them.

I believe in the very simplest dialogue. I have seen nearly all of Shakespeare's plays. This is the great writer. But take *Julius Caesar* and you will find tremendous inaccuracies from an historical point of view; but these are not important. The most important thing is that you get the feeling of history. The actual facts, very few people know. If you find out from some obscure historian that Aurelius had curly hair, does it matter if the actor playing him has straight hair? But you cannot change the actual event.

We have tried to use the most simple and primitive English, void of cliche and slang. I think we were successful up to a point with *El Cid*. Unless you have a poet, a man really steeped in words, who knows the value of words and the language of words, you are better off with the minimum of dialogue. The words don't make the picture, anyway. If you asked anybody, however devoted they are to films, what a character said they will never be able to tell you; but I guarantee you they will be able to tell you what the character did, where he was going, or what the pictorial movement was. It is the image that really drives home a point. The words are only there to supplement the picture. Shakespeare needed the words to create the image. His stage was not like our stage. For us, the image is always there.

One must be very careful of words. A word can destroy an image. There is constantly a need to be careful what words to exclude, rather than add. The word is on the soundtrack, it is away from the picture, it is vital that what you see is real, rather than what you hear.

I have made films for four hundred thousand dollars and for sixteen million dollars; and I have enjoyed making both. I shall not make another "big" film for a little while. The final arbiter, for all its size and complexity, has to be you, it is in front of you, you see it, and only the way you see it is the way you want it to be. A director who is not physically A1 cannot make this kind of film. I have a rigorous doctor's report on myself before I get involved in one of Mr. Bronston's epics: I must be fit, able and willing.

My next film—much smaller in physical size—I am setting up with my own company. It is a war story, *The Unknown Battle*, for which the Norwegian Government has given us fantastic co-operation because it is one of their great stories, and the British Government which was closely concerned has given us a great deal of help in research.[1] *Men in War* and *God's Little Acre* I had also done with my own companies. The new film derives from two books, *Skis Against the Atom* and *But for These Men*, and Ben Barzman is again associated with me as writer.

I believe in the nobility of the human spirit. It is that for which I look in a subject I am to direct. I do not believe that everybody is bad, that the whole world is wrong. The greatness of Shakespeare's plays is the nobility of the human spirit,

---

[1] Released as *The Heroes of Telemark* (1965).—R. K.

even though he may destroy the character. And the same with Greek tragedy. Or a modern drama like *The Longest Day*, in which the united human spirit was destroying something that was going to destroy the world. Why is the American Western film such a success throughout the world? It is because a man says "I am going to do something"—and does it: we all want to be heroes. This is what drama is. This is what pictures are all about. I don't believe in anything else.

SAMUEL FULLER
(1912-   )

In *Pierrot le Fou* Samuel Fuller defines the cinema in terms that seem torn from the pages of a Fuller scenario—lean, direct, disturbing and almost threatening. At first this article seems to call up a different image, film as a summation of the earlier arts, a combine which runs from Mayakovsky to McCarey. But, while Fuller goes on at length about the virtues of using film to bring great literature, music and art to the millions (the man seems closer to Thalberg than his critics might admit), his own work is far removed from this. In fact, the Fuller of *Run of the Arrow, Shock Corridor* and *The Naked Kiss* does not emerge here until the end, when the article suddenly begins to spout phrases like "a form of expression that seizes the creator," "youth burning with ideas" and "excitement . . . squashed like a gnat," overheated imagery in the most fervid Fuller tradition. Originally a reporter, Fuller was associated with the old *New York Journal* and during the 30's traveled around the country covering murder trials. His war experiences with the First Army in Africa and Europe proved central to his later film work, with the schematized dramatic conflicts of the war film dominating even his non-battlefield productions. Fuller's stylistics are as full-bodied as his narratives, and the sheer filmic energy of his best work is hardly surpassed in the post-war American cinema. Yet it is to England and France that Fuller must look for his laurels, as even American auteurists have been slow to put their praises into print, except, of course, for Peter Bogdanovich, who is currently serving as producer of Fuller's latest project, *The Big Red One*.

WHAT IS A FILM?

SAMUEL FULLER

In Kassel, Germany, there is a collection of paintings, among them almost a score of Rembrandts including *Jacob Blessing the Sons of Joseph*.

A play dramatizing Rembrandt's moment of inspiration and hours of execution of *Jacob's Blessing* could be produced on the stage. A novel could describe the rebellion in Rembrandt. A poem could illustrate what prompted him to paint *Jacob's Blessing*. A composer could create a symphony of Rembrandt's thunder with a brush. A series of color photographs could bring out the details of the dying patriarch. A sculptor could carve Rembrandt painting *Jacob's Blessing*. An actor could narrate the scene of Joseph summoned to his father's deathbed and bring tears to thousands of listeners.

But only a movie can combine all these elements and bring the film viewer right to the heart of the matter to watch the creation of *Jacob's Blessing;* to share Rembrandt's intimate attitude toward life; to become involved with his outcries so that they become our outcries; to learn what manner of man he was to others and to himself; to live with him and his common-law-wife in their squalid garret; to experience his joy when he discovered the meaning of the Mennonites and to be there when he mixed colors to match emotions so that light and darkness take shape before our eyes.

What a moment for any man, woman and child! When art can dramatize and hypnotize, entertain and educate, inspire and reveal, grip imagination and convey a sense of reality, play sacred emotions and interplay blinding colors—that is art in its purest form and that form is the film.

What other medium can take us into the eye of a character, probe through his mind, catch a look that would take a dozen words to describe?

From *Cinema*, July 1964. Reprinted by permission of Samuel Fuller.

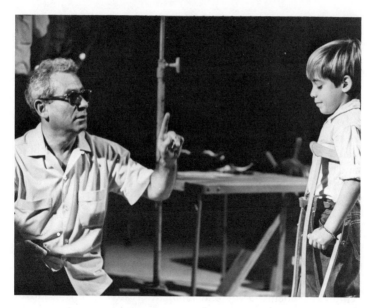

Samuel Fuller directing *The Naked Kiss.*

Novels, biographies, autobiographies, plays and histories are of the highest forms of art because they enable the reader to digest contents within the confines of his own privacy and to make up his mind on his own terms and time whether to reject or accept the ideas in the works. A film is not in competition with the written word. A film inspires feeling for the written word. The success of *Gone with the Wind* on the screen created a phenomenal reader interest in the Civil War resulting in astronomical sales of written matter on the subject, new book clubs, special magazines dealing with that war, and an avalanche of books that were published immediately after Appomattox finding new life in republication.

My Fair Lady—soon to be released as a film based on the smash Broadway show based on Bernard Shaw's *Pygmalion* based on W. S. Gilbert's comedy *Pygmalion and Galatea* which was also told by William Morris in *The Earthly Paradise* based on John Marston's 1598 play *Metamorphosis of Pygmalion* based on Ovid's story *Metamorphoses* based on the Greek legend of the sculptor of Cyprus who fell in love with his ivory statue of Aphrodite, gave life to the statue and married it—will do more for the English language than all the works mentioned because the professor of phonetics in the film will reach millions of people.

Irving Stone's *Lust For Life* was a best seller but the film based on his book has jockeyed more people to be interested in Van Gogh and in art than volumes of text books and thousands of critiques. Watch the interest Stone's *Agony and Ecstasy*, soon to be made as a film, will arouse in the world of art because Michelangelo, on the screen, will invite the viewer to witness the birth and execution of the huge statue of *David* from a single block of marble.

Song Without End introduced Liszt to millions of new ears and Harry Sukman's Academy Award bridging of *Hungarian Rhapsodies, St. Francis Preaching to the Birds*, concertos and symphonic poems *Dante* and *Hamlet*, created such a beautiful blend that viewers were influenced enough to stock their libraries with music by the Hungarian composer.

Hamlet starring Laurence Olivier animated high pressure among film viewers for all the works of Shakespeare including his folios and quartos. Shakespeare is a standard on sale the year round, but Olivier's *Henry V* was responsible for those unfamiliar with his works to buy old and new editions of Shakespeare. One bookseller admits to such a fabulous demand that film viewers have become experts, and can intelligently denounce altered passages as corrupt and offer their own interpretation to the presence of a word rare in Shakespeare's day and often obsolete.

The Barretts of Wimpole Street, a film based on the romance of Robert Browning and Elizabeth Barrett Browning, excited moviegoers to demonstrate interest in the poems of Byron, Shelley, Keats, etc., and taught them an affection for verses and an awareness of lyrical beauty to the ear from the rapture of John Crowe Ransom to the cyclonic snatches of Vladimir Mayakovsky.

The Life of Emile Zola launched a parade of filmgoers to the stalls for works by Balzac, Baudelaire, Borel, Rimbaud and France's greatest novelists and experimental poets who influenced modern literature. Hundreds of thousands of viewers of the film showed an interest in France that would make any teacher happy from a lecturer at Oxford to a tutor at P.S. 143.

One day the greatest educational medium will be the film. Millions of children will watch a moment in history told through drama so gripping that dates of events will become dates of exciting moments, instead of numbers to crowd their reluctant minds. The Hamilton-Burr duel, witnessed through the eyes of a boy who overhead the challenge and crossed the river to New Jersey to watch the fight, would send armies of children in all parts of the world to their text books to check facts, argue points, re-live the duel through the boy they saw in a movie. Imagine what the life of Henry Hudson on film, told through high adventure, would do for students studying American, British, Canadian history? One man, one river, one movie—and one hundred minutes later an example on the screen of how truly important the art of film can be would be proved. One day a series of movies—not documentaries, but movies brimming with humor, action, suspense, mystery, love, battles, evil and good—will be made dramatizing the story of the world as we know it from the beginning of time to the present; and this series, dubbed in all languages to be seen by anyone who goes to the films, will educate while it informs all the communities in all countries.

There is no art medium that can accomplish this and reach as many people as the art of the film.

Beethoven is always inspiring. At times his music can bring tears. So can a scene in a movie. What moment in the arts can bring a choke as does the moment in John Ford's *The Informer* when Gypo Nolan says to his Sinn Fein colleagues "I didn't know what I was doing"? To stir emotions is the goal of the artist. Rodin's *The Kiss*, Vinci's *The Last Supper* and the Louvre's *Tomb of Philippe Pot* treat directly with emotion. One cannot look at these works without tasting excitement, for the true artist brings something into existence that causes us to weep with grace or smile through tears. Pope said art was a steward that lives on managing the riches of nature. If that is true, then art is the midwife of nature. A landscape on canvas, a phrase on paper, a melody in the ear, "Good night, sweet prince" spoken on a stage, or the old priest's last wish fulfilled in Leo McCarey's film *Going My Way* when his 100-year-old mother arrives from Ireland, are works of human activity addressing humanity in different forms.

It is not enough that the artist carries his happiness with him. He must share it freely with the whole of mankind and there is no better channel than through the youngest of all the arts, the film.

Artists will always be jealous of one another and the tournament of talent can be as cruel as the ashes of defeat or nonrecognition; but the yellow sickness of envy, in the long run, serves to drive the artist on to be better than the one responsible for the jaundice in the soul. The same competition, fierce and often fatal, exists in the art of making a film.

There are novelists, dramatists and poets who do not consider the film a form of art. Needless to say, the majority of these creators are suffering from old-fashioned sour grapes. Most of them would give their last adjective to write a movie; the rest continue to deride the medium, reminding one that the cave man with the club probably derided his neighbor's engravings of Ice Age elephants on the walls of the cave. All right, then, what *is* art? It is emotional impulse indispensable to artistic expression. And no other expression fired the imagination as the movie. The mirage in *Lawrence of Arabia* is representational truth of a new interpretation—new because it is seen, felt and contributes to the viewer's intimate communion with realism and the rhythm of creation. To describe a mirage is one form. But to live it emotionally when it is part of a drama conveys to us sound, form, color, shape—a criterion of the work of art. If movies were made during the Biblical days imagine the fabulous knowledge we would have today of the people in those days, of their true habits, true outcries, true customs, true desires.

Art is the talent to exercise a form of expression that seizes the creator who did not look for it. It happened. At times it is a blessing, at other times a curse, but always it remains a monster of talent draining the artist from the beginning and continuing to plunge young and old into a world of their own, a world hard to accept or understand by those outside the compass of the artist.

What about the artist? What about those three prongs so important in the making of a movie? First there is the writer, then the director, finally the actor. The producer does not belong in this category since his responsibility is to produce the money to finance the film, or to hire the talent to make it, or to supervise the talent an executive producer has selected.

The writer is the Gibraltar, the base of the *pousse-cafe* of varied talents, the artist without which no camera will turn until words have been put on paper. Stories are the Fort Knox of movies. And a good story has always entertained people, back to the scribblings on cave walls in France. In the last decade a number of writers have become writer-directors, for they want to follow through their original thoughts, dialogue and pieces of business from typewriter to the shooting stage.

But what about the new writer? The new blood? The youth burning with ideas? Why is he not encouraged to help further the art of the film? A creator, new or old, should be artist, not pawn; should be given the chance and encouragement to uncover the rich vein of ideas that prompted him to turn his life and future to moviemaking. There are too many defeatists mourning for the good old days and, of course, the good old days began when time began. Enthusiasm of youth is the heartbeat of movies. New ideas are bred daily, new experiments fail and succeed, old barriers are broken down. A true artist does not rush into a board of directors' meeting but charges into a world of exciting ideas. There is no shortcut to talent. But, unfortunately, there are ways to bypass it, such as the great shotgun out of Wall Street booming away to drown out the cries of virgin artists. Despite a small group of moviemakers determined to put on film their original ideas, so many are echoing the call of the film world by replacing "What's the story about?" to "What's the business statement of the characters?"

If shortcuts are taken and new ideas discouraged, the creator will approach his inspiration with the feeling that to make a movie is a trade like repairing autos and his art will become a job because the excitement has been squashed like a gnat.

Youthful creators are eager to spread their enthusiasm but there are too many hurdles to overcome and they find that entertainment is no longer an emotion to sell, but cold business served on a supervised platter. True, the selling of a movie is a business, but the making of one, the actual creation of one, should remain an art.

The spirit that makes movies an art is being stifled but will never die. Today film creators feel the cold wind of economy. Studios are being divided like Caesar's Gaul into three parts: panic, fear, insecurity. "Be practical" is the battle cry of the backers. But the artist, unlike the banker, can't play "Heads I win, tails you lose."

This is not the only hurdle. There is censorship. Not the censorship of pornography. The creator instinctively censors himself. But the censorship of the man with the money. He will encourage the artist to come up with something different but automatically find fault with it because it *is* different. He has a censorship of emotions. That could be a death-blow to the artist. Not all producers are members of this club. Some really produce the inspiration, but generally they depend on someone else's works be it an original story, a novel, a play, an autobiography, a history or a musical play. There is nothing wrong in that. As a matter of fact, the keystone of financing movies is the producer who selects a story and is responsible for its purchase to be developed into a screenplay. But in the course of this a producer will often change the inspiration of the original work causing the creator's enthusiasm to commit suicide. Some will argue that producers have improved works they've recommended to New York to be purchased for Hollywood movies. True. But that is a rare miracle. The unfortunate hurdle the creator has to overcome is the movie moujik, the fine example of an operator who entices talent to destroy it. These moujiks are the real enemy of the creators making movies. These moujiks are the "packagers" who know friends who know friends who have friends that will put up money to back a picture. These moujiks are men who serve camouflaged arsenic-on-the-rocks to neophyte writers and directors and actors and whose attack on art has become so dehumanized that it is a miracle films are made at all under their supervision. This breed will pass. History has recorded their prototypes through the ages.

Another hurdle to overcome is the critic. Like death and taxes, the art world will always have them. Unless a critic, in his review, inspires the writer, director, actor, or composer with new reflections for the next idea, his review is utterly meaningless in the true sense of the critique. When a critic lacks the honest and creative imagination to bring clay figures to life he lacks the inspiration to inspire creators. It is a startling fact that if many of the film critics never had the chance to unbind themselves, films would still be made. What a dictatorship of ego when a man not only reviews a film, but seeks and finds pride in his own selection of words and ultimately enjoys his own musical phrases. An artist's Hell will always be paved with the skulls of critics and the bones of censors but despite them, the true creator will win eventually because art always had the artist and those who sponged on his talent. The spongers are the forgotten ones. Who remembers Jefferson's critic or Voltaire's pitiful censor? Demosthenes phrased it neatly: "The readiest and surest way to get rid of critics and censure, is to correct ourselves."

JOHN
FRANKENHEIMER
(1930-   )

Like Sidney Lumet, Franklin Schaffner and Delbert Mann, John Frankenheimer was part of the "golden age of television," a director of such series as *Playhouse 90* and the *DuPont Show of the Month*. When the star of live New York television began to dim, these men transferred their operations to Hollywood and began directing a similar string of ambitiously dramatic features. Often quite talky, the films made use of scripts by writers like Chayefsky, Inge, Serling, Vidal and Axelrod, men who were part of the same migration of TV and post-war Broadway writing and directing talent. The best of them soon adapted their talents to the older medium, and retained only the most useful elements of their earlier style. Frankenheimer was among those who successfully made the transition, and it would seem that the live-action values of his television experience contributed significantly to the success of such films as *The Manchurian Candidate* and *Seven Days in May*. In the early 60's American film criticism was in a pathetic state, and Frankenheimer in a prescient suggestion offers the French as a model to be studied. Although he does not mention the "new wave" by name, it is the work of critic-directors like Godard, Truffaut and Chabrol to which he refers. Unfortunately, while the general level of American film criticism may have improved somewhat since 1964, the creative interaction between filmmakers and film critics which he describes here has simply not yet come to pass.

CRITICISM AS CREATION
JOHN FRANKENHEIMER

A really creative critic is indeed a rare creature—even rarer, perhaps, than the creative artist. And his criticism often follows his personal bent. Hazlitt wrote superbly about acting, George Bernard Shaw wrote about the sort of play that ought to have been acted in preference to the play he had seen. Max Beerbohm wrote idiosyncratically about himself.

While I realize there is room and need for many different kinds of criticism, I have certain thoughts about what I might call the ideal film critic. I was quite surprised recently when a leading film trade publication reported that 85 per cent of the patrons of neighborhood theaters want straight-out factual reviews. They want to know the plot, who the stars are, and whether the movie is a frivolous comedy or a rugged adventure. They are not interested, apparently, in comments on the film.

This may be an informational service that the daily newspapers must give, but it is not my idea of film criticism. I have been very fortunate in the reviews I have received as a director but I don't feel that, if the reviews had been less favorable, they would have had much influence on my approach to the films I've directed since. I couldn't let destructive criticism affect me for very long or I would not be able to function as a creative artist. Of course, as all men do, I have an ego and it can be bruised for a while after reading a bad review. But I must be able within a short time to erase any damage or I could not survive as a creator. A man can be ruined by criticism, especially if it is what I call destructive or noncreative criticism. Hardy stopped writing novels after the critics' reception of *Jude the Obscure* and Tennyson was driven to altering his poems at the reviewers' bidding; he even contemplated leaving England.

The medium in which I work constantly reminds me of my

From *Saturday Review*, December 26, 1964. Copyright 1964 by The Saturday Review. Reprinted by permission.

John Frankenheimer and Burt Lancaster during the shooting of *Birdman of Alcatraz* (1962).

own limitations. But I must keep my ego, even a degree of arrogance, so that I can always strive to make the great movie, the ultimate expression. With such high hopes, it can only pain me to face what I consider to be irresponsible criticism. The ideal critic, at least one whom I would take seriously, must be able to communicate with me in cinematic terms. I should be able to sit down with that man and talk to him about specifics. He should be able to speak to me in English, not in cinematic jargon, about the actual making of a movie.

Henry Canby used to say about reviewing that he asked himself three questions: What was the creator trying to do? How well did he do it? Was it worth doing?

I welcome any critic who will honestly ask himself these questions about my work. But, for his answers to have much validity for me, he has to be aware of my intention, my execution, and the value of what I was doing, not only in general esthetic terms but in a specific filmic sense as well.

I think a further clarification of this point is the differentiation I once made between bad and terrible films. To make a terrible movie requires high skill and high ambition. Almost anybody can grind out a bad film. But what may only be a hair-breadth line between great and terrible is the result of the scope and complexity of elements that have to go into every motion picture. To make the whole great, everything from story to screenplay to cast to cameraman to cutting has to be great in turn. For example, when a critic reviews a foreign film and he doesn't understand the language in which it was made, an entire area of judgement is cut off from him. In this case, all that really matters are the images. If the picture is beautiful, that's likely to be enough. The dialogue may be awful, the actor's interpretation of the lines may be all wrong, but that entire aspect of the film is withdrawn from critical appraisal.

Up to this point I haven't yet completely delineated my ideal critic. There are, of course, individual men and women here and abroad writing about films whose views I do respect and whose opinions are of interest to me. It's the general level of criticism, and American criticism especially, that concerns me. I think the thing that most disturbs me about American film criticism is its lack of involvement with those people who are directly and creatively making movies. I do realize that it is difficult to achieve such a relationship in America for a number of reasons. Historically our movies have survived or sunk on the basis of their being popular entertainment. The movies and the intelligentsia—whoever they may be—never really got together. Very often, when an American-made movie does get artistic acclaim, it is so many years after it has been made that it is too late for the criticism to have any effect on the state of the cinema; e.g. *Citizen Kane*. We still retain to a certain degree the provincial attitude that we are not the center of artistic film excitement, even though we will certainly acknowledge the ultimate artistry of Chaplin and Griffith. I think the American critic is often quite unsophisticated about the product of his own country. An English drama critic once said, "Few things in journalism are simpler than condemnation. Young men often begin this way; they grow out of it, learning that nothing is more ingenuous than extreme sophistication." I think quite a lot of the critical writing in the United States expresses the point of view of youth.

It might be helpful at this point to consider French as opposed to American film criticism. For example, in France there is much more of an involvement of the critic, not only as a reviewer but as a creative intellectual force (perhaps too much so) with the film as a contemporary expression. He communicates with the makers of the film, the directors, cameramen, film editors. There is a dialogue going on between the makers and the critics of films, and this is what makes for real and pertinent criticism. The crossing of mind and mind and perhaps the influence of both upon each other is a healthy thing. A good director must love to make movies and there has to be an element of love in the relationship of the critic to the film. It is interesting to note that several French critics have become moviemakers and a few today even combine both vocations. Here, as in France, there should be a sense of immediacy in the entire *milieu* of the film critic. There should be tremendous excitement about what is going on here and now in this place and in this time.

If the state of the film does not engender excitement in the critic, he should react not with sarcasm and extreme sophistication but with something more akin to anger, which correlates very often with love. He should try to promulgate an atmosphere in which better pictures will be made. What I would like to see—and I'm sure some of my peers would disagree vehemently with me—is a love-hate relationship between the critic and the director. This would give me, as a creator of films, great stimulation.

There is, however, another field in which I feel the critic has a vital job to do. This is in helping to create, not only an informed public opinion, but a public love of the cinema; to help to form a generation of moviegoers who love the film not only as entertainment but as a unique art form. It is not an easy task because here the critic must tread the fine line between appreciation and cultism. I know that many will say that this can be done only on the level of the art film, on the plane of so-called high culture. But I would hope that this isn't necessarily the case. I believe that our greatest art form is the film. It belongs to our century, to our time. It is the only art form that so totally involves the onlooker, where in fact he cannot escape being involved. I would never encourage any cinema worship, but there are certain very real changes in attitude that might be brought about by the creative critic.

If the critic could influence the youth—that group which seems most to influence the taste of the nation—to want to see better movies, I am quite sure that more good movies would be made. Unfortunately, in America today so much money is involved in the making of a film that it must do very well at the box office even to make back the original investment. As creators in this field, we are dependent on the public and need a true climate of acceptance for our best efforts. I do not mean by this that my concept of the critic's job today is to give good movies good reviews. It goes far beyond that. I think that we need some great propagandists for the film as entertainment *and* art. I know that what I ask of the critic is extremely difficult. He must be able to communicate not only with me on my terms but with the public on its terms. I communicate through my films but I think that in many ways the film is the art form that most needs verbalization. Most people use films only as a means of escape. A good critic should stimulate them to discuss films, to argue about them, to become excited about them. His function in making final judgements about films is really much less important. I can't begin to say how this should be done or even if it can be done. If criticism could achieve this, then I feel that it would be a truly creative instrument.

GENE KELLY
(1912-   )

It has become relatively more common recently for screen personalities to promote themselves to director—Clint Eastwood being one very visible example. But in the 40's and 50's comparatively few were making the move, screenwriting, editing or even producing being a much more likely starting point. Dick Powell and Cornell Wilde were able to make the transition successfully, and often proved more interesting behind the camera than in front of it. But the films of director Gene Kelly have never quite achieved that special grace which radiates from the best work of dancer-choreographer Gene Kelly. A Broadway hoofer who achieved his greatest success in the original production of *Pal Joey*, Kelly won a Hollywood contract that soon established him as MGM's top song-and-dance man. As the spark plug of Arthur Freed's most expansive musical extravaganzas, Kelly raced through *Anchors Aweigh*, *The Pirate*, *An American in Paris* and many others, developing a personal approach to film dancing which made lavish use of the technical resources of the cinema in general and MGM in particular. The three films he co-directed with Stanley Donen (*On the Town, Singin' in the Rain, It's Always Fair Weather*) pointed the way to an integration of dance and narrative generally along the lines he indicates here, but somehow Kelly's later solo efforts have been considerably less interesting. When the chance came to direct *Hello, Dolly!* he seemed swamped by a scenario that reduced dancing to an afterthought, and the hoped-for *fin-de-siècle On the Town* never materialized.

SOME NOTES FOR YOUNG DANCERS
GENE KELLY

Many young dancers are puzzled by terms like "film dancing" or "cine dance." "What does it mean?" they want to know. "Isn't dancing the same, no matter where or how it's performed?" Technically, yes, and from the performer's standpoint, yes. But choreographically the staging and the concepts are, or should be, different.

To begin with, dancing loses much on film: it loses its third dimension the same way photographed sculpture does. But it loses even more than sculpture. Lost is the living, breathing presence and personality of the performer, and gone are the kinetic forces that make the strongest interplay between audience and dancer.

Has film dancing any advantage? Yes, of course. The modern movie musical gives us many. Because of the marvelous things film can do, we can take a dance into the streets, up in the air, on top of buildings, anywhere our imagination chooses. We can use film techniques (flashback, dissolve, etc.) to enable the dancer to say, "I was," instead of always, "I am." And we can take advantage of the dramatic story to build mood and character for the dance.

But with these advantages come added work, added difficulties, and, of course, added planning. It is now incumbent on the choreographer to see that the dance belongs in the film and is part of it. Otherwise, it is merely stage dance photographed. The dance must come out of (1) plot situations, (2) character development, or (3) incidents that enhance one of these two. When we study the best film dances, we see they have at least one of these ingredients—often all three.

But we should also look at the exceptions to the rule. If the

From *Dance Magazine*, September 1965. Reprinted courtesy of *Dance Magazine*.

Barbra Streisand with Gene Kelly on the set of *Hello, Dolly!* (1969), a singer's musical directed by a master of the dance musical.

story is about the theatre or the ballet, of course it must be stage dancing photographed, because that is what the story asks for. But even then the work can be enhanced by film techniques, as witness *The Red Shoes*. That story was about a ballerina in a ballet company. The performance took place on stage, but by the use of film techniques we looked into the thoughts and emotions of the dancer while she was dancing. We saw the girl in real life and the same girl in a ballet.

As to the dancer himself, if he is to play an acting role on film or TV that requires dancing, he must be able to master a variety of styles. It is obvious that if he is a truck driver in the story, he cannot get out of his truck and stand in 5th position. His movements must not take him out of the characterization. His movements even have to fit his costume. It follows that the "Bluebird" variation wouldn't be very suitable for the truck driver. And likewise, if the hero be D'Artagnan or Prince Charming, the movements assigned to the truck driver wouldn't fit them, nor their characterizations, nor costumes. The chore-ographer must choose a style and movement that will be suit-able—he must create from the character.

Now these problems exist for the performer in a stage char-acterization too, but the lines are not as rigidly drawn. The camera lens makes everything so cruelly real. What might be a lovely group of costumes in a stage set could look like a Hal-loween party through the lens. A romantic change of mood as the stage lights dim perceptibly could, through the camera, look like a power failure.

It's true that officially these problems belong to the art di-rector, the scenic designer, and the costume designer. But any experienced choreographer knows that he had better make them his problems too, or his hard work may lose its effect.

I suggest to young dancers that they can benefit greatly by studying dancing in motion pictures, not just from the point of view of observing techniques, but also to learn to judge how successfully the dancer on the screen has carried out his char-acterization—or how unsuccessfully.

· · ·

There's another whole field of dance photography which in-terests me, but which, amazingly, has barely been touched in this technical age. That is the photographing of all our leading dancers so that the next generation can see how they danced. My own generation has done very poorly at this, and I really hope that the coming generation will do much better. Just think how thrilling it would be if we could today see some footage of Nijinsky! Let's hope that fifty years from now young dancers will have available to them a dance film library that until now has been denied to us.

ARTHUR PENN
(1922-   )

In discussing *Bonnie and Clyde* in terms of "private morality and public violence" Arthur Penn was reacting to the
storm of outrage directed at the film from critics like *The
New York Times*' Bosley Crowther. The film's violent
excesses, including point-blank shootings and a notorious
slow-motion massacre, proved a watershed in the history of
graphic violence on the screen, the beginning of an era in
which public outcry would focus less on sexual escapades
than on violence and brutality. With America's chief filmic
watchdogs, the Production Code Administration and the
Legion of Decency, both on the ropes in the mid-60's,
Bonnie and Clyde appeared as a test case for "redeeming
social value" as the ultimate censorial yardstick. Over the
next few years this yardstick began to warp inconveniently
as communities were first greeted by Peckinpah and *A
Clockwork Orange*, then assaulted by *Street Fighter* and
The Texas Chain Saw Massacre. Penn himself seemed to
enjoy the controversy, and *Bonnie and Clyde* does fit
neatly into his own hotly debated body of work. Originally a New York stage and television director, Penn
first attracted attention with *The Left-Handed Gun*, and
with the exception of *The Miracle Worker* all of his subsequent work has evoked heated reaction both pro and con.
Today his supporters find such films as *Mickey One*,
Alice's Restaurant and *Little Big Man* among the few
American films worthy of comparison with Bergman, An-
tonioni and Godard—a concept which, in the dark days of
the 60's, would have been regarded with considerable
skepticism by the likes of Bosley Crowther.

BONNIE AND CLYDE:
PRIVATE MORALITY &
PUBLIC VIOLENCE

ARTHUR PENN

I don't think the original Bonnie and Clyde are very important except insofar as they motivated the writing of a script and our making of the movie. Whether they are violent or not violent, whether we are sympathetic to them or not sympathetic, doesn't matter. They were a part of an event, they were there when it was happening. So we hung our movie on them, but we don't confine it to them. This is not a case study of Bonnie and Clyde: we don't go into them in any kind of depth. They were the outlaws, they were the sports of nature, they were thrown off by the events of their day, and they did something about it.

At that time, there was no national police force: they were all state-confined police forces. When Ford made the V-8, which was sufficiently powerful to out-run the local police automobiles, gangs began to spring up. And that was literally the genesis of the Clyde and Bonnie gang. What happened was that they lived in their automobile—it was not unusual for them to drive seven and eight hundred miles in a night, in one of those old automobiles. They literally spent their lives in the confines of the car. It was really where they lived. Bonnie wrote her poetry in the car, they ate ginger snaps in the car, they played checkers in the car—that was their place of abode. In American Western mythology, the automobile replaced the horse in terms of the renegade figure. This was the transformation of the Western into the gangster.

Meanwhile, these very rural people were suffering the terrors of a depression, which resulted in families being up-rooted, farms being foreclosed, homes being taken away, by the banks, the *establishment* of their world, which in part was represented by the police. In the context of our film, Bonnie and

From *Take One*, Vol. 1, no. 6 (1967). Reprinted by permission.

Arthur Penn and Faye Dunaway on location for *Bonnie and Clyde*.

Clyde found themselves obliged to fulfill some kind of role which put them in the position of being folk heroes—violators of the status quo. Retaliators for the people. And, in that context, one finds oneself rooting for them and, unfortunately, we find ourselves confronted with the terrible irony that we root for somebody for a relatively good cause who, in the course of that good cause, is called upon to commit acts of violence which repel us.

When a man is in authority—in uniform (I'm now quoting Mack Sennett) it's twice as funny when he slips on a banana peel than when he isn't. And that seems to me to be the essence of what we are dealing with here—which was that violence directed against other people (let us say other people who shared Bonnie and Clyde's given social status) would not be funny—it would not be that hidden Freudian impulse in all of us which is to, somehow, bring the forces of authority at least one rung down the ladder. And if, in this case, Bonnie and Clyde brought them several rungs down the ladder, it was, perforce, funny. It's regrettable that we find it funny, but it's funny. When the President says something rather banal, it's funny. When somebody else says it, it's not very funny.

I don't think it is funny to see the policemen killed, although that doesn't mean there isn't a funny result visible in rather horrible things. I went through a long war, which was rather horrible and funny. There is no question about it: the character of humour in violence is an immediate and constant correlative. They are there, and they are there in almost equal quantities—that was my personal experience. In the films we were attempting to recreate that. The murders get less and less funny, and more and more particular because they begin to be identified with the murderers and, in that sense, we begin to understand the motivation for the murder. The killing gets less impersonal and, consequently, less funny.

With respect to *Bonnie and Clyde* and my other films (*The Left-Handed Gun, The Miracle Worker, Mickey One, The Chase*), I would have to say that I think violence is a part of the American character. It began with the Western, the frontier. America is a country of people who act out their views in violent ways—there is not a strong tradition of persuasion, of ideation, and of law.

Let's face it: Kennedy was shot. We're in Vietnam, shooting people and getting shot. We have not been out of a war for any period of time in my life-time. Gangsters were flourishing during my youth, I was in the war at age 18, then came Korea, now comes Vietnam. We have a violent society. It's not Greece, it's not Athens, it's not the Renaissance—it is the American society, and I would have to personify it by saying that it is a violent one. So why not make films about it.

I don't think one has to make a pre-judgement and say that, because I have strong pacifist tendencies, I must therefore report only pacifist behaviour. I think that would be hypocritical. In point of fact, being of a pacifist character or nature perhaps makes me more acutely aware of the character of violence as practiced among human beings, and it somehow interests me more. I find myself drawn to demonstrating it—to dealing with it. Maybe because I'm a coward: I mean, I wouldn't do any of these things—I don't like to fight, but I am intrigued by watching people fight and seeing it happen.

What I meant in *Mickey One*, for instance, was that we live in a violent time—we make a kind of bargain with violence in our own lifetime. We are in a violent era. And I have to emphasize that I don't mean "violence" only pejoratively—not only in its negative aspects. It's violent to get in an airplane and be in Montreal in an hour—it's a violent experience, it's an assault on the senses. It's an assault on the senses to get in an automobile and drive: it's an assault on the senses to do so many of the things that we do. It is the character of the modern world.

This is something that is really taking place in this society that people are not talking about, but that everyone is cognizant of. In the same way, we have all this stuff about pot and about LSD—all the mind-expanding drugs—all of that is going on. The cinema is always ten years behind the times. Cinema doesn't deal with it and yet kids thirteen and fourteen are talking about it—they're smoking pot. Let's face it: it should be dealt with, it's a part of the mores and customs of our time.

I'm getting less interested in the stage and more interested in the cinema. The Broadway stage is designed for a tiny little audience which can afford to pay ten dollars to go to see *How to Succeed in Business*. They consequently, are not a serious audience—one does not do serious work there. That doesn't mean that it's not a nice place to work, because you can make a good living there while you go out and make movies that don't necessarily make a lot of money.

Let's face it, there are no serious plays on Broadway. The

so-called serious play has the air of being stately and literary, but it does not really assault any of the fundamental values of its audience. Movies do—they move in on a highly personal level in the way that a book or a poem does. Plays don't do that. If we were dependent upon that audience that goes to Broadway, we would all be disappearing into one little frame of film in about five years—I mean, the theatre in New York is disappearing into the musical comedy, and that's it. You go in there, work for six or seven weeks—if the thing is a hit, you get a royalty for the rest of the run. Then you go off and make a movie.

There is a body of history and mythology about Bonnie Parker and Clyde Barrow which includes various estimates of their sexuality. We chose, among other things, the characteristic of *relative* impotence in Clyde as a condition not dissimilar from what my personal sense is of what their life was like in that period in the Southwest. It's a peculiarly puritanical society—a peculiarly rigid, moralistic society—and we were trying to distinguish between the rigid morality which could very well render somebody impotent at the interior, private level while at the same time he could exceed all limits of external morality and still feel at one with himself. It seems to me not too uncharacteristic of some of the things that are visible in the south of the United States today: a church-going, highly moralistic, highly puritanical society, which has integrated and made a part of itself a kind of violence against other human beings which, viewed from the outside, seems absolutely intolerable. It was that kind of disparity—between a private rigidity and a public violence—which we were trying to delineate in the film.

GENE SAKS
(1921-   )

Perhaps no other film director is so completely identified with Hollywood versions of Broadway successes as is Gene Saks. Originally an actor (he can be seen in *A Thousand Clowns, A Shot in the Dark,* and various other films), Saks became a director of Broadway comedies and musicals (*Enter Laughing, Half a Sixpence*) and describes here his first Hollywood experience, *Barefoot in the Park*. All of Saks' films have been adaptations from Broadway, occasionally of works he had originally directed on the stage. His great success with *The Odd Couple* and *Cactus Flower* was somewhat tempered by the reception of *Last of the Red Hot Lovers* and *Mame,* although these last two may have been more the victims of unfortunate casting than anything Saks had control over. Like the work of Herb Ross (who followed him from Broadway to Hollywood in 1969), Saks' films are visually undistinguished and concerned primarily with dialogue delivery. Note here the discussion of his relation with the (unnamed) cinematographer, Joseph La Shelle, one of the most important directors of photography in 60's Hollywood and a particularly close associate of Billy Wilder. "After awhile . . . I dared to suggest that he move the camera in or back," Saks remembers, a surprisingly deferential remark from a director of moving pictures. There is of course a similarity here to the story of Elia Kazan and his association with Leon Shamroy on *A Tree Grows in Brooklyn* (q.v.). But Saks remains primarily a producer's director, a writer's director, an actor's director. Given adequate support he can transfer his material to the screen without loss; but when he is poorly served by his collaborators there is little he can do.

"WELL, HOW DO YOU LIKE DIRECTING MOVIES?"

GENE SAKS

Ever since the first week of shooting my first picture I've been asked, "Well how do you like directing movies?" "Fine," I'd say, "I like it." Or at more eloquent moments, "Very interesting; it certainly is an experience!" I may even have said "It's a fascinating experience." I hope I didn't, but those were hectic days. I just might have.

Until now I couldn't stop long enough to sit down and give any thought to a more satisfactory answer. The fact is, it was like being thrown in the water without knowing how to swim. It's a bad time to give interviews.

Besides, since I had just come out from New York with only stage experience I was a bit defensive and sensed all sorts of implications in the question, like: "Don't you like it better than directing in the theatre?" "Isn't it more challenging?" "Wouldn't you rather live in Los Angeles?" "Cold in New York, isn't it?" And when we came to New York to shoot on location my New York friends asked the same question and the implications were: "Aren't you going to do plays any more?" "Are you going to live out there permanently?" And, "Have you sold out?"

But now that the first rough-cut preview is past and I have the knowledge that I did swim back to the boat, I can look less self-consciously at the question and see that it was generally asked without ulterior motives, and that people might really be interested in knowing my feelings about directing a motion picture in relation to directing a play, and whatever random thoughts I might have had about directing my first picture. Fair enough.

I love it. It was one of the best experiences of my life. I think this is true because despite the strangeness of a new medium, I

From *Action!*, March-April 1967. Reprinted by permission of the Directors' Guild of America.

could recognize my own work on the screen when I saw those first dailies. I was almost surprised to see that that was the way I had intended it. I no longer felt that I was in a different world. I knew that the most important things were still a good script and a good cast, and that despite its frightening powers, or lack of powers, the camera was still secondary to the two things I knew best—the actor and the story.

Being an actor, the art of acting has always been my first concern and interest. As a director, I've always given more attention to the acting than any other phase of a production. I suppose I feel that it's the area in which I have the most to give. My feeling is that there is no difference between good screen acting and good stage acting. If a performance is really good it will be good in both media. It may be effective in one medium and not the other, but this does not mean it is necessarily really good acting. Both on the stage and on the screen certain things can be gotten away with at certain moments, but a really first-rate performance can stand up either place. In the theatre I can be reached twenty rows from the stage though I cannot distinctly see the actor's face. I can feel his presence and what is happening to him even if his back is to me. He should make me feel the same involvement if the camera is close-up on his face.

However, the extent of his impact on me, given these two choices, is not in the power of the actor. It is in the power of the director, and the only place the director has this power is on the screen. In fact, on the screen he has an overwhelming number of choices, while on the stage he is, by comparison, severely limited. The usual practice, I imagine, on the screen, is to come in close to the actor's face for the moments of greatest importance. But I think important moments can be as effective from far away—as Fred Zinnemann chose to do in the trial scene of *A Man for All Seasons* when he placed the camera even further away than if the action were on stage in a theatre. This "long shot" was used at one of Paul Scofield's most important moments. For me it made the moment even more moving and eloquent. By keeping the camera back, I could see the entire hall with all the spectators, and I felt as if I were one of them, sitting on one of those wooden benches watching that trial.

This is actually an instance of using a stage picture in a movie. The relationship of the audience is similar to what an audience in the theatre would see, sitting where the fourth wall of that courtroom would be. Conversely, I have often tried to make the stage plays, especially the musicals I have directed, move like movies. I've tried to make scenes fade in and fade out by moving the scenery, dimming or raising the lights and even making the actors, at times, back off stage as the lights fade and the scenery moves off to appropriate musical underscoring. In this sense the theatrical instinct both on stage and on film are not so different.

With all its advantages, film has great restriction for someone accustomed to working only in the theatre. The restriction I felt most strongly at first was that of the camera lens cutting off my peripheral vision. If I sit in the tenth row of the orchestra in a theatre, I see both sides of the 32-foot proscenium opening, but the camera sees a picture of much less breadth. When actors are spread more than a few feet apart I must cut back and forth from one to the other (as my eye automatically does on stage). So I had to get used to keeping actors closer together or spreading them apart in depth rather than width. Before long I accepted this and learned to look through the camera before each shot. When I didn't, I regretted it.

I began work by rehearsing the cast two weeks on a taped floor plan of the set, much as live television was done a few years ago. Since I was doing a stage play (*Barefoot in the Park*), certain characteristics were inherent. It was many times more verbal than most movies. Scenes were often longer. Action was restricted to a small set, often in the same room. I was completely at sea as to where to put the camera and finally decided to concentrate on making the actors behave as I thought they should and then showed it to the cameraman and told him what I had to see. Thankfully, he saw what I saw. If he didn't see it, I'd keep adjusting the actors or the action until he did. After awhile, I got to know the geography of the set so well that I could sense where the camera would have to go from the demands of the action of the scene. Later I even dared to suggest that he move the camera in or back, or shift the angle a bit to make a picture that pleased me more. But generally, I learned that he had a very good sense of where to put the camera and when and how fast to move it.

At first, the waiting to light between setups came as a welcome respite and gave me a chance to think and plan ahead, but as I gained confidence in my ability, the waiting became annoying, though never as annoying as to the actors or the producer. Somehow I could always use that time to think about the next scene or to work with the actors.

The challenge of what to say to an actor between takes is enormous, and the actor must be made aware that he can do it better each time no matter how spontaneous or good the last take felt. Or if he feels he's failing, he must be given confidence by a new idea that will catch his imagination. Not easy while the technicians stand there waiting and the Assistant Director looks worried because you're ten pages behind. You keep thinking "Should I settle for that second take? It was pretty good." I don't think you should, because you don't get another chance tomorrow night as you do in the theatre. Each performance of a play brings you another chance. I have restaged scenes three months after a Broadway opening. I've always felt that given enough time, I could make the most impossible scene work, whether it be by rewriting, restaging, or changing the actor's performance in some way. I always feel there is an eventual solution on the stage.

Manipulating a play with a live audience night after night in a tryout is an important part of the total work in a play. Its importance cannot be measured. The interplay of the actor and the audience is absolutely essential in comedy. The actor can control the audience response in a way that can never be accomplished by the director in the cutting room. As far as I can see, at this point, spacing for laughs on film, based on reactions from a few previews, is not very reliable and extremely limited since it can be used only at points where there are cuts.

The movie director must make his scene work before any audience sees it.

To me, the two most important moments for a film director are the moment when he says "Print" and the moment the following day when he makes his choice of takes after seeing the "dailies." Then the director is most alone and most vulnerable and I found these moments the most difficult, because in choosing, you say, "I alone make this decision; I alone take the responsibility for it." These are as really "moments of truth" as any I can imagine, and there is nothing in the theatre to equal them for power or responsibility.

IDA LUPINO
(1918-   )

Daughter of the noted British music hall star Stanley
Lupino, Ida Lupino studied at the Royal Academy of
Dramatic Art and came to Hollywood in 1934. Although
she appeared in such important films as *Peter Ibbetson* and
The Gay Desperado, Lupino did not reach her full potential as an actress until the *film noir* 40's, particularly in
Raoul Walsh's *They Drive by Night, High Sierra* and *The
Man I Love.* The studio troubles which she describes here
may indeed have interrupted her acting career, but no
doubt also hastened her move into direction. When Ida
Lupino began directing she did not have to handle assignments dictated by studio programs, and instead she was able
to develop her projects through her own company. As
a result her films display the obsessions and consistencies
of a true *auteur*, obsessions unique in the immediate post-
war film scene. What is most interesting about her films
are not her stories of unwed motherhood or the tribula-
tions of career women, but the way in which she uses
male actors: particularly in *The Bigamist* and *The Hitch-
Hiker*, Lupino was able to reduce the male to the same
sort of dangerous, irrational force that woman represented in most male-directed examples of Hollywood *film
noir*. After a long hiatus in television she directed *The
Trouble With Angels* for Columbia (1966), a film she fails
to mention here. Feminist film historians have been slow to
pick up on Lupino, but they would do well to study her
strangely personal work—even that last, rather saccharine
retelling of *Mädchen in Uniform*.

ME, MOTHER DIRECTRESS
IDA LUPINO

On the set they all call me mother—the actors, the cameramen, the assistant directors, the grips, everybody. Not "that mother," just plain "mother." They started years and years ago when I had my own independent company and we made a policy of discovering and using young talent. Some of the kids, like Sally Forrest, who starred in *Not Wanted* for me nearly twenty years ago, were so young, it was natural for them to call me "mom" or "mother." From that time on the name was picked up by everybody so that now if somebody on the set should call me "Ida" or "Miss Lupino" I wouldn't know what to do.

I love being called mother. For when I am working I regard my production company, motion picture or television, as a very special kind of family: the producer, the writers, actors and the crew—we talk and feel and work things out together. We do everything together. We are indeed one big family—the happier the better.

I would never think of treating my cast and crew as anything else. I would never shout orders to anyone. I hate women who order men around—professionally or personally. I think it is horrible in business or in the home. I've seen bossy women push their men around and I have no respect for the gal who does the shoving or the man who lets himself get pushed around. I wouldn't dare do that with my old man. When we were married they said it would last three months. It's now seventeen years. It's because I don't ever order him around. I learned that. And I don't do it with the guys on the set. I say, "Darlings, mother has a problem. I'd love to do this. Can you do it? It sounds kooky but I want to do it. Now, can you do it for me?" And they do it—they just do it.

From *Action!*, May-June 1967. Reprinted by permission of the Directors' Guild of America.

Ida Lupino.

That goes for the leading man and the leading lady, too. I don't ever say, "Do this. I want you to stand here. I want you to do that." Having been an actress, I know what it is like to have been put into an uncomfortable position. If someone had come up to me and asked, "Does this feel comfortable?" it would have made all the difference in the world.

I would never think of indulging in what has come to be known as the woman's right to change her mind. As soon as I get a script I go to work on it. I study and I prepare and when the times comes to shoot, my mind is usually made up and I go ahead, right or wrong.

If I get a script in time, I prepare on a week-end. I go out on the backlot or to the sets on Saturday and Sunday, when it is nice and quiet, and map out my set-ups. I do that every time it's at all possible.

I went out on the backlot at Universal awhile back to prepare a *Virginian*, but I had forgotten those studio tours, you know, twelve thousand people traipsing all over the place over the week-end. There I was on the set, dripping wet in the killing heat, wearing no makeup, looking like a witch searching for an old house to haunt, and these tours started coming through. The bright young know-it-all guide would happily tell his eager charges, "And there, ladies and gentlemen, is the famous actress-directress Ida Lupino preparing for *The Virginian*." I tell you, I wanted to die.

I was in dire need of a friend and luckily I found one—a studio policeman. He sympathized with my need to work in peace and anonymity and so he'd keep track of the tour trams and when one was headed my way he'd rush over and, like a latter day Paul Revere signal, "The tourists are coming." Then I'd duck behind a building and hide.

I never planned to become a director. The fates and a combination of luck—good and bad—were responsible.

For about eighteen months back in the mid forties I could not get a job in pictures as an actress. Along with Annie Sheridan and Humphrey Bogart and John Garfield (we were all under contract at Warners) I was on suspension. It seems we were always on suspension, because we wouldn't do some of the shows we were asked to do. I don't know whether it was Jack Warner or who it was, but all I knew was that when you turned down something you were suspended and you stayed suspended. But I was the only one who had a radio clause in my contract, so I was able to keep alive as a radio actress. I was working every solitary week doing radio—Silver Theatre, with Boyer on his show, with Tyrone Power and C. B. DeMille on his LUX theatre.

Then Collier Young and I formed our own production company, called it "Film Makers." We co-wrote a screenplay about unwed mothers titled *Not Wanted* and put it before the cameras. We had just started shooting when Elmer Clifton, our director, suffered a heart attack. We were much too poor to afford another director so I stepped in and took over.

Those were thrilling days for us. We co-wrote and co-produced and I went on to direct each successive film. We discovered new talent and we did the kind of film that is "new wave" today. We tackled topics that were pretty daring at the time—unwed mothers, under the table pay-offs in amateur tennis, a hitchhiker's cross-country crime spree—thirteen murders, bigamy and polio. We would shoot those films in about thirteen days and at a budget of less than two hundred thousand dollars and they were "A" pictures. We were doing fine. But we made one fatal mistake.

We got talked into going into the distribution business. I opposed the move every step of the way. "We're creative people, we're picture makers," I argued. "We know nothing about distribution. Let's stay away from it." But I was outvoted and pretty soon we were out of business.

While we were still in operation a darling cameraman named George Diskant came over to do one of our films, *The Bigamist*, with Joan Fontaine and Edmund O'Brien and Edmund Gwenn. He said, "Ida, I'm in with a group called "Four Star" with some old buddies of yours, David Niven, Charles Boyer and Dick Powell. Why don't you come over and go into television?"

"Television," I screamed, "Really George, you're out of your mind."

Well the next thing I knew, David Niven called me up and said, "Lupy Kupy, I know you're against television, but come over and do a guest spot on our show anyway." I said, "Oh, Niv, I can't. The whole thing scares me."

He said, "Come and do just one."

So I went over and did this one shot. And the next thing I knew Dick and David said, "Now, look, you must be the guest who came to dinner—stay with us." So I stayed with them for two years. I was the guest who never left and became the fourth star of "Four Star Playhouse" and loved every minute of it—and never missed directing.

Then, during a summer hiatus, Collier Young asked me to direct Joseph Cotten in *On Trial*, and having been inactive as a director for so long I could not believe the offer. "Are you sure Mr. Cotten wants me?" I asked. And the answer was "yes." It was *The Trial of Mary Surratt* and I hadn't directed for so long I was nervous, so nervous.

That was my first directorial job after having acted for two and a half years. Then I did "Screen Directors Playhouse," then "Adam and Eve." I didn't direct any of those. I can't direct myself. I have to have somebody else do it. When that was over my husband had a new series and strangely enough, he and the producer asked me to direct the pilot. "No," I said, "I can't possibly do that. I'd be far too nervous directing you, Howard." He said, "I want you to do it." So I went ahead and did it and the show sold. Then I went on to do "Thrillers" and "General Electrics" and "Have Gun—Will Travels" and "Sunset Strips" and "Tates" and "Hong Kong," "Untouchables" and "Hitchcocks" and "Sam Benedicts" and "Novaks."

I did so many Westerns and action shows I was looked upon as a director who could not direct a *man and a woman* story. For a long time I couldn't get a job directing a love story. I could do a lot of soul searching and conjecturing on *that* state of affairs, wonder out loud why the male producers around town did not think a woman knew about love. It took Stanley Rubin of General Electric Theatre to get me to direct a love story between Anne Baxter and the present governor of California, Mr. Ronald Reagan.

Speaking of love stories and love scenes, I was offered a script awhile back that I still can't believe. I was asked to direct it, not act in it. It was something. And I'm no prude. I'll go to and enjoy a picture like *Room at the Top*. If you want to show a man and a woman in their relationship, fine, as long as it is done with taste. But if you want to show filth, I'd sooner starve, I won't do it. I don't see any reason for the rage of the moment where everybody has to be either bottomless or topless. Why, I don't know. There are so few pictures that you can go and see and take the kids. For instance, *Night Games*. You know, I don't know. I practically lost my lunch.

Now then, getting back to that script offered me. In one of the opening scenes, a party scene, a bunch of teen-agers are all, you know, fine. Flying. They run out of ice, so, one of the boys goes into the bathroom to fetch some out of the bathtub. But when he gets there, a young boy and a young girl are making love atop the cubes in the tub. Without interrupting them the boy reaches under and scoops out some cubes and puts them in the ice bucket and leaves. Then I got rather sick to my stomach.

I've had some offers to direct out of the country—in Spain, Italy and Greece—all thoroughly acceptable scripts. But I have my old boy and my daughter and I love them and life is too short for me to leave them and go flipping off for five or six or seven months. I just won't go.

I'll do all of my directing close to home. What I'd really like to do is pick up in 1967 where we left off some ten or so years ago, with an independent company, discovering new talent, writing our own scripts and making good provocative pictures at the right price. I am now polishing an original screenplay called *Murders and Minuets*, a suspense story that I'm really excited about. When I'm satisfied with the script I'd like to direct it. That's what we did for a decade and that's what I want to do again.

That's film making.

EDWARD DMYTRYK
(1908-   )

There has been surprisingly little written in Hollywood
about the creative function of film editing, except perhaps
on the most idealized level. The grim realities of production
have so confused responsibilities here that in print most directors concentrate their attentions on the script, the actors,
the camera—on anything but that question of "the cut."
Yet none would deny the role of editing in the success of
any film. The problem lies in the production end of the
studio system itself. "We'll fix it in the editing," is a powerful and sometimes chilling cry, for it implies that the
"mistakes" of writer, director or actors can be turned inside out by the proper manipulation of scissors and glue.
Unfortunately it is all too often some producer, distributor
or star who wields the shears. Edward Dmytryk began in
film as an editor, cutting the films of Paramount's finest
directors throughout the 30's. In 1935 he began directing
B-pictures on the side, and he emerged in the 40's with a
reputation for briskly paced, low-budget thrillers. *Murder,
My Sweet* and *Crossfire* established him as a major director,
but Dmytryk's career unraveled when he was imprisoned
as one of the "Hollywood Ten." On his release he re-
nounced his earlier political alliances and was soon rein-
stated as a top director, working during the 50's on such
major projects as *The Caine Mutiny* and *Raintree County*.
But Dmytryk's films by this point had grown impersonal
and mechanical, the taut personal style of his 40's classics
now a thing of the past.

THE DIRECTOR AND THE EDITOR
EDWARD DMYTRYK

Back somewhere in the dim, distant mid-thirties at Paramount, Baron Rothschild was being shown the studio. He was brought to my cutting room for a briefing on the most mysterious art in pictures. After about half an hour he said, "Well, it would seem that this is where pictures are really made." I modestly agreed with him. Then, I became a director . . .

Naturally, my opinions were soon modified. But if anyone expects a completely non-biased attitude toward cutting, he can stop right here. I think cutting *can* be an art, I think it *can* be creative, I think editors *are* underpaid, I believe they *are* greatly undercredited. But I think most of the problems are caused by the nature of the job, or the nature of the cutters themselves.

First, let me get one huge source of controversy out into the open; the question of "right"—right of first cut, right of creative judgment, etc. In our own guild, the annual meetings invariably erupt with cries of, "Let's fight for the right to control the cutting of our pictures." It's been interesting to note that these cries almost always come from our youngest, least experienced members, men who would probably strangle in their own trims if they were placed at the bench and told, "There, go ahead, cut!"

I don't believe I've ever heard one acknowledged, top-flight director, young or old, ask for the right to cut his pictures; he's already got it. That's one of the interesting things about our business; anyone who truly deserves the managements' confidence, almost invariably has it. And the same thing holds true for editors. But first . . .

Cutting *is* a mysterious art. Excluding, of course, those who came up through the ranks (and slowly enough to really learn

From *Action!*, March-April 1969. Reprinted by permission of the Director's Guild of America.

Edward Dmytryk (without hat) on location in Louisiana swamp for *Alvarez Kelly* (1965). Director of photography Joseph Mac-Donald with hand on camera (right).

what it was all about) most directors are somewhat in awe of the cutter. Then, too, they feel they are somewhat at the cutter's mercy—and so they are. It is a fact of nature that we tend to distrust, often fear, the strange or unfamiliar. If we are in a position to do so, we will often put it down, even if our well-being depends on it.

To most directors, cutting is a mystery. They know what

they want to see up there, but they don't know how to go about getting it. They are, as I said, largely in the cutter's hands. And often, the cutter is the one person they know least of the entire company. They work closely with the cameraman, the assistant director, the actors and the crew—they establish a rapport. But during shooting they usually get to see the editor about fifteen minutes a day. To a certain extent, they remain comparative strangers until the end of shooting.

It's difficult to freely trust your lifeblood to a stranger. This is why, when possible, a director will hang on to a cutter he knows and trusts for dear life. However, in these days of freelance endeavours, this has become a progressively rarer situation. Under such conditions, the editor is often unconsciously "put down." His salary is a case in point. In my opinion, based on his contribution, I would say that he deserved at least as much as the cameraman. I've never seen bad photography ruin a really good picture; *Open City* is a case in point. I have seen bad cutting ruin a really good picture, and good cutting restore it—not once, but a number of times.

Now, to get back to "right." To me, this must go along with talent. The best directors make "their" pictures (even though they may, sometimes, have to fight a little). The best cutters make "their" cuts, and almost always without contractual guarantees. In my entire career as a cutter I was only once interfered with—told exactly where and how to cut. The result was a catastrophe, and recognized as such by the director and the studio executives. A producer was the heavy in this case.

Among other things, this experience taught me that one of a cutter's chief talents must be the ability to interpret the director's and/or the producer's desires. Not too infrequently, these are expressed in a kind of double-talk (not all directors are articulate). Some of my toughest moments as a cutter were concerned with trying to figure out just what the hell the director did want. However, having once decided on an interpretation, I set about achieving it in my own way. The result is what counts, and no good director is going to argue with a good result.

Now, I think all good directors know what they want on

the screen, and it is the function of good editors to see that they get it. I do not think they can, except on infrequent occasions, improve on the director's conception. The poor cutter can, and frequently does, diminish it. At best, what sometimes happens is that the director will have a sequence he's not quite sure of. He will cover it literally from all angles, then say to the cutter, "Go ahead. See what you can do with it." And that is a good cutter's delight.

Beyond that, nothing can stop a cutter from showing a sequence cut his way, even if it isn't what the director had originally conceived. For my part, though I always go over every sequence with my cutter before he picks up the scissors, I always have an understanding that if he can add something brilliant he will earn my gratitude. But I must be convinced his way is better than mine. And, once or twice, it has been.

It will be noticed that I use the adjective "good" a lot. This is a "thing" of mine. I do not believe you can carry on a discussion of this sort on the supposition that all cutters are good—all directors are good. It just isn't so. Of all the crafts in films, I believe the art of editing has fewer top-flight practitioners than any other. I can't think of ten cutters I would leave my film with, secure in the knowledge that they would, by themselves, get the best out of the film I gave them.

This paucity of top-flight cutters is due to several causes.

First, some of the most creative cutters move up the line to directing or producing, though it is by no means true that a fine cutter will necessarily make even a fair director. (I've known several excellent editors who have failed as directors though their editorial skill remains unchallenged.)

Second, and I think most important, is that cutting is no longer attracting the more gifted people. Since the establishment of an arbitrary eight-year apprenticeship, I have known a number of talented young men who have opted for other fields because they simply did not want to wait that long for an opportunity. This ruling seems incomprehensible to me. Even a doctor, to whom I may have to trust my life, does not have to apprentice himself for eight years before he can practice. But a cutter?

As a side note: my own son chose to start as an assistant director, though he would have liked to go into the cutting room. After the minimum time as a second assistant, he became a first assistant (not to me—I'm against nepotism) and now earns more than a cutter of years' standing. If he had gone into cutting, he'd still have years of apprenticeship ahead of him, at an apprentice's salary.

I have known young men who, after six months in the cutting room, could do a better job than some twenty-year veterans. After all, experience can sharpen brilliance, but never create it.

Third, communication. The very nature of the job discourages the kind of relationship which should exist between the director and the cutter. I mentioned earlier the mistrust some directors have, often subconsciously, of the whole process of cutting. This, of course, is due to insecurity. Yes, Hortense, many directors are insecure, too.

The best way to eliminate that insecurity is by adequate communication. Now, the director, by definition, is the busiest man in the company. He usually sees the editor at the end of a long, busy day when he looks at the rushes. Sometimes the cutter will wander out on the set and spend a half-hour or so— even then he rarely has a chance to say more than "Hi."

Is it any wonder that most directors feel the cutter is half a stranger?

Actually, this whole problem was beautifully met once, to the benefit of studio, directors, producers, cutters and pictures. That was at Paramount, through the '30s and '40s. George Arthur set up a department (later ably carried on by Chuck West) which broke new ground, but since has been discarded, as have a number of other good practices in the reorganization of our film studios.

According to Arthur's plan, editors stayed on the set with the directors, to be used or not, as the directors saw fit. In the best instances, they advised the director on the need for additional shots for optimum cutting effect, the elimination of some angles of no real value, sometimes actually worked out the camera set-ups (as in the case of some stage directors, unfamiliar with films), headed second units and, generally, acted as bouncing boards for the directors' ideas.

In the worst instances, they had a lot of time on their hands, but were still able to get far better acquainted with the director and his ideas regarding the film. A man called a "first cutter," really a top assistant, put together the first cut under the supervision of the editor. When the shooting was completed, the editor could take over the actual final cutting or, as happened in some instances, simply continue supervising.

The advantages are obvious. During that period Paramount developed a far greater number of excellent cutters than any other studio, more cutters moved on to higher positions or greater responsibilities, and the director-cutter relationship was never at a higher level. Nor, incidentally, were the salaries at any other studio nearly as good.

To borrow an old saw—most directors feel pretty lonely up there. In my experience, most would like to have somebody to bat the ball with. A cameraman has his own duties, and is usually not a story man. An assistant is generally the second busiest man on the set. I often used a so-called "dialogue director" purely for this purpose. His job was not to direct dialogue—he would have been fired if he had tried—but to act as a "creative assistant." At least five of my dialogue directors went on to directing or producing.

I have always thought that no one could fill this spot better, more usefully, more economically than a creative cutter. Then, an editor's desire for a creative outlet could be fully realized, and a film could truly become "ours" and not "mine" or "mine" and "mine."

ROGER CORMAN
(1926-   )

Roger Corman has for twenty years been one of the most
active of Hollywood independents, first as a producer-
director associated with American International Pictures,
and more recently as a producer-distributor with his own
company, New World Pictures. Between 1955 and 1970
Corman directed some forty-eight features, nearly all on
phenomenally small budgets. His genius from the start was
as a producer, putting together deals, raising money, and
getting his films made on the tightest possible schedules—as
tight as two and a half days in one case. Corman's first films
were westerns, those perennial subjects of low-budget film-
making, but soon he moved over into science fiction and
horror, building an underground reputation with films like
It Conquered the World and *Attack of the Crab Monsters*.
In 1960 he began work on a more elaborate series of hor-
rors, the Vincent Price-Edgar Allan Poe cycle that finally
won him serious critical attention—not all of it good—from
French and British critics. *The Wild Angels* was chosen
to open the 1966 Venice Film Festival, perhaps the peak
of Corman's critical acclaim, but he cut back his own directorial output after this (it had been as high as six or eight
films a year at one point). Since 1971 he has expressed little
interest in directing, and instead devotes his energies to
New World Pictures, perhaps the most successful of the independent operations to spring up in Hollywood in the 70's.

THE YOUNG FILMMAKERS
ROGER CORMAN

The close of the last decade has given us all much to think about in political, social and economic terms which has a bearing on the changing state of the motion picture industry. It is evident that the greater percentage of motion picture audiences are in the under-30 age bracket. We have seen that films which appeal to them on a wide level can be big box-office—particularly if they also draw in their parents and other veteran filmgoers. It is not surprising, therefore, that our attention is drawn to the phenomenon of the increasing emergence of young filmmakers and would-be filmmakers. Where do they come from, what do they know, and do they have any staying power?

First of all, I'd like to preface my thoughts on the subject with the comment that my sympathies are pretty much on the side of young filmmakers—if only because it still comes as somewhat of a shock these days when I see myself referred to as a *veteran* filmmaker. I did not find it easy to get a start in the motion picture business myself and once I had established myself as a profitably independent filmmaker I found it enjoyable and stimulating to back a number of young filmmakers who have since gone on to further successes. Among the young directors I gave a start to were: Irv Kershner, Francis Coppola, Monte Hellman, Peter Bogdanovich, Dan Haller and Bruce Clark. They had various backgrounds, mostly including some film school background. Francis Coppola and Bruce Clark were star UCLA film school graduates. Francis Coppola has since, of course, become a notable director and innovator within the organization field and will in turn no doubt introduce young filmmaking proteges of his own. Bruce Clark has just finished *The Ski Bum* for Joe Levine only a year or so after writing,

From *Journal of the Screen Producers' Guild*, June 1970. Reprinted by permission.

Roger Corman (left) directing Peter Fonda in a scene from *The Wild Angels* (1965). Corman's assistant, Peter Bogdanovich, holds script at right.

directing and producing his first professional feature film for me. Dan Haller was the art director on one of my most successful cycles of horror films and since my backing him as a director has most recently completed *Pieces of Dreams* starring Robert Forster for United Artists. Peter Bogdanovich was an enterprising young journalist and film critic when I first met him and hired him to write, direct and produce a horror film, *Targets*, starring the late Boris Karloff. Monte Hellman had a UCLA film school background and a deeply serious commitment to filmmaking as a valid art form. He is now preparing a major film at Cinema Center. Nevertheless, despite some considerable differences in experience and viewpoint I would say that all the young filmmakers I selected had one thing in common—a wide knowledge of films and a considered personal response to what they had seen.

This will be found to be equally true, I believe, of the rising generation of filmmakers. Aspiring young filmmakers today grow up in what essentially might be called a Film Culture. There are film departments in colleges all over the country, the study of film and filmmaking is by no means limited to faculties in California or New York universities. Where ten years ago there might only have been a rather shaky film society supported by a few devotees there are now flourishing film departments. Or, to look at it from another point of view, the young student who as little as ten years ago would have been writing a novel or producing plays now turns to filmmaking. He grows up, I would say, quite unlike the perhaps solitary film addict of a decade or so ago, because film as the culture reflecting the attitudes and concerns of contemporary society, the idea that film is the most *relevant* art form and commercial enterprise, has become the common assumption of the entire campus, so to speak, not the fanatical conviction of the few. Therefore, the young filmmaker, student or otherwise, today shares a certain common background with his contemporaries. The common point of reference between, let us say, an arts major, a graduate in biochemistry, a college drop-out and a rock musician is very likely to be contemporary films. One would expect and hope, therefore, that young filmmakers are increasingly in a position to know what their contemporaries, the audience by and large for whom they will be making films, respond to in the cinema.

Perhaps it should be added, however, that there is a possible danger or disadvantage that appears at times to result from growing up in a film culture in the way I have described. First of all, with regard to film school training, there is the obvious point that as film becomes a more and more popular option among college students it will attract a number of young people who want to coast along easily, doing something pleasant; so that not every graduate of a Film School is going to reflect the quality or usefulness of its training. However, the most dedicated and ambitious of young student filmmakers cannot but benefit from film school training and the increasing competition amongst young filmmakers. The other, and more insidious danger, is that young filmmakers who grow up with every opportunity to learn about filmmaking, both its rudimentary essentials and new experimental directions, to criticize the accepted working conventions and collaborate with each other in ways to revise or even reject them totally, are rather likely then to expect to be given opportunities to make films. The young filmmaker, I suspect, will always be better advised to hold the conviction of the rebel—that the Establishment is not going to step down automatically in favor of youth because the Establishment (whoever they may be at any given time) wants to go on making films, and making films profitably, too.

A question which is probably going to be brought up time and time again in the near future is whether the new generation of filmmakers, starting to work at a transitional period in the motion picture industry which is seeing considerable changes in the old *star* and *studio* system, will have any staying power. I believe a large percentage of them will prove to have such tenacity and versatility. Those who are dedicated enough and determined enough. Others will undoubtedly find their level in other areas, such as television or commercials.

With reference to future trends in the industry and the way in which these may affect young filmmakers I believe that there will continue to be a valid need for studios for certain kinds of work, but that the majority of films in the future will be shot on natural locations. My last two films were shot entirely on location. So aspiring young filmmakers can gain valuable experience by shooting their first films, short subjects or otherwise, on natural locations, on or around the campus, anywhere, because they will be shooting in conditions essentially similar to what they will later hope to be handling professionally. I believe also that there is great potential in new channels for reaching audiences, not Pay TV, but some kind of cartridge or cassette to play in the home.

Finally, there is the question of whether the young filmmaker is likely to become an innovator. Hopefully some of them will. With a greater acquired knowledge of what has been done in films before, they may learn to distinguish between true originality and the pleasurable experience of simply seeing or doing something oneself for the first time. There is the possibility that much can be achieved through cumulative experience: filmmaking may well follow the natural laws governing other arts and sciences, namely that a masterpiece, an apparent breakthrough of some kind, is not born out of the blue but is in part made possible by previous achievements.

It may also be true that there are very few conceptual filmmakers. By this I mean conceptual ability as applied to film, the ability not simply to find a good subject, a great story or idea, but to see also how to deal with it in an unexpected way, the ability to grasp how a strong statement or point of view can be made cunningly, so that an audience will adopt it as their own. I would say that Stanley Kubrick's *Dr. Strangelove* was an example of this kind of ability. On the whole, I think you could give a young filmmaker a fight in a bar, say, to shoot and he would be likely to find it difficult as a *pure action* scene. You could probably tell a non-film school, non-Film Culture director, to shoot a fight in a bar and he'd do it with ease. Young filmmakers are liable to be more conceptually ambitious, but whether they can fulfill that ambition is another question. I cannot emphasize too strongly that the essence of film is *movement*—acquiring a film sense is largely a matter of recognizing this, developing a sense of rhythm in visual terms. The watchword of the under-30's is very much against linear thinking, demonstration by verbal logic. If the emergent young filmmakers really are learning to think visually their contribution to film may be a very vital one.

WILLIAM FRIEDKIN
(1939-   )

One of the most complicated of all filmmaking tasks is the creation of an elaborate action sequence, a project involving the seamless integration of a series of highly specialized skills. Quite frankly the problems involved are more often logistical than aesthetic, and the overall operation can easily take on the aspect of a major military maneuver—especially when there are vehicles involved. On *Ben-Hur* Andrew Marton was faced with recreating a well-known literary scene, with the added responsibility of accurate period reproduction, but William Friedkin's problems with *The French Connection* were quite different. While there was no popular text to adhere to, a "classic" sequence had to be constructed from scratch, and then played out not on a closed set but in the wintertime streets of the borough of Brooklyn. Friedkin's lucid, almost clinical analysis is a model of its kind, and reflects the organizational skills so clearly demonstrated in the film, the kind that wins awards from fellow directors who have faced similar problems themselves—although the very seamlessness of the operation makes the "direction" invisible to the typical audience. *The French Connection* was the film that firmly established Friedkin's reputation, which previously had rested on a lot of television work and such films as *The Night They Raided Minsky's*. Its success allowed Friedkin his choice of projects, and interestingly enough he has in the past six years labored over only two films, both among the most complex productions of the 70's, *The Exorcist* and *Sorcerer*.

ANATOMY OF A CHASE
WILLIAM FRIEDKIN

About two and a half years ago, Phil D'Antoni told me the story of *The French Connection*. It was then a book he had just optioned, based on the true story of an important narcotics investigation that took place in New York City between 1960-1962. I thought it was a terrific story filled with fascinating characters.

The narrative as set forth by Robin Moore contained all the raw material for an exciting screenplay, except for a chase sequence. It was on this point that D'Antoni and I were in full agreement: What we needed most of all was a powerful chase. In fact, our thinking frankly followed formula lines: A guy gets killed in the first few minutes; checkerboard the stories of the cop and the smuggler for approximately 20 minutes; bring the two antagonists together and tighten the screws for another 10 minutes or so, then come in with a fantastic 10-minute chase. After this, it was a question of keeping the pressure on for another 20 minutes or so, followed by a slam-bang finish with a surprise twist.

D'Antoni, of course, had been the producer of *Bullitt*, which offered what was probably the best car chase of the sound film era. It was because of this that I felt challenged to do another kind of chase, one which, while it might remind people of *Bullitt*, would not be essentially similar.

I felt that we shouldn't have one car chasing another car. We had to come up with something different; something that not only fulfilled the needs of the story, but that also defined the character of the man who was going to be doing the chasing—Popeye Doyle, an obsessive, self-righteous, driving, driven man.

At this point, I should say that the chase sequence in *Bullitt*

From *Action!*, March-April 1972. Reprinted by permission of the Director's Guild of America.

William Friedkin setting up the *French Connection* chase in the streets of Brooklyn.

is perhaps the best I've ever seen. When someone creates a sequence of such power, I don't feel it's diminished if someone else comes along and is challenged by it to do better. The chase in *Bullitt* works perfectly well in its own framework, and so, I feel, does the one in *French Connection*. When a director puts a scene like that on film, it really stands forever as a kind of yardstick to shoot at, one that will never really be topped. That will always provide a challenge for other film makers.

CONCEPT

After I had agreed to direct the film, D'Antoni and I spent the better part of a year working on what turned out to be two unimaginative, unsuccessful screenplays.

The project was eventually dropped by National General

Pictures, and lay dormant for about 10 months. During that time, D'Antoni and I continued to work on it. I had been involved in production and post-production work on *Boys in The Band*, so my own involvement then was a kind of sideline.

Every studio in the business turned the picture down, some twice. Occasionally, we would get a glimmer of hope, and during one such glimmer, we contacted Ernest Tidyman, who had been a criminal reporter for the New York *Times*, and had written a novel called *Shaft*, the galleys of which D'Antoni had read and passed on to me. Tidyman had not written a screenplay before. But we felt, because of what we read of *Shaft*, that he had a good ear for the kind of New York street dialogue for *The French Connection*.

Tidyman agreed to work with us on an entirely new script. Up to this point, we had a storyline that was pretty solid, but we had nothing in the script that indicated the kind of chase we eventually wound up with. We had spent a year and gone through two screenplays without indicating what the chase scene would be—because we didn't really have one.

One day D'Antoni and I decided to force ourselves to spend an afternoon talking, with the hope that we could crack this whole idea of the chase wide open. We took a walk up Lexington Avenue in New York City. The walk lasted for about 50 blocks. Somewhere during the course of it, the inspiration began to strike us both, magically, at the same time. It's impossible for either one of us to recall who first sparked it, but the sparks were fast and unrelenting.

"What about a chase where a guy is in a car, running after a subway train—"

"Fantastic. Who's in the car?"

"Well, it would have to be Doyle."

"Who's he chasing?"

"Well, that would have to be Nicoli, Frog Number One's heavy duty man."

"How does the thing start?"

"Listen, what would happen if Doyle is coming home after having been taken off the case and Nicoli is on top of Doyle's building and he tries to kill him?"

". . . and in running away, Nicoli can't get to his car."

"Doyle can't get to his."

"Nicoli jumps on board an elevated train and the only way Doyle can follow is by commandeering a car."

"Terrific."

And so on.

During that walk, D'Antoni and I ad-libbed the entire concept of the chase to one another, each building upon the other's thoughts and suggestions. The next afternoon, we met with Tidyman and dictated to him our mutual concept. Tidyman took notes, then went off and put the thing in screenplay form. At this point, the chase was all we needed to complete a new draft of the script.

The original draft of the chase ran about five or six pages of screenplay. It was very rough and hadn't the benefit of research to establish whether or not what we were proposing was possible.

The script in its new form was at that time submitted to 20th Century-Fox, namely David Brown and Dick Zanuck, who decided to make the picture.

It then fell to me to determine how we could go about shooting this sequence, which we always considered to be the most important element in the film. First, we had to contact the Metropolitan Transit Authority of New York City. This was done by our associate producer, Kenny Utt, together with production manager Paul Ganapoler. They had a series of meetings with Jules Garfield, the public relations representative for the Transit Authority, who agreed in principle to our concept, but told us that there were numerous inaccuracies involved in what we were proposing. He said that everything having to do with the operation of the elevated train was inaccurate. We were suggesting that the runaway train crash into a stationary train that was just outside the station, but it was not possible for such a crash to occur because of safety precautions. He said that if we would agree to more accurate details, he would allow us to use the facilities of the Transit Authority.

Utt, Ganapoler and I met, together with representatives of the Transit Authority Engineering, Safety and other departments, all of whom criticized the sequence as written. They indicated to us what would be more accurate. Happily, their suggestions were more exciting than what we had conceived.

For instance, I discovered that it was impossible for an elevated train to screech to a sudden halt. If the motorman, when threatened by a gunman, had a heart attack and took his hands off the forward mechanism, it would operate as a kind of safety brake, or deadman's brake, and would cause the train to come slowly to a stop.

I also learned of a device called a trip-lock, which is placed at intervals along the tracks. This is a small yellow hammer that lowers to allow the smooth passage of a train when the signal light is green. If the signal is red, the trip-lock is in an upraised position. If a train goes through a red light, the trip-lock raises and strikes the wheels and causes them to gradually slow down. This makes the train come to a gradual stop, rather than a sudden brake.

One thing the Transit Authority people were adamant about: There would be no crashing of the two trains. We agreed to this. We ultimately came up with a suggestion of a crash, not one that is graphically presented.

I worked with the TA people for several weeks. Then I went ahead and wrote a new sequence that was considerably longer than the first and more accurate in terms of what would actually happen, given the fictional circumstances that we devised. This sequence was approved by the Transit Authority and we had a go-ahead.

EXECUTION

As everyone knows, most films are not shot in sequence. Our chase scene was shot entirely out of sequence, and over a period of about five weeks. It did not involve solid day-to-day shooting. One reason was that we were given permission to use only one particular Brooklyn line, the Stillwell Avenue, running from Coney Island into Manhattan. After numerous location scouting trips with Utt and Ganapoler, we found a section of the Stillwell Line that we thought would be ideal, stretching from Bay 50th Street to 62nd Street.

It seemed right because the Marlboro housing project was located just two blocks from the entrance of the Bay 50th Street Station. The project was perfect for Doyle's apartment building, and it stood directly across the street from the Stillwell tracks.

Together with Utt, Ganapoler, my cameraman, Owen Roizman, and the First Assistant Director, Terry Donnelly, I proceeded to plan a shooting sequence. We knew that in shooting in the middle of winter, we might run into a number of unforeseen problems. But no one could have guessed at some of the ones we were eventually hit with.

I decided to divide the shooting into two logical segments: The train and the car. They had to be shot separately, of course, but at times we had to have both for tie-in shots.

I had hoped for bad weather because it would help the look and the excitement. But, of course, I also hoped for consistent light. We told ourselves that even if the light was not consistent, we had to shoot anyway; our schedule and our budget demanded it. I would try to accommodate the cameraman if the light was radically different from day to day.

If we had a weather report saying the light was going to be different on one day from what it was on the preceding day, we would try to schedule something else. This occurred on a number of occasions. As it happened, the New York winter of 1970-71 was not a mild one. Although there was little snow or rain, there was a great deal of bright sunlight. It was painfully cold through most of December and January, when the chase was filmed.

Very often it was so cold—sometimes five degrees above zero—that our camera equipment froze, or the train froze and couldn't start. One day, the special effects spark machine didn't work, again because of the cold. Once the equipment rental truck froze. We seldom had four good hours of shooting a day while inside the train.

One day, after having filmed for six consecutive days with bright sunlight, there was time when we had to shoot a sequence with the car running underneath the tracks. In the morning, after everyone had arrived at location, a massive snowstorm began. Needless to say, we didn't shoot any chase that day.

A part of our concept was that the pursuit should be happening during a normal day in Brooklyn. It was important that we tie in the day-to-day activity of people working, shopping, crossing the street, walking along, whatever. This meant that while the staging had to be exciting, we had to exercise great caution because we'd be involving innocent pedestrians.

The Transit Authority allowed us one section of express track on the Stillwell Avenue Line from Bay 50th Street to 62nd Street, a total of eight local stops and about 26 blocks. But there was a catch: We could only shoot between the hours of 10 in the morning and three in the afternoon!

This was the time between the rush hours. Quitting at three o'clock was a hardship, because it meant we would only have half a day to shoot with the train. Starting at 10 was also a problem, because we had to break at 1 p.m. for a one-hour lunch. This meant, in effect, that we had really less than five good hours of shooting each day. It also meant that we would have to be so well planned that every actor, every stuntman, and every member of the crew knew exactly what was expected of him. It meant that I would have to lay out a detailed shot-by-shot description of what was going to wind up on the screen, before I had shot it.

THE BEST-LAID PLANS

Some days we planned to film under a section of elevated track and arrived to find that section of track being repaired. So we had to change our schedule and try to shoot something else in the script.

Five specific stunts were planned within the framework of the chase. These were to occur along various points of the journey of the commandeered car. They were to be cross-cut with shots of Doyle driving fast and with the action that was going on in the train above.

A word about the commandeered car. It was a brown, 1970 Pontiac, 4-door sedan, equipped with a 4-speed gear shift. We had a duplicate of this car with the back seat removed so we could slip in camera mounts at will. The original car was not gutted, but remained intact so that it would be shot from exterior.

The entire chase was shot with an Arriflex camera, as was most of the picture. There was a front bumper mount, which usually had a 30- or 50-millimeter lens set close to the ground for point-of-view shots. Within the car, there were two mounts. One was for an angle that would include Gene Hackman driving and shoot over his shoulder with focus given to the exterior. The other was for straight-ahead points-of-view out the front window, exclusive of Hackman.

Whenever we made shots of Hackman at the wheel, all three mounted cameras were usually filming. When Hackman was not driving, I did not use the over-shoulder camera. For all of the exterior stunts, I had three cameras going constantly. Because we were using real pedestrians and traffic at all times, it was impossible to undercrank, so everything was shot at normal speed. In most shots, the car was going at speeds between 70 and 90 miles an hour. This included times when Hackman was driving, and I should point out that Hackman drove considerably more than half of the shots that are used in the final cutting sequence.

While it was desirable to have Gene Hackman in the car as much as possible, we hired one of the best stunt drivers from Hollywood, Bill Hickman, to drive the five stunts. Consulting with Hickman, I determined what the stunts would be, trying to take advantage of the particular topography of the neighborhood.

THE FIVE STUNTS

(1) Doyle's car driving under the tracks very fast. He looks up to check the progress of the train. A car shoots out of an intersection as he crosses it. Doyle's car narrowly misses this

car, spins away and cuts across a service station to get back underneath the elevated tracks.

(2) From within Doyle's car, as he pulls up behind a truck we see a sign on the truck, "Drive Carefully." The truck makes a quick left turn without signaling, just as Doyle tries to pass him on the left, causing a collision and spinoff.

(3) Doyle approaches an intersection while looking up at the tracks. As he glances down, an enormous truck passes in front of him, obscuring his view of a metal fence. When the truck pulls away, the fence stands directly in his path. This particular fence was not part of the Stillwell Avenue route. It was something we discovered while location-scouting beneath the Myrtle Avenue Line, another elevated branch several miles away from Stillwell Avenue. I decided to switch locales because of this fence which suddenly prevented a car from continuing beneath the tracks.

(4) Doyle speeds through an intersection against the light. As he does so, a woman with a baby buggy steps quickly off the curb and into his path. Doyle has to swerve and crash into a pile of garbage cans on a safety island.

(5) Doyle turns into a one-way street the wrong way to get back underneath the elevated tracks. Over his left shoulder, we see the train running parallel to Doyle, a half-block away.

On the first day of shooting the chase, we scheduled the first stunt, which was to be Doyle's car spinning off a car that had shot out of an intersection. I had four cameras operating. Two were in a gas station approximately 100 yards from where the spin-off would occur. One was on the roof of the station with a 500mm lens, and another had a zoom lens on the ground, hidden behind a car. Two more cameras were on the street, directly parallel to the ones in the gas station, also about 100 yards from where the spin-off was to occur.

What we hoped would not happen, happened, causing this shot to be much more exciting than Hickman or I had planned. The stunt driver who was in the other car mis-timed his approach to Doyle's car (with Hickman driving), and instead of screeching to a halt several feet before it, mis-cued and rammed it broadside!

Both cars were accordions, and so on the first shot of the first day of shooting the chase, we rammed our chase car and virtually destroyed it on the driver's side.

Fortunately, Bill Hickman wasn't hurt. The driver of the other car wasn't hurt. Each of them walked away shaken and mad, but safe and sound. And I was able to pick up the action after the crash and continue it with Doyle's car swerving off and continuing on its way.

Naturally, right after this spectacular crash occurred, all four cameramen chimed out "Ready when you are, B.F."

We were forced to call our duplicate car into service on the first day of shooting, and on all subsequent days when we had to shoot events that would conceivably occur before the crash.

To achieve the effect of Hackman's car narrowly missing the woman with the baby, I had the car with the three mounted cameras drive toward the woman, who was a stunt girl. As she stepped off the curb, the car swerved away from her several yards before coming really close. But it was traveling approximately 50 miles per hour.

I used these angles, together with a shot that was made separately from a stationary camera on the ground, zooming fast into the girl's face as she sees Doyle's car and screams. This was cut with a close-up of Doyle as he first sees her, and these two shots were linked to the exterior shots of the car swerving into the safety island with the trash cans.

The only other "special effect" was the simulated crash of the trains. Since we couldn't get permission to actually stage a crash, we achieved the effect by mounting a camera inside the "approaching" train, which we positioned next to the train that was waiting outside the station. We had the "approaching" train *pull away* and shot the scene in reverse, undercranking to twelve frames per second. Just after what seems to be the moment of impact, we included an enormous crashing sound on the sound track, completing the illusion.

For many of the shots with the car, the assistant directors, under Terry Donnelly's supervision, cleared traffic for approximately five blocks in each direction. I had members of the New York City tactical police force to help control traffic. But most of the control was achieved by the AD's with the help of off-duty members of the police department—many of whom were involved in the actual case.

Working with Donnelly were second assistants Peter Bogart and Ron Walsh, plus trainees Dwight Williams and Mike Rausch.

Needless to say, the cooperation of New York City officials was incredible. We were given permission literally to control the traffic signals on those streets where we ran our chase car. We rehearsed a shot in slow motion five or six times before I was satisfied that all safety conditions were met and that the coordination was there.

Then we prayed a lot, and kept our fingers crossed.

For one particular shot, we used no controls whatever. This was shot with two cameras mounted, one inside and outside the car. The inside camera was on a 50mm lens, shooting through the front window; the outside camera was on a 25mm mounted to the front bumper. I was in the car. Bill Hickman drove the entire distance of the chase run, approximately 26 blocks, at speeds between 70 and 90 miles an hour. With no control at all and only a siren on top of his car, we went through red lights and drove in the wrong lane!

This was, of course, the wrap shot of the film. I made two takes and from these we got most of the point-of-view shots for the entire sequence.

COMPLETION

The question I'm most asked in interviews about *The French Connection*, is how the chase was filmed. As is obvious from the above notes, it was filmed one shot at a time, with a great deal of rehearsal, an enormous amount of advance planning, and a good deal of luck.

But at least 50 per cent of the effectiveness of the sequence comes from the sound and editing. The sound was done entirely after the fact. Several months after the completion of shooting and what looked like a good cut, I went back to New York City. With sound man Chris Newman, we made all the sounds for the elevated train. Then I returned to California and with Don Hall, the sound supervisor at 20th, made all the sound for the car on the Fox back lot.

We treated the recording of the individual effects with the same care and attention to detail as we did the photographing of the picture. The use of effective sound effects is, I feel, as important as the picture.

Individual frames or shots or still photographs from the chase are unimpressive. The manner in which all the elements are combined, and how sound effects orchestrate the scene—that makes it effective.

I can't say too much about the importance of editing. When I looked at the first rough cut of the chase, it was terrible. It didn't play. It was formless, inspite of the fact that I had a very careful shooting plan which I followed in detail. It became a matter of removing a shot here or adding a shot there, or changing the sequence of shots, or dropping one frame, or adding one or two frames. And here's where I had enormous help from Jerry Greenberg, the editor.

As I look back on it, the shooting was easy. The cutting and the mixing were enormously difficult. It was all enormously rewarding.

MICHAEL RITCHIE
(1939-   )

Michael Ritchie's account of his experiences on *Smile* differs from William Friedkin's *French Connection* essay in many of the same ways that the films themselves differ. While Friedkin's film was practically storyboarded in the old Hitchcock tradition, Ritchie applied the documentary techniques of the *cinéma vérité* to govern his much less formal approach. On his best films his camera seems an organic part of the action, and he is unafraid of extensive overshooting—on *Smile* more footage was exposed than on any of Erich von Stroheim's legendary productions. Once a director of television documentaries, Ritchie approached his theatrical features in the style of the Maysles Brothers, emphasizing the presence of the filmmaker as a way of minimizing the distorting impact of that presence. But Ritchie is after all a director of fictional films, and while *Gimme Shelter* deals with a real rock concert, *Smile* focuses on a beauty pageant staged solely for the purposes of the filmmakers. His two films with Robert Redford, *Downhill Racer* and *The Candidate*, are perhaps his most satisfying in this regard, concentrating on a single individual instead of attempting to picture an entire community, something attempted with uneven success in *Smile*. Although at times Ritchie employs more traditional techniques, as in *Prime Cut* and *The Bad News Bears* (to date his only real commercial success), his true metier seems to be this odd mixture of fictional and documentary strategies. If there is one style particularly suited to our television-ridden age, Ritchie seems to be the master of it, and given the right sort of scripts he could easily become a leading figure in 1980's Hollywood.

THE PRODUCTION OF "SMILE"
MICHAEL RITCHIE

The production of my latest feature film, *Smile*, came about in a rather interesting way. I live up in Mill Valley, California, about an hour's drive south of Sonoma County, where the action of *Smile* takes place. About two years ago, because I had a friend up there, I was invited to become a judge in the "Miss Sebastopol Apple" contest. I went up there and had a great time. After that I was invited to be a judge in other, similar pageants.

I've always loved the "Miss America" and "Miss Teenage America" pageants and the others of that type and, because of my enthusiasm for such events, I got the idea of doing a film about "a week in the life of a pageant"—but also one that would show what happens to the rest of the town during that period. Unlike *American Graffiti*, which concentrates only on the kids, I wanted to show the interlocking relationships of the kids and the adults, similar to the way Peter Bogdanovich handled it in more serious terms with *The Last Picture Show*, where all the relationships of the community became clearer as the separate stories criss-crossed each other.

So, with this idea based on my experiences in the pageants and some characters who were amalgams of people in real life, I went to David Picker, who was then an independent producer for United Artists. I started to tell him my idea, but when I was five or ten minutes into the telling, he stopped me and said: "You've got a deal. Go out and make the film. Hire anybody you want to write it and when the script is finished let me see it."

So we finished the script and sent it to him in New York, where he was at the time. Two hours after he received it, he called me up and said: "You've got to start July 7th." And that

From *The American Cinematographer*, October 1975. Reprinted by permission.

was it. I've never had a project happen that easily before. *Downhill Racer* was a series of confrontations between some of the studio people who wanted to make it and some who didn't—people who thought the script was good and people who didn't. But this was almost like an incident out of the old Hollywood, where King Vidor writes something on the back of an envelope and says: "I think I'll call it *The Big Parade.*" It was that kind of experience and it was thrilling. I'm very grateful to David Picker for the opportunity to make the film that way. He was the Executive Producer and I was allowed to get together my own production company.

Tim Zinnemann was the Associate Producer on the film and wore three or four hats. It was the first time I'd worked with Tim, but he was terrific and made it possible to get the picture made for a million and a quarter dollars—which is today's variation of the old million-dollar movie, allowing for inflation. We had, within that budget, the opportunity to spend the money any way we wanted to and, to me, one of the most important things was getting Conrad Hall, ASC, as the Director of Photography. So we bent in other areas in order to be able to afford Conrad, and I'm glad we did.

Somehow, Hall had acquired the reputation, going back to the *Butch Cassidy* days, of being a little bit slow, of being a perfectionist and so forth. But Tim Zinnemann, who had worked with him on *The Day of the Locust*, which was no quickie production, nevertheless said: "Hey, that picture went at the pace that John Schlesinger wanted it to go, and Conrad is as fast as you ask him to be."

That proved to be exactly my experience in working with him. Connie was extraordinary, and no matter how fast we moved it all looked wonderful. There was no variation in photographic quality between the day that we got seven set-ups and the days that we got 45 set-ups. It was all perfect within the look and consistency that we wanted.

Of course, we always had to be aware of the dollars in making the film, because there just was no room for going over budget. I mean, we would have lost the picture if it had gotten out of hand.

The way the pageant was staged in *Smile* reminds me of those MGM musicals, where Mickey Rooney would say to Judy Garland: "Hey, we've got a lot of kids here with a heck of a lot of talent. We've got a barn. Why don't we put on a show?" And that's exactly what we were doing in the Veteran Memorial Auditorium in Santa Rosa, California. We were gearing our rehearsals and shooting toward putting on a live show for 1,500 paying customers who could come in and see a two-hour pageant complete with a winner crowned.

None of the girls knew who was going to win. We kept the last pages of the script away from all of the actors. Nobody but David Picker, myself and the writer knew who the winner was going to be. The audience was going to help select the winner and all of the girls would be sharing in the excitement and nervousness of the competition, all the things that would happen in a real pageant. The guys in the crew were, too. They were discussing and arguing about who they thought was going to win, taking side bets, the whole thing.

During the intermission we went out and counted the audience ballots, mixed them in with our own story needs and wrote up the sealed envelopes. Then I went in and whispered to Conrad Hall and the additional two operators we had shooting, just what the order of winners would be, so that the cameramen could swing their lenses toward the right girls.

The reactions of the girls show a spontaneity that we couldn't have gotten in any other way. It's like the kind of thing you get at the Academy Awards, when people get Oscars and they're so stunned they walk off the wrong way. You can't stage that; it has to happen in real life.

We had a reason for making the audience pay to see the show, and it certainly wasn't to feed the coffers of the production. I'd had an experience with free crowds when I was making *The Candidate*. We said: "Come and See Robert Redford." The crowd that showed up was mostly teenagers and we didn't want that for this film. We wanted the kind of audience that actually turns out for a state-level finals pageant, and that includes a lot of important people in the community—mothers and fathers and grandmothers.

So we went to the Santa Rosa Arts Council and arranged to do this as a benefit for them. We said: "You get us the audience and you sell the tickets and you keep the proceeds." They were delighted. They made several thousand dollars off the film and we got an audience that had exactly the look we needed.

Lighting that pageant was enormously difficult for Connie Hall because he had to do one lighting job for the whole auditorium—backstage, front stage, orchestra pit, the back of the auditorium, group shots, close shots, whatever—for three cameras which would be roaming at will all over the place.

We held a dress rehearsal on the afternoon of the pageant and I had a "battle plan." I showed every one of the units where they had to be, but I couldn't physically be with all the units, I had to move back and forth from one unit to the other. All of the camerawork was hand-held, except for the zoom shots made on the PSR camera. We shot seven-and-a-half hours of film during that two-hour pageant and Connie was all over the place—God bless him. The curtains would open on a new talent act and he'd suddenly be there, standing behind the girl on a ladder. Then the curtains would close and moments later —like the Roadrunner—he'd be down in the orchestra pit. It was extraordinary. The amazing thing was that even though the entire pageant had to be filmed with a single lighting set-up, some of that footage was among the best photographically that we have in the entire film.

Connie had an overall visual concept for the picture that we talked about before, and it involved keeping all the colors to soft pastels. There were no hard colors. We worked very hard on the coordination of the costumes and the locations to keep that pastel look. We wanted it to be soft and for the teenagers to look beautiful, even though certain aspects of the comedy were very hard and abrasive and there were even pratfalls. So everything throughout the film was shot with very light diffusion. This worked out fine for the release prints, because the CRI, being a dupe negative, tends to pick up a bit of contrast, but since we had started off with this soft diffused look, the contrast did not become bothersome.

Another thing that Conrad Hall did—and he made tests of this, because he'd never tried it before—was to not use fill light on the exteriors, but instead to take care of the harsh shadows and the bright blue skies by underdeveloping one stop to create a thin negative and then print up. The thinness of the negative takes out the harsh shadows, but it means that you don't have to use fog filters or pre-fog the film or do any of the other things that people are fooling around with these days.

I don't say that this method would work for *The French Connection,* where a kind of dark and dirty look was desirable, but where you want real colors, where you want to have the faces of girls look soft and pink, rather than tan and ruddy, this technique is absolutely perfect. Conrad did tests outdoors with one of the girls and we would try various levels of underdevelopment and overdevelopment with and without diffusion, and the differences were extraordinary.

He didn't use the kind of diffusion he used on *The Day of the Locust,* which looks marvelous. That was quite a different kind of film and he was going for much more stylized effects. Our film being comedy, we wanted photography that wouldn't make people stop and say: "Wow, what a great shot!" It would just seem very truthful and the girls would look pretty and the town would appear like a charming bit of Norman Rockwell Americana.

We never did a moving camera shot or a zoom shot that was not motivated by the action. No one is aware of the camera moves. That's something of a "first" for me. I had hand-held shots in *The Candidate* which I wanted everyone to recognize as hand-held shots, because I wanted a kind of newsreel photographer's point of view. We had zap zooms in *Downhill Racer* because we wanted to go an almost stylized sports action way—since the action of sports is often treated with zap zooms. But we didn't do any of that in *Smile*—no rack focus, none of those things. I won't say I haven't been guilty of using those techniques in the past, but they all have their place. This idea was to be John Ford Simple—which is not really that simple, because I don't let scenes run on without editing, fixed on a two-shot, the way, let's say, Francis Coppola does a lot, or the way John Ford did in his classic time. The reason is that I believe the best performance is a combination of many performances of an actor. In other words, "Take One" may have something that will never be as good again; whereas, "Take Twelve" will have something that is far superior to "Take One"—and you can go on and on. The secret of film is being able to put together all those moments and create a performance that never existed. The idea of saying: "I'm going to do it all in one shot," doesn't do anything but impress a film student who is looking at it for the 438th time. The audience doesn't care. Editing is the language of film and it's there to help performances and to help the director. I think part of the problem is that there are some cameramen who work so long to make one angle absolutely perfect that they try to talk you out of taking the scene from another angle. On the set they'll say, "What a shame to break it up," or "You don't have to break it up, do you?"

There have been times when I've been tempted to go along on that score and play the entire scene from one angle. But always, just for protection, I've said to myself: "I'd better do another angle, or shoot a couple of close-ups, or whatever." Thank God I've said that, because if you do a scene from one angle only, very often when you see it on the screen it just hangs there, and you say, "My God, where do I go from here?" Fortunately, on *Smile*, Conrad never once said to me, "Why do you have to break it up?" I know that he was acutely aware of the importance of editing to the creative process.

On that subject, one of the negative things that is happening in the film industry is, that because of economic factors, directors are being required to rush their films into the theatres and there is less and less time in the editing room. This accent on speed is also very evident on the set and it is especially hard on the cameraman. Whereas, the director, if he has that freedom in his contract, can try different things with the editor in the cutting room and not stop until he thinks he has arrived at the best possible way to do something, the cinematographer is always having to compromise on what he might really like to do. He may say to himself, "Boy, if I had another two hours I could really make that look great." But there are all those dollars riding on the sound stage.

On the other hand, there are cameramen who are so instinctive that in 20 minutes they can do as good a job as they would do in three hours. Then again, that often depends upon the type of film that is being made. I'm sure that Conrad would not have liked to have to do *The Day of the Locust* as fast as he had to do *Smile* (33 days), but, at the same time, I never heard him complain about not having enough time on *Smile*.

I would work again with Connie any time and anywhere, because it is tremendous when a director and a cameraman are "in sync" the way we were and have a give and take that goes beyond the cinematography. Throughout the entire filming, he maintained a constant awareness of my problems and a willingness to contribute to the solution of them.

INDEX

(Numbers in italic refer to photographs.)

INDEX

INDEX

INDEX

INDEX